LETCHWORTH
The First Garden City

LETCHWORTH
The First Garden City

Mervyn Miller

Phillimore

First published 1989
Reprinted 1993

Published by
PHILLIMORE & CO. LTD.
Shopwyke Hall, Chichester, Sussex

ISBN 0 85033 715 1

Printed and bound in Great Britain by
BIDDLES LTD
Guildford and King's Lynn

Contents

List of Illustrations

List of Colour Plates

Acknowledgements

It was in April 1974, whilst working for the newly formed North Hertfordshire District Council as their Principal Planning Officer, that I first discovered the wealth of information chronicling the early development of Letchworth, the First Garden City. I also used the resources of the then newly opened First Garden (Heritage) Museum, including a collection of many thousands of drawings and photographs bequeathed by the late Mrs. Barry Parker, to form a permanent record of work by her husband and Raymond Unwin. It is most appropriate that the Museum is now housed in the former Parker and Unwin Offices on Norton Way South, Letchworth. A further major, and largely untapped, source of Garden City history lay in the records of First Garden City Limited, the original developers, now held by the Letchworth Garden City Corporation. It was the late Horace Plinston who made available this material, including unique correspondence between the Company and their consultant architects, to enable me to complete a Ph.D. study on the life of Raymond Unwin, awarded by the University of Birmingham in 1981. Through my adviser, Professor Gordon Cherry, and the Planning History Group, I have made many valuable contacts with colleagues in the field over the past 15 years and many of them have provided encouragement in preparing my research for publication. Invaluable comments and encouragement were given by the late Sir Frederic Osborn, the late Sir Nikolaus Pevsner, and Lewis Mumford.

Locally, too, many with early Garden City connections have provided valuable counsel, particularly the evening class students who have attended my lectures on the Garden City movement over the past 12 years. The personal advice of the late Hugh Bidwell, and his widow Margaret, and Mrs. Barbara Barry Parker, daughter-in-law of the architect, have been most valuable. At First Garden City Heritage Museum, Doreen Cadwallader provided access to a wide range of subject matter related to the early history of Letchworth, particularly when I was arranging the 75th Anniversary Exhibition at the Museum. More recently, Robert Lancaster, the current Curator, has provided enormous assistance and has specially reprinted many of the photographs to be found in this book. At the Letchworth Library, Kenneth Johnson has been a fount of knowledge on fine details of Garden City history. The Hertfordshire County Archivist, Peter Walne, has custody of Howard's papers, and kindly allowed me to reproduce some original diagrams from *Tomorrow*. At the Letchworth Museum, Gilbert Burleigh has provided information and photographs relating to the latest excavations east of Green Lane. Finally, I must also record my thanks to former colleagues in the North Hertfordshire District Council Planning Department for the opportunity to develop a detailed appreciation of Letchworth during my period as Principal Planning Officer.

This book is the latest in a series about the development and social life of Letchworth which began in 1913 with C. B. Purdom's *The Garden City*. With my interest in planning and architectural history, it is perhaps inevitable that I have emphasised the revolutionary nature of the Letchworth experiment in its early years, putting Howard's theories into practice as far as was practicable under prevailing conditions. In the interwar period Letchworth became more of an 'ordinary extraordinary town', and events, particularly in its social life, paralleled those experienced in settlements elsewhere of comparable size. The unique nature of the Letchworth experiment came to the fore once again in the heroic struggle, most ably led by Horace Plinston, to prevent the estate being sold off in separate parcels to the highest bidder. The foundation of the Letchworth Garden City Corporation in 1963 was a truly momentous event. I am indebted to the Garden City Corporation for generous assistance over the incorporation of a colour section which will highlight the attractiveness and continued relevance of the Garden City environment. Particular thanks are due to the Corporation's Chief Executive, Andrew Egerton-Smith for confirming the sponsorship and for making available, through Peter Carrick Associates, illustrations of the Corporation's 'Section 32 Projects'. Local newspapers have been helpful in tracing photographs of events which occurred up to 25 years ago and are credited in the list of illustrations. I must, however, mention Alan Millard of *The Comet*, who produced splendid prints at very short notice, without which the illustration section would have been the poorer. In addition, Peter Hodge prepared illustrations from material where historic interest inevitably outweighed technical quality.

Turning now to the production of the text, no praise could be too high for Mrs. Rena Brent who has coped magnificently with the task of transcribing the text of the book from tapes, and the lengthy chore of editing and correcting. Without her hard work, the book would not have been a practical proposition. Kay Monk gallantly compiled the index. Finally, I should like to record my gratitude for my son's patience and understanding over the priority given to preparation and writing the book during the past six months. It is to him that this book is dedicated.

June 1989   MERVYN MILLER

Illustration Acknowledgements

The author wishes to thank the following for permission to reproduce illustrations: First Garden City Heritage Museum, 2, 6, 9a, 12, 15, 16, 20, 23, 25, 27a, 28, 30, 44, 50b, 55, 57, 62, 63, 65a & b, 66, 67, 68a & b, 69b, 71, 72, 73a & b, 75, 76, 78, 81, 82, 86, 89, 92, 94a & b, 95; Hertfordhire County Record Office, 3a & b, 11, I; Letchworth Museum, 17, 18, 19; Joseph Rowntree Memorial Trust, 22; Original drawings by Mervyn Miller, 43, 46; Margaret Bidwell, 50a; Mrs. Barbara Barry Parker, 83, 91; Letchworth Library, 96, 102; *Comet* Newspaper, 105, 108; *North Herts Gazette*, 104, 106; Letchworth Garden City Corporation/ Peter Carrick Associates, 109, 110, 114, 115, 116; Pentangle Design Group, 112, 118, XII; Leicester County Museum and Art Gallery, II; Francis King, IX; Peter Carrick Associates, XIV. The remainder of the historic material is from the author's collection and the remaining photographs, both monochrome and colour, are by the author.

For Sam

Chapter One

Coketown Rebuked

It [Coketown] was a town of red brick, or of brick that would have been red if the smoke and ashes
had allowed it; but as matters stood it was a town of unnatural red and black like the painted face
of a savage. It was a town of machinery and tall chimneys, out of which interminable serpents of
smoke trailed themselves for ever and ever, and never got uncoiled. It had a black canal in it, and
a river that ran purple with ill-smelling dye, and vast piles of buildings full of windows where there
was a rattling and a trembling all day long, and where the piston of the steam-engine worked
monotonously up and down like the head of an elephant in a state of melancholy madness. It
contained several large streets all very like one another, and many small streets still more like one
another, inhabited by people equally like one another, who all went in and out at the same hours,
with the same sound upon the same pavements, to do the same work, and to whom every day was
the same as yesterday and tomorrow, and every year the counterpart of the last and the next.

Charles Dickens, *Hard Times* (1856)

The Victorian industrial city elicited both praise and condemnation from many contemporary observers, not least the novelists and social analysts.[1] The work of Dickens was matched
by that of Mrs Gaskell, who encapsulated the geographical and class division of society in the
title *North and South*. Henry Mayhew was amongst the first to publish detailed observations of
slum life, and the practice culminated in Charles Booth's massive *Life and Labour of the
People in London*, in the last decade of the 19th century. The purpose of this chapter is to
summarise the diverse reactions to urban environmental problems, of which such a keen
social observer as Ebenezer Howard (1850-1928), the founder of the Garden City movement,
would have been acutely aware. The context and the extent to which the Victorian city
acted as catalyst will be discussed here, but more specific influences on Howard's concept
will be described in Chapter Two.

The Health of Towns   The Victorian industrial city simultaneously represented both the
triumph of economic progress and the tangible reflection of social and environmental
consequences beyond the concern of *laissez faire* enterprise. Already, by 1801, 20 per cent of
the population of England and Wales lived in towns with more than five thousand
inhabitants, and by 1851 the proportion had grown to 54 per cent, rising to 72 per cent by
1891. In addition the population was growing rapidly and the largest cities and towns were
attracting a great proportion of the increase, both by inmigration and natural increase.
London, with a population of 900,000 in 1801, expanded to 2,263,000 in 1851, reaching
3,900,000 in 1891. Important provincial cities rapidly expanded, primarily as a consequence
of early industrialisation: in 1851 Liverpool had a population of 375,000; Manchester,
367,000; Birmingham, 232,000; Leeds, 172,000; Bristol, 137,000; Sheffield, 135,000; and
Bradford, 105,000. The population of England and Wales doubled from 8,873,000 in 1801
to 17,927,000, and doubled yet again by 1911.

The local government structure, particularly during the early part of the century, was
both ill-equipped and unwilling to regulate this massive urban expansion; between 1851
and 1911 rudimentary controls were introduced to alleviate some of the worst evils of slum
housing, disease and overcrowding. Prior to 1830, a few towns established Improvement
Commissions through private Acts of Parliament. The Liberal Reform Government of the
1830s introduced rationalised Parliamentary constituencies and local government, laying

1. Coketown personified — *Over London by Rail* — based on an etching by Gustave Doré (1832-83). The railway symbolised both the advance of the industrial revolution and the degradation of the urban environment.

the foundations for civic pride, but much of this focussed on the status of the city centres, and municipal aggrandisement.

National concern for public health arose following the widespread cholera epidemics of 1831-3, which claimed 32,000 victims, a further 62,000 in 1848-9, and a recurrence with 20,000 in 1853-4. Edwin Chadwick (1800-90), as Poor Law Commissioner, prepared reports on public health in the late 1830s, and a Select Committee on the Health of Towns reported in 1840.[2] In 1842 the Poor Law Commission reported on the Sanitary Conditions of the Labouring Classes. These reports identified the relationship between disease and polluted water supplies, arising from the lack of sewage and waste disposal facilities, and burial practices, and the contributory effect of overcrowded, particularly basement, housing was recorded.

Initially there was no positive government response. A Royal Commission, often known as the Health of Towns Commission, was appointed in 1843, to which Chadwick contributed significantly. A private propaganda organisation, the Health of Towns Association, was founded in the following year. The Metropolitan Association for Improving the Dwellings of the Industrious Classes, dated from 1841, and the Society for the Improvement of the Condition of the Labouring Classes from 1844.[3] Both were constituted as charitable trusts, with articles of association, limiting dividend to five per cent. They relied on investors of an altruistic outlook, willing to accept a modest return for funding reforming work, which included the construction and management of blocks of model tenements. In the 1860s the extensive work by the Improved Industrial Dwelling Company, and the Peabody Trust, brought into common use the term 'five per cent philanthropy'. Between them the nine major Trusts had by 1905 housed 123,000; their model was to prove a fruitful basis for Howard to expand as the development mechanism for his Garden City concept in the closing decade of the century.

Public Health Legislation 1848-75 The need for government intervention was under-lined by the recurrence of cholera in 1848-9. Whilst tentative efforts at control of building standards had been reflected by local Building Acts for 208 towns in England and Wales between 1800-45, and the London Building Acts, first codified in 1774, had been extended and consolidated in the 1844 Metropolitan Building Act, it was not until the passing of the 1848 Public Health Act that national standards were enacted. This was a landmark in its creation of a central Board of Health, and its empowering of the formation of local Boards. The emphasis of control was placed on water supply and drainage, and the passing of plans for buildings was introduced. The fundamental defect was its permissive adoption — by 1854 only 182 local Boards had been formed, but the pace quickened following the 1858 Local Government Act which extended powers to include constructional strength and stability, and space around buildings. Following the report of the Royal Commission on the Sanitary Administration of England, the Local Government Board was established as the central government department with responsibility for public health, and, subsequently, housing and town planning, whilst a further Public Health Act in 1872 established sanitary authorities with obligatory powers. These measures were consolidated in the Public Health Act of 1875. Model bye-laws followed two years later and the scene was set for the proliferation of the 'bye-law' suburb — healthier than the chaotic network of slum courts and alleys, but to the aesthetically sensitive a deadly reflection of unthinking conformity with prescribed standards, and further inducing the uncontrolled outwards sprawl of the major urban areas.

Legislative concern extended to the closing of unfit housing from the 1860s. The Artizans' and Labourers' Dwellings Act of 1868, sponsored by William Torrens, aimed at introducing compulsory powers of demolition and repair, and building of replacement dwellings. In the event it was emasculated, but it highlighted the principle of the owner being publicly responsible for the condition of his property. Some years later, the Home Secretary, R. A. Cross, promoted the Artizans' and Labourers' Dwellings Act, 1875, under which unhealthy areas could be cleared as a whole, and the land acquired for redevelopment by other bodies, including the housing trusts. There was, however, no obligation to rehouse, and the legislation was sometimes used for more lucrative commercial improvement, as in the case of Corporation Street, Birmingham.

Practical Exemplars Some industrialists were quick to learn the benefits, and sub-sequently advertising value, of model communities which housed a contented and productive workforce. Already in 1800, Robert Owen (1771-1858), a visionary industrialist whose name was to be linked with several Utopian schemes over the next three decades, was constructing housing for his workers at New Lanark,[4] a secluded valley 30 miles south-east of Glasgow. His stern moral proselytising was reflected in the dour rectitude of the community buildings, which today evoke the imagery of a closed society in which company domination of social life loomed large. Owen's *Report to the County of Lanark* (1820) advocated a series of agricultural and industrial villages, based upon unity and mutual cooperation, qualities which were to figure prominently in Howard's vision three quarters of a century later, but the notion of centralised control had, fortunately, disappeared. As will be discussed in Chapter Two, Howard's skill lay in tempering the extremism of Utopian concepts without sacrificing their essential principles.

By the 1860s a mainstream of model industrial villages had emerged which laid the foundation for further advances in the closing decades of the century. Landowners possessed the ability to control the laying out of their estates subject, as already noted, to few controls. In 1847, Colonel Edward Akroyd began construction of housing at Copley, on the outskirts of Halifax in West Yorkshire.[5] Although back-to-back, the varied terraces with mullioned windows and roof lines punctuated by gabled dormers, set a pattern for both local and more distant successors. Sir Titus Salt, a Bradford textile manufacturer who had made his fortune from alpaca, built a palatial complex of mills four miles north-west of the city, with housing to the south. The name 'Saltaire' was a combination of its creator's name with the River Aire on which the development was located. Construction took place from 1851-76. The village was notable for including a substantial park, and the architects, Lockwood and Mawson, were responsible for varied terraces of housing in an Italianate style, an Institute, Church and Almshouses for retired employees. Not to be outdone, Akroyd founded a second village, Akroyden, situated on the hillside to the north of Halifax. The main feature was an immense double quadrangle of Gothic-style housing, for which George Gilbert Scott (1811-78), one of the most eminent Victorian architects, acted as consultant, and also designed an impressive church nearby. Akroyd's workforce found the houses to be unduly like almshouses. Akroyd himself lived nearby and aimed at merging social classes, an objective embraced by the Garden City movement, and particularly by Henrietta Barnett (1851-1936), at Hampstead Garden Suburb.

The Aesthetic Adventure   By the late 1880s, reaction against conventional Victorian values in the arts and industry was manifested through the Arts and Crafts Movement, spearheaded by the reforms in architecture and applied design advocated by John Ruskin (1819-1900) and William Morris (1834-96). Both had approached the shortcomings of the industrial society through their concern for the future of architecture and the arts, but they soon drew out the interdependence of aesthetics with social and economic factors.[6] Ruskin's prolific output of 'political economy' included passages which vividly anticipated the improved environment and integration of town and country advocated by the Garden City movement: both Howard and, much later, Lewis Mumford, selected the following quotation, allegedly from Ruskin's *Sesame and the Lilies* for its figurative power in evoking the ideal settlement.

> Providing lodgments [for working people] means a great deal of vigorous legislation and cutting down of vested interests ...; thorough sanitary and remedial action in the houses that we have, and then the building of more, strongly, beautiful in groups of limited extent ... walled round so that there may be no wretched festering suburb anywhere, but clean and busy streets within, and the open country without, with a belt of beautiful garden and orchard around the walls, so that from any part of the city perfectly fresh air and grass and the sight of the horizon may be reachable in a few minutes walk. This is the final aim.[7]

Ruskin's imagery invokes Raymond Unwin's subsequent realisation of the built form of the Garden City. Morris perhaps provided a more strategic overview. In January 1884, lecturing in Leicester for the Socialist League, Morris hinted at the synthesis of social and environmental factors with which the Garden City movement, and subsequently town-planning, would be centrally concerned — 'honourable and fitting work', 'decency of surroundings'; and 'leisure'. 'Decency of surroundings' included

> 1. Good lodging; 2. Ample space; 3. General order and beauty. That is 1. Our houses must be well built, clean and healthy. 2. There must be abundant garden space in our towns, and our towns must not eat up the fields and natural features of the country. 3. Order and beauty means that not only our houses must be stoutly and properly built, but also that they be ornamented duly: that the fields be not only left for cultivation, but also that they be not spoil by it any more than a garden is spoilt: no one for instance be allowed to cut down, for mere profit, trees whose loss would spoilt a landscape: neither on any pretext should people be allowed to darken the daylight with smoke, to befoul rivers, or to degrade any spot of earth with squalid litter and brutal wasteful disorder.[8]

Rarely have the comprehensive goals in environmental planning been so succinctly and eloquently stated in the intervening century. Morris, of course, sought to attain such goals through revolution. Howard, who appears to have been indifferent to aesthetics, advocated 'the peaceful path', but could scarcely have been unaware of Morris's pronouncements. Raymond Unwin certainly was not, for in the early 1880s he joined the Socialist League as one of Morris's most active young acolytes. The aesthetic vision, in the closing decades of the century, was already beginning to appear not only in individual houses, but in a series of communities with direct significance for the ultimate built form of Garden City.

Bedford Park, Port Sunlight and Bournville

Arts and Crafts architecture was first widely seen through the work of Philip Webb (1831-1915), who had designed the Red House for Morris himself in 1859-60, and more extensively through the buildings of Richard Norman Shaw (1831-1912), who in the 1870s evolved a richly eclectic architectural style, based on the revival of country Queen Anne, with picturesque massing highlighted by the white painted sash, casement and bay windows, all three often mixed on the same building, with lively roof lines broken by numerous tall chimneys, and features such as gables enriched by tile hanging. The style formed the basis for Bedford Park, a middle-class suburb developed in west London from 1875 onwards, in which the street grid was purposefully fragmented to preserve mature trees, giving an informality and individuality to the grouping of houses designed by Shaw and others.[9] This visual harmony of the garden suburb was disrupted in the late 1880s by a revolutionary tall white roughcast house, with stone mullioned windows, impudently commanding views across the village green. The architect was C. F. A. Voysey (1857-1941), one of the most influential of the younger Arts and Crafts followers, whose widely published designs for 'the smaller middle-class house' were to exert a profound influence over suburban and model Garden City housing, from the 1890s.

The final decade of the century witnessed the development of two of the most influential of the model industrial communities, which in many respects set environmental standards for the 20th century, creating a lineage developed through the Garden City movement, Hampstead Garden Suburb, the pioneer 1909 Housing and Town Planning Act, and ultimately through local authority housing schemes prepared under the 1919 Housing Act. The begetters, W. H. Lever (1851-1925), and George Cadbury (1839-1922), both assisted the Garden City movement during the crucial transition from theory to realisation.

Lever expanded a family grocery business into an industrial empire based upon Sunlight soap, brand leader by 1887 after only three years on the market. In 1888, he acquired a site on the west bank of the Mersey, between Birkenhead and Bromborough Pool, a pioneer model village built by Price's Patent Candle Company in 1853-8. North of his new factory he commenced construction of a model village named Port Sunlight in honour of his most profitable product.[10] Lever attended to its development with paternal pride, to realise 'a conveniently planned and healthy settlement laid out with all possible artistic thought on

sound business lines'. He also built model housing at Thornton Hough, outside the gates
of his newly acquired manorial seat. He promoted the revival of the black and white
Cheshire vernacular architecture, designed by William and Segar Owen. Their housing
was of strikingly individual character, with elaborate and beautifully crafted timber studwork above a stone base. This set the pattern for most of the early housing, although further
consultants were employed, including London-based architects such as Ernest Newton
(1856-1922) and Edwin Lutyens (1869-1944). The site with its waterlogged channels
distorted the layout of housing quadrangles but showed off picturesque grouping to advantage. Lever eschewed individual gardens in favour of open frontages, in which no individual
shortcoming would spoil the corporate image. Allotments were provided in the inner
quadrangles away from public view. The housing designs introduced a middle-class concept
for working-class housing. Lever soon realised the publicity value of his settlement which
was regularly visited by leading politicians, and English and European Royalty. The
village was always, in effect, on parade, which created an uncomfortable impression of
perpetual Sunday best. Lever had acquired a taste for town planning, and in 1909 endowed
Liverpool University with a Chair in Civic Design. The following year a revised plan
transformed Port Sunlight into a Beaux-Arts exercise, with the creeks filled in to create
vistas for formal set pieces such as the Lady Leverhulme Art Gallery.

Bournville was much less self-conscious, perhaps reflecting Cadbury's unassertive Quaker
beliefs, which contrasted with Lever's loudly proclaimed non-conformist evangelism.[11] In
1879, Cadbury's chocolate factory moved five miles from the centre of Birmingham to
benefit from the purer air of Bournbrook, near Selly Oak. Although advance housing for
the works foremen was constructed, in a Victorian Italianate style, it was not until 1895
that development got fully under way, when Cadbury and his architect W. Alexander
Harvey began to plan a complete village. Harvey was influenced by Arts and Crafts
architects such as Voysey and M. H. Baillie Scott (1865-1945). His designs for informal
terraces and semi-detached cottages rejected the more self-conscious artiness of Lever's
village. The layout had affinity with Bedford Park, and community buildings and recreation
areas were integrated, rather than standing out as formal set pieces.

Cadbury stressed the amenity, economic and recreative role of the individual garden, and
plots were generously sized, allowing for a high proportion of the individual family
requirement for fruit and vegetables to be provided. Economy of construction allied to the
prevalent high quality of materials and craftsmanship produced housing designs which
were widely influential at Earswick, Letchworth, and in the early L.C.C. Cottage Estates,
from the turn of the century onwards. In contrast to Port Sunlight, Cadbury made available
up to half of the housing for non-Bournville employees, which promoted social integration
and diminished the paternalistic character of the community.

Public Housing Initiatives   Although there were isolated examples of local authority
housing built from the 1840s, it was not until 40 years later that there were moves towards
more positive intervention. The Royal Commission on the Housing of the Working Classes
(1884-5), under the Chairmanship of Sir Charles Dilke and in which the Prince of Wales
participated, received wide publicity. It revealed a situation in which street improvements
had increased problems of overcrowded slum housing. As a Parliamentary Reporter,
Howard would have been familiar with the findings. A decade later, he was official reporter
of a Commission of Inquiry into Labour.[12] In 1888, Charles Booth began his monumental
study of urban conditions, published as *Life and Labour of the People in London*, a 17-volume
work which revealed overall that 35 per cent of the 900,000 population of East End London
were in the three lowest classes of poverty. Later examination of the remaining districts
confirmed that the findings were not restricted to the East End.

In 1888, further legislation created the London County Council, the first of the Metropolitan Authorities, with effect from 1 January 1889. Composed of an alliance of Liberals and Socialists, the new Council pressed for improved housing legislation and in 1890 the Housing of the Working Classes Act consolidated existing measures, and added powers which enabled authorities to undertake housing for a demonstrated need, independent of their involvement in slum clearance.[13] A Housing Branch was created within the L.C.C. Architects Department, under W. E. Riley (1852-1937), which carried forward the pioneering work of the private trusts in its Boundary Street estate at Bethnal Green (1894-1900). A 1900 amendment to the legislation enabled local authorities to purchase land outside their own districts for housing schemes, and the L.C.C. acquired 39 acres at Totterdown Fields, Tooting, for their first cottage estate, soon followed by the White Hart Lane, Tottenham scheme (1904-14).

The scene was set for the first 'Municipal Bournville', and this action was commended by Raymond Unwin at the first Garden City Association Conference, held in September 1901, appropriately hosted by Cadbury. The dawn of the new century thus appeared to herald a broad consensus on solutions to the housing problems created by the previous one. Although the underlying principles of the Garden City movement, and concurrent moves towards improved housing and planning legislation were ultimately different, the imagery of the housing, drawn from Bournville and refined through the work of Unwin and the L.C.C. architects, was shared.

Chapter Two

An Ideal City Made Practicable

Ebenezer Howard (1850-1928) Let Ebenezer Howard introduce himself:

> I was born on January 29th 1850, within the sound of Bow Bells in the City of London at 62 Fore Street. My father's name was Ebenezer and he had several confectioners' shops round London. My mother was a farmer's daughter with good common sense, nothing brilliant about her . . . Fore Street has undergone many changes since 1850 but it is still one of those city streets where important looking warehouses stand cheek by jowl with confectioners and similar shops.[1]

The City of London was still a Dickensian mixture of counting houses and tea shops during Howard's childhood. His father was never an astute businessman, and some commentators have claimed that this influenced Howard's advocacy that the Garden City development company should undertake commercial activity. Early on Howard received a poignant lesson in the contrast between city and country life, for he was sent away to a dame-school in Suffolk aged $4\frac{1}{2}$, and subsequently to Cheshunt, then a small coaching town in Hertfordshire on the Cambridge Road. The latter left 'a latent memory of fair landscapes and wholesome enjoyment would become active when long afterwards the possibility arose of making a first Garden City in one of the choicest Counties in England'.

Having completed his education at Stoke Hall, Ipswich, at 15, Howard began work for Greaves and Son, City Stockbrokers, the first of several clerical posts. He gained expertise in shorthand by taking down the sermons of Dr Joseph Parker, of Poultry Chapel, one of the most eminent non-conformist ministers, who stated that if Howard had a vocation it would be as a preacher. The usually published

2. Ebenezer Howard. The father of the Garden City points proudly to a plan of Letchworth, his first creation.

photographs of Howard do give the impression of a rather muddling old gentleman, a down at heel yet defensively respectable City clerk of the type immortalised as Mr Pooter in George and Weedon Grossmith's *Diary of a Nobody*. Yet he had a capacity for deep contemplation and an aptitude for unexpected actions, both of which stood him in good stead when formulating and advocating the Garden City concept.

In the United States In 1871, at the age of 21, Howard emigrated to the United States with two companions, possibly finding that both his intellectual and spiritual non-conformity were too constrained by City life and work. He travelled way out West, settling, appropriately, in Howard County, Nebraska, as a homestead-farmer, for two months — the failure of which venture he attributed to the lack of cooperation by his companions and neighbours. The journey to Nebraska was not without incident, for crossing the River Missouri by ferry Howard met Colonel William Cody, alias 'Buffalo Bill'

> who was much interested in my rifle . . . of the singer pattern . . . converted from an Enfield muzzle loader to a breech loader . . . I was much struck with his Winchester rifle . . . capable of firing 10 or 12 shots with one loading.[2]

The young Ebenezer survived the rigours of Western life — riding 30 miles in one day without a saddle to obtain treatment for a septic hand at a military camp. After being given a saddle for the return journey, and having quaffed 'a restorative which doubtless contained whiskey' he galloped off 'in so cheerful a frame of mind', breaking his right stirrup, and was promptly thrown off, happily unhurt. He retreated eastward to Chicago, Illinois, the hub of the fast developing mid-west, recovering from a disastrous fire which had destroyed most of the central business district in 1871. Howard worked for Ely and Burnham, law stenographers until 1876, and became acquainted with Christian Science and Spiritualist circles after work. The redevelopment of Chicago left its impact as he witnessed the growing American obsession with piling up increments in land values as the central business district was recreated in skyscraper form. Significantly, generous parks were also being laid out along the shore of Lake Michigan and the urban fringe, and Chicago was known as the Garden City of the mid-west. Its suburbs were growing rapidly. Twelve miles from the central 'loop', the great American landscape architect, F. L. Olmsted (1822-1903), had prepared a master plan for Riverside, one of the most prestigious suburban communities, with an informal layout, individual houses in generous plots, and landscaped parkway roads. Olmsted was, of course, best known for Central Park, New York, a lung of verdant landscape in mid-town Manhattan, a concept which was to be prominently featured in Howard's own Garden City diagrams.

Parliamentary Reporter Howard returned to England in 1876, although he subsequently revisited the U.S.A. to try to market his own improvements to the Remington Typewriter. A spare-time inventor, he worked on mechanical projects, culminating, towards the end of his life, in a complex shorthand typewriter. He joined the firm of Gurney and Son, official Parliamentary Reporters, and settled down to a career meticulously noting down details of lengthy debates, graduating to Committees and Government Commissions. He was to reject Parliamentary procedure for bringing the Garden City to fruition. He was, neverthe-less, impressed at the broad agreement on key problems such as housing and labour, but equally frustrated by the inability of Parliament to devise far-reaching and comprehensive solutions.

In August 1879 he married Elizabeth Anne Bills, daughter of a Nuneaton innkeeper. She proved to be an ideal partner, running a household on a slender income, supporting his activities apparently unconcerned by the increasing domination of his extra-mural interests

over family life. In the early 1880s the most significant was the Zetetical Society, a debating
club, which examined social and religious questions, and whose membership included
the socialists Sidney Webb (1859-1947) and George Bernard Shaw (1856-1950), founder
members of the Fabian Society in 1884. Howard spoke on Spiritualism as early as 1880; the
Society stimulated his broadening outlook.

Towards Utopia   Howard's reading spanned early socialist literature. He never referred
to Karl Marx, but was familiar with Socialist principles through H. M. Hyndman, the
founder of the Social Democratic Federation. He also drew on the work of the anarchist
Peter Kropotkin, who visited London in 1881, and discussed the merits of decentralised
economic decision-making and self-government in his *Factories, Fields and Workshops*.[3] In
1883, Howard read Henry George's *Progress and Poverty* (1879), which examined the question
of land reform, arguing that the artificially high values of city centre properties placed an
undue financial burden upon the working class. A tax upon land values would help to
recoup the value created by the community, which under free market conditions benefited
landowners. This concept was to become one of the shibboleths of planning, and, to Howard,
revealed the necessity of ensuring that land values increased by development were put into
trust for communal benefit.

Howard acknowledged the influence of three distinct projects, from which he formed his
own amalgam, 'A unique combination of proposals' which underpinned *Tomorrow: A Peaceful
Path to Real Reform* in which the Garden City concept was described in 1898. These were:

> (1) The proposals for an organised migratory movement of population of Edward Gibbon Wakefield
> and of Professor Alfred Marshall; (2) The system of land tenure first prepared by Thos. Spence [sic]
> and afterwards (though with an important modification) by Mr. Herbert Spencer; and (3) the model
> city of James Silk Buckingham.[4]

Wakefield had, in 1849, written of the necessity for overseas colonisation to be based upon
a representative spectrum of society, rather than the social misfits who had been consigned
to Australia, and Howard adapted the concept to the dispersal of population from the
teeming industrial cities. Marshall was an eminent economist who had, in 1884, written of
the desirability to decentralise population from central London to country estates cand
attract industries, to the mutual benefit of both the capital city and the new satellites.
Thomas Spence, a late 18th-century radical from Newcastle-upon-Tyne, advocated parish
ownership of land as a universal tenure, and his concept was revived by H. M. Hyndman
in 1882. Howard wished to convey the rights to his model community after the purchase of
the Garden City estate: he inherently distrusted nationalisation which represented the
substitution of one superior landlord for another, without community accountability.
Herbert Spencer had postulated that all men were equally entitled to use the earth, but
could not work out an equitable system of compensating existing owners which would be
remunerative to the community as a whole.

Howard credited a diverse group of philosophers and reformers with near discovery of
the Garden City including Thomas More, Morris and Ruskin. Two Utopian community
concepts were of significant importance in shaping the Garden City — James Silk Buckingham's *Victoria* (1849), and Dr Benjamin Ward Richardson's *Hygeia* (1876).[5] It was from
the former that he drew most direct inspiration. Buckingham described his proposals in
National Evils and Practical Remedies. Their basis was a Model Town Association, formed and
incorporated by Royal Charter, through an Act of Parliament. The development was to be
wholly privately financed, however. A site of 10,000 acres (4047 ha.) was to be purchased,
on 1,000 acres (404.7 ha.) of which Victoria, a town of 10,000 inhabitants, would be
constructed. Its layout was a square plan form, with major diagonal and radial avenues.
The outer square contained 1,000 small houses, rented for £5 p.a.; the second, workshops;

and larger houses, rented at £300 p.a., were located in the inner squares, together with public buildings. The whole settlement was to be illuminated by a central towering beacon. The development company would not only manage the estate, retaining ownership of all buildings, but would also be the sole employer, operating a strict eight-hour day, providing free medical services, nurseries, public baths, kitchens and laundries. It would raise £3,000,000, divided in £20 shares, at least one to be held by every resident. £1,000,000 would be used to create industrial and agricultural enterprises, and Dividends were to be limited to ten per cent. Howard was strongly influenced by Victoria, not least by its crisp finite form, which he transposed to circular geometry. He decided to attract industry to leased sites, considering that the development company might initially have insufficient resources for direct involvement. Buckingham's requirement for even the humblest residents to invest £20 in the community would have excluded those in greatest need of rehousing and Howard dropped this. However, the partnership element was fundamental to the Co-Partnership movement which subsequently developed a substantial amount of housing at Letchworth, and many model suburbs. Richardson's pamphlet *Hygeia or the City of Health* was based on his October 1875 lecture to the Social Science Congress in Brighton. He proposed a city with 100,000 population, 20,000 houses, built on a 4,000-acre (1618 ha.) site, giving an average density of 25 persons per acre (61 p. p. ha.). The layout included three main tree-lined boulevards, below which ran an underground railway. Elaborate street cleansing mechanisms and houses built of glazed brick, with arches to permit maximum air circulation, would ensure a minimum mortality rate, the late 19th-century public health yardstick.

Both Buckingham and Richardson had taken their settlements out into the country and had proposed a self-contained built area in the centre of their estates. Agricultural enterprise figured prominently in Victoria, fusing town and country in a functional symbosis, whilst the countryside was brought into the streets of Hygeia. Howard was also well aware of the contribution to the urban park movement by Sir Joseph Paxton (1803-65),[6] and of the clean division between urban development and landscape found in parts of Bath and around Regents Park in London. The 1880s saw mounting agricultural depression, worsened by increasing imports of cheap cereals from America, as a consequence of Free Trade. Rural depopulation increased, swelling the urban population. As a counter attraction, smallholding communities represented a significant theme in Utopian philosophy. In the 1840s a group of Chartist land colonies were begun by Fergus O'Connor (1794-1855), beginning at Heronsgate, near Chorleywood, Hertfordshire.[7] O'Connor overstretched his resources, his land company was declared illegal by a Commons Select Committee in 1848, and was compulsorily wound up in 1851. He died a broken man, but his settlements weathered the vicissitudes and served as models for the 'back to the land' movement of the late 19th century. Howard included smallholdings in his agricultural belt, which potentially assisted the integration of town and country more positively than the larger farms, and all would benefit from the accessibility of a ready market.

The Catalyst   It was an American Utopian novel by Edward Bellamy which provoked Ebenezer Howard to formulate his own proposals. Published in 1888, *Looking Backward* described the transformation of Boston by A.D. 2000 into a centralised consumer-oriented urban community, through technological advance and co-operation. As with Hygeia, there was generous planting, large open squares, statues and fountains, and electrical power had created clean industry. Howard evidently read the book at a sitting, carried away by its eloquence and conviction.

> The next morning as I went up to the City from Stamford Hill I realised, as never before, the
> splendid possibilities of a new civilisation based on service to the community, and not on self-interest,

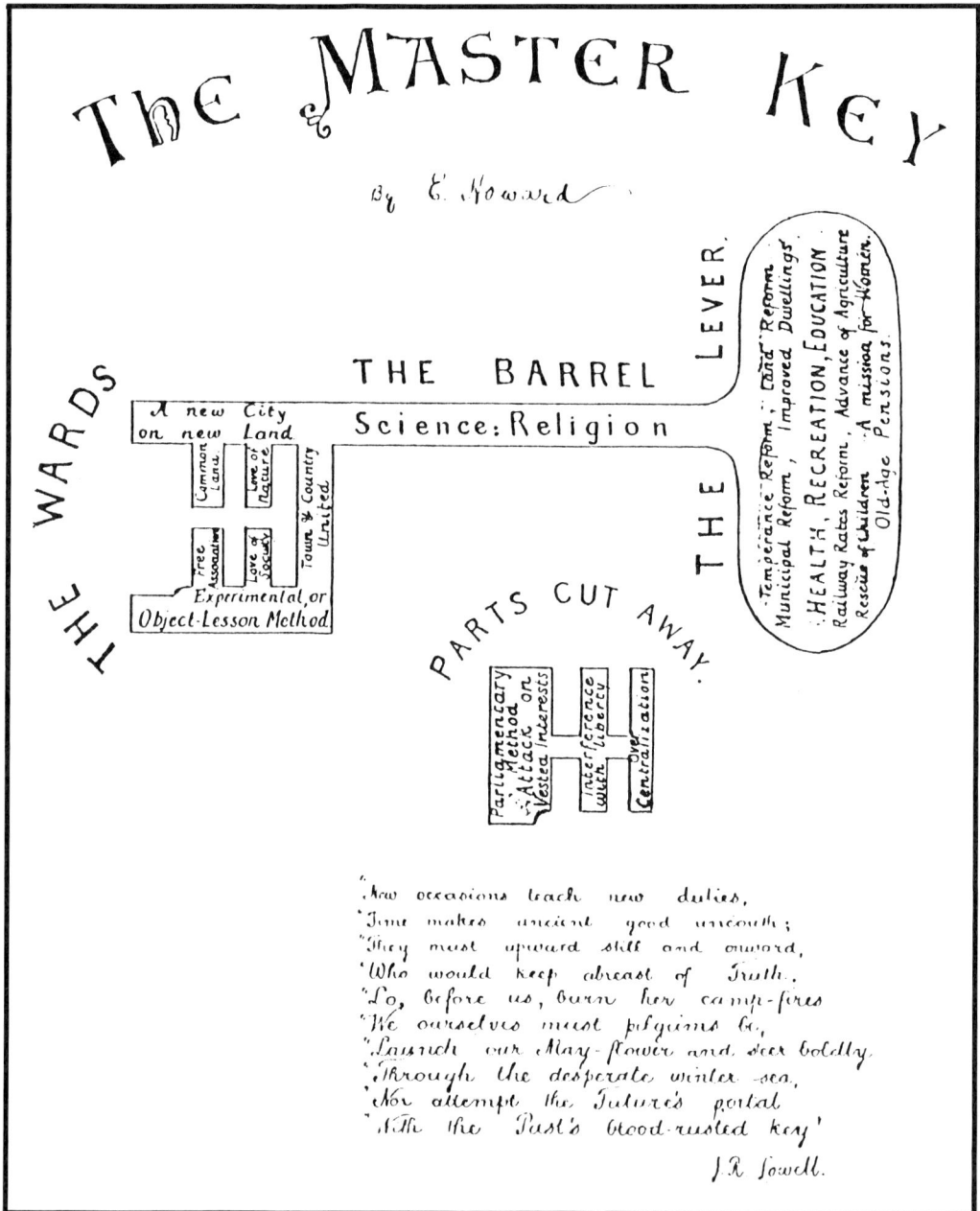

3a. & b. Howard's sketch diagrams. a) The Master Key. The concept of cutting away Parliamentary method as an obstacle to progress undoubtedly led to the decision to omit this diagram from publication.

b) Ward and Centre. Howard had included the Biblical command 'Go up and possess the land' — this was struck through 'omit this' in pencil.

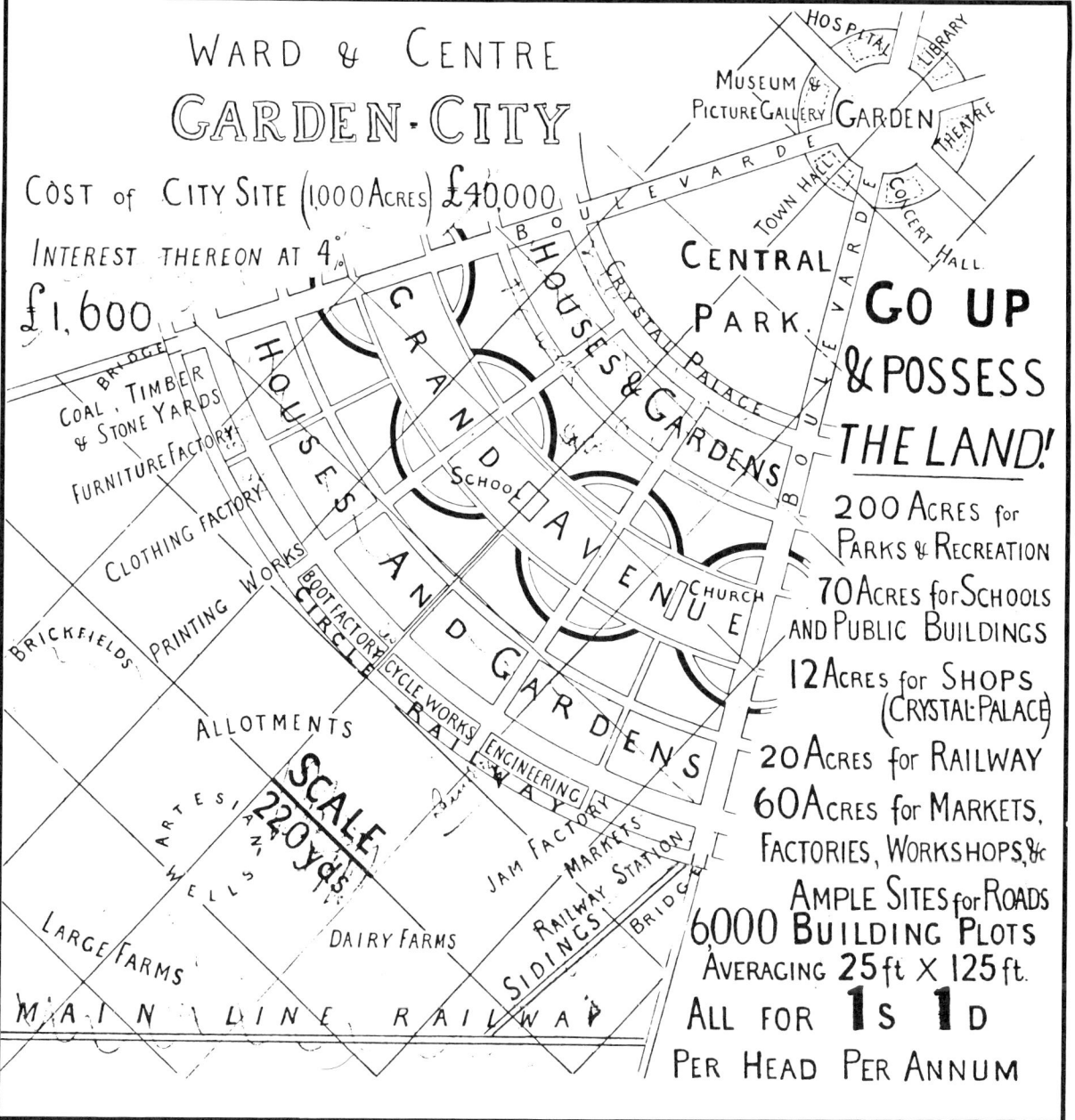

WARD & CENTRE
GARDEN·CITY

COST OF CITY SITE (1,000 ACRES) £40,000

INTEREST THEREON AT 4%

£1,600

HOSPITAL
LIBRARY
MUSEUM & PICTURE GALLERY
GARDEN
THEATRE
TOWN HALL
CONCERT HALL

CENTRAL PARK

BOULEVARDE

CRYSTAL PALACE

HOUSES & GARDENS

GRAND

HOUSES

AVENUE

AND GARDENS

School

Church

BRIDGE
COAL, TIMBER & STONE YARDS
FURNITURE FACTORY
CLOTHING FACTORY
PRINTING WORKS
BRICKFIELDS
BOOT FACTORY
CIRCLE RAILWAY
CYCLE WORKS
ENGINEERING
ALLOTMENTS

SCALE
220 YDS

ARTESIAN WELLS

JAM FACTORY
MARKETS
RAILWAY STATION
SIDINGS
BRIDGE

LARGE FARMS
DAIRY FARMS

MAIN LINE RAILWAY

GO UP
& POSSESS
THE LAND!

200 ACRES FOR PARKS & RECREATION

70 ACRES FOR SCHOOLS AND PUBLIC BUILDINGS

12 ACRES FOR SHOPS (CRYSTAL PALACE)

20 ACRES FOR RAILWAY

60 ACRES FOR MARKETS, FACTORIES, WORKSHOPS, &c

AMPLE SITES FOR ROADS

6000 BUILDING PLOTS
AVERAGING 25 ft × 125 ft.

ALL FOR 1s 1d
PER HEAD PER ANNUM

at present the dominant motive. Then I determined to take such part as I could, however small it might be, in helping 'to bring a new civilisation into being.[8]

Howard guaranteed the English publication of Bellamy's book, by taking 100 copies, largely given away to friends. The publication elicited a very different response from William Morris, who retreated into guild socialism with *News From Nowhere* (1890), in which he described a communal society living in a federated network of villages, the poetic epitome of decentralisation.[9]

As the 'nineties dawned Howard's concept took shape. Drafts and diagrams were discussed with family and friends. He was heartened by the evidence given by all parties, including the trades union leaders Ben Tillet and Tom Mann, to the Royal Commission on Labour (1892-4) at which he was the official reporter. Yet his distrust of government remained and he wrote a long chapter, 'The Master Key',[10] illustrated by a diagram in which he summarised the pre-requisites for the new society, to be achieved through the 'experimental object-lesson method'. The key was to be fashioned by cutting away the redundant parts in order to fit and turn the lock — Howard cut away Parliamentary methods which he felt would support vested interests against social progress. He noted that 'it is in practice long after a majority are distinctly agreed on the passing of a measure that it at length emerges in a frequently mangled [*sic*] shape from this complex piece of machinery'.

In the event the chapter and diagram were omitted, though references to 'The Master Key' remain in Howard's introductory chapter to *Tomorrow*. Diagrams which were published were also modified[11] — the sketch of the 'Ward and Centre' of Garden City was originally embellished with land costings and the Biblical exhortation to 'go up and possess the land!'; this was struck through in pencil 'omit this'. The early 1890s were a period of social unrest, with Morris's Socialist League fragmenting into revolutionary anarchist groups. Evidently, Howard was persuaded that discretion would ultimately prove to be the better part of valour. Likewise, his land requirement for his prototype varied — Howard originally specified 9,000 acres (3642 ha.), reduced to 6,000 (2428 ha.) on publication. The name ranged through 'Unionville' and 'Rurisville' before the clarity of 'Garden City' was adopted. On the cluster diagrams showing 'the Social City', 'Christos', with possible overtones of blasphemy disappeared in favour of 'Gladstone', commemorating the Grand Old Man of politics, whose Premiership dominated the 1890s. Finally the manuscript was ready for publication. Swan Sonnenschein, of Paternoster Square, London, a firm noted for socialist literature including the English Edition of Marx's *Das Kapital*, issued the book in October 1898. *Tomorrow a Peaceful Path to Real Reform* at last appeared in print.[12]

The Prototype Described   Howard described and illustrated his prototype with the precision of an inventor. He introduced the concept with chosen quotations from contemporary observers and illustrated it with 'The Three Magnets', one of the most famous of all planning diagrams succinctly summarising his physical, social and economic objectives. Over magnets representing 'Town', 'Country', and his new community, 'Town-Country', he superimposed the advantages and disadvantages of each. Terms such as 'Social Opportunity', 'Lack of Society', 'Gin Palaces', and 'Hands out of Work', have acquired Victorian overtones but do not obscure Howard's overall objective of combining the advantages of both town and country living and eliminating their disadvantages. If he achieved this ideal, the people would, given free choice and mobility, flock to the town-country magnet like iron filings. With mounting enthusiasm he wrote

Town and country *must be married, and out of this joyous union will spring a new hope, a new life, a new civilisation.* It is the purpose of the work to show how a first step can be taken in this direction by the construction of a town-country magnet; and I hope to convince the reader that this is practicable,

THE
THREE MAGNETS.   Nº 1.

TOWN

Closing out of Nature. Social Opportunity.
Isolation of Crowds. Places of Amusement.
Distances from work. High money wages.
High Rents & Prices. Chances of Employment.
Excessive Hours. Army of Unemployed.
Fogs & Droughts. Costly Drainage.
Foul Air. Murky Sky. Well-lit Streets.
Slums & Palaces. Palatial Edifices. Crowded Dwellings.

COUNTRY

Lack of Society. Beauty of Nature.
Hands out of work. Land lying idle.
Trespassers Beware. Wood. Meadow. Forest.
Long Hours. Low Wages. Fresh Air. Low Rents.
Lack of Drainage. Abundance of Water.
Lack of Amusement. Bright Sunshine.
No Public Spirit. Need for Reform.
Deserted Villages.

/THE PEOPLE.
WHERE WILL THEY GO?

TOWN–COUNTRY.

Beauty of Nature. Social Opportunity.
Fields and Parks of Easy Access.
Low Rents. High Wages.
Low Rates. Plenty to do.
Low Prices. No Sweating.
Field for Enterprise. Flow of Capital.
Pure Air and Water. Good Drainage.
Bright Homes & Gardens. No Smoke. No Slums.
Freedom.   Co-operation.

WARD AND CENTRE
GARDEN-CITY

N.B.
A DIAGRAM ONLY.
PLAN MUST DEPEND UPON
SITE SELECTED

SCALE

GARDEN-CITY

AGRICULTURAL LAND 5000 ACRES   POPULATION 32,000
CITY. 1,000 ACRES

GARDEN CITY AND RURAL BELT

DIAGRAM

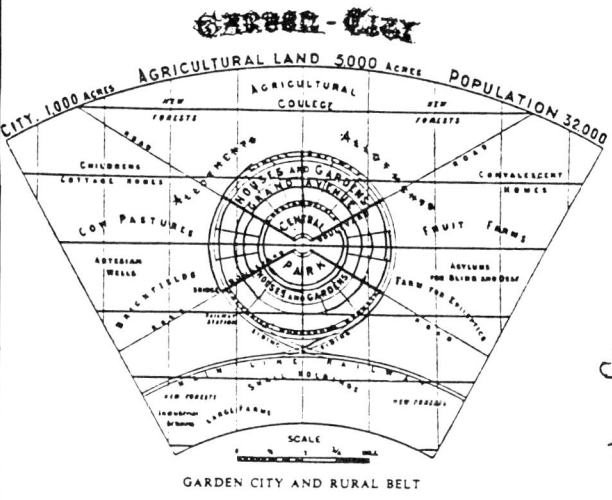

ILLUSTRATING CORRECT PRINCIPLE
OF A CITY'S GROWTH - OPEN COUNTRY
EVER NEAR AT HAND, AND RAPID
COMMUNICATION BETWEEN OFF-SHOOTS.

COUNTRY
GARDEN CITY
POPULATION 32,000
CENTRAL CITY
POPULATION 58,000
CONCORD
POPULATION 32,000
COUNTRY
INTER-MUNICIPAL RAILWAY
HIGH ROAD

4. Diagrams from *Garden Cities of Tomorrow* (1902). (*Top left*) The
Three Magnets: possibly the most famous of Howard's diagrams
summarising the objectives of the movement in a brilliant analogy.
(*Top right*) Ward and Centre: the diagram indicates that Howard
had envisaged formal crescents of housing like those at Bath or in
Regents Park. (*Bottom left*) Garden City and Rural Belt: the idea of
reserving a permanent rural belt from development, yet serving
the new settlement, was one of the most radical ideas. (*Bottom
right*) The Correct Principle of a City's Growth: the diluted social
city cluster inevitably weakened its message.

here and now, and . . .. on principles which are the very soundest . . . from the ethical or the economic standpoint.[13]

He asked his reader to visualise the purchase of a 6,000-acre (2428 ha.) estate, costing £240,000, or £40 per acre, an average for first class rural land.[14] Capital would be raised by a development company which would hold the estate in Trust 'first as a security for the debenture holders, and secondly . . . for the people of Garden City . . . which it is intended to build thereon', and the articles of association would limit the dividend to five per cent, with any surplus covenanted for community benefit. The proposal followed the traditional method of buying cheap land, for development and, through periodic revaluations, raising additional capital to complete the scheme. With the addition of the dividend limitation it was, in fact, five per cent philanthropy writ large. 1,000 acres (404.7 ha.) in the centre would be developed for the town area, in circular form, nearly $\frac{3}{4}$-mile radius. The Garden City would house 30,000 residents, with an additional 2,000 in the surrounding agricultural belt, which was to be preserved permanently from urban development. It would form a productive adjunct to the Garden City providing building materials, from brick earth or stone quarries depending on the geology of the chosen site. Smallholdings and allotments, hospitals and institutions, and facilities for recreation would be included. A main line railway which would feed a circular loop serving the peripheral industrial belt which, with the benefit of extensive use of electricity, would present clean working environment far removed from the dark satanic mills of Coketown.

The circular form of the Garden City would be divided by six broad radial boulevards, each 120 feet wide, into wedge-shaped local wards. Concentric circumferential avenues sub-divided each ward into blocks, with cross roads named after such great literary figures or inventors as Milton and Shakespeare, Kelvin and Edison. Examination of *Tomorrow* reveals comparatively little detail of its built form or about housing provision. The major part of the latter was to be provided in 5,000 plots, with an average width of 20ft by 130ft depth, long narrow slices of land comparable with conventional bye-law terraced development. However, the built area was to be sub-divided into two by a central Grand Avenue, shown flanked by curving sectoral crescents, suggestive of Regents Park, Hove or Bath. The Grand Avenue was to be 420ft wide, forming an internal green belt more than three miles long, an additional 115-acre park, within which would be six school sites, one for each ward, surrounded by playgrounds and gardens, with other sites for churches and local community buildings. Reaching Fifth Avenue, a name immediately suggestive of the prestige develop-ment near Grand Central Station, New York, the character changed from residential on one side, to an immense 'crystal palace', housing all commercial, shopping and exhibition facilities, on the other. Paxton's original Crystal Palace, wonder of the Victorian age at the Hyde Park Exhibition of 1851, had been rebuilt at Sydenham Hill, on the south flank of built-up London, and long remained a popular cultural and exhibition centre. Howard extended the concept to include shops. His annotated copy of *Tomorrow* included photographs of the imposing Galleria Vittore Emmanuele in Milan (1865-67), and William Moseley had proposed a 'Crystal Way', for London, submitted in evidence to the Select Committee on Metropolitan Improvements in 1855.[15] Parallels with many famous arcades and sub-sequently with modern covered shopping centres are readily discernible, particularly that built at Milton Keynes, the last major state new town, in 1980. The crystal palace encircled a 145-acre (58 ha.) Central Park, with six major public buildings at the hub — museum and gallery; hospital; library; theatre; concert hall; and town hall. The overall character had a formality associated with Baroque plans such as Karlsruhe or L'Enfant's brilliant plan for Washington D.C. A network of main radial avenues running from a central square with an imposing public building was also to be found on Christopher Wren's 1666 plan for rebuilding the City of London. Howard sensibly warned that the final layout must

5. The Wren Plan for rebuilding the City of London, 1666. Wren's layout, with its combination of grid and radial roads, helped Unwin to formulate the layout for Letchworth. The resemblance between the area around 'The Exchange' (A) and the centre of Letchworth is striking.

6. The Social City, *Tommorrow* (1898): a group of slumless, smokeless cities, forming a cluster with a total population of 250,000, comparable with Milton Keynes in the 20th century.

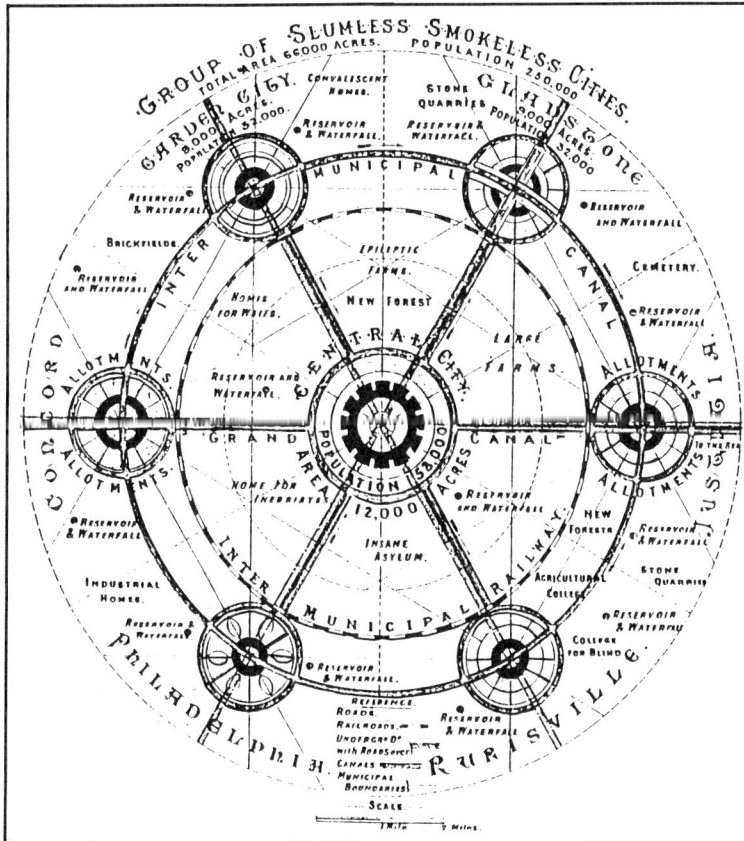

depend upon the site selected. There was little suggestion, however, that the Garden City would consist predominantly of small houses, with little formal urban character.

The individual Garden City was only to be one element in the larger Social City cluster of six Garden Cities,[16] each of 32,000 population, around a larger 'Central City' of 58,000 population, all linked by inter-urban rapid transit and, in the original version, by canal. The federated Social City would have the benefit of a range of services and leisure activities available to a population of 250,000, without the congestion associated with a single town of that size. Howard stated that, as each Garden City approached completion, its development company would float a subsidiary to acquire a new site nearby, thus building up the overall complex. He did not describe the effect of bidding up the cost of the land through this process, but such was his confidence in his overall objective that he acquired the site for Welwyn Garden City as agricultural land a mere 15 years after the commencement of Letchworth.

The remaining chapters dealt with the revenue of the estate and its administration.[17] Howard envisaged that the whole of the revenue would be raised through his scheme of 'rate rents'. Fair rents from the land and property would, he believed, be more than sufficient to pay the interest on the purchase price of the estate, to provide a sinking fund to pay off the principal, to construct and maintain all infrastructure normally provided by public authorities, and, after payment of limited dividends, to provide a large surplus for community purposes which might even provide old age pensions or personal accident or health insurance. Individual leases would include covenants by the landlord to apply the whole of the income to secure the financial objectives stated above. The administration of the City was to be in the hands of a Board of Management, to be elected by the tenants. Howard never entirely formulated a satisfactory control structure and this was perhaps his greatest weakness. He shied away from the political role of the Board, although he provided details of every function of its administrative structure. Whilst industry would be privately financed, and could range from the customary capitalist enterprises to co-operative ventures, shopping together with varied social services were described as 'pro-municipal undertakings', envisaged largely as non-profit making trusts. Howard also felt that housing could constitute such an activity, although he stated that the Company might be overstretched if it attempted this from the outset,[18] thereby anticipating the difficulties encountered in developing Letchworth. Other organisations such as building societies, cooperative societies, or even trade unions might enter the housing field. Finally, Howard reassured his readers that it was to be regarded as neither a Communist nor a Socialist experiment.[19] He was well aware of the many failures which had beset earlier ideal communities, and of the controversy of the emergent Socialist movement, notwithstanding the success of the Fabian 'progressives' in the L.C.C. coalition. He had written his specification for a group of 'slumless, smokeless cities', and had described the prototype Garden City in detail.[20] He made sure that review copies of *Tomorrow: A Peaceful Path to Real Reform* were widely distributed, and in Autumn 1898 he doubtless awaited public reaction with keen anticipation.

Chapter Three

Utopia Limited

Mixed Reviews Quite prophetically Gilbert and Sullivan chose the title *Utopia Limited* for one of their last Savoy Operettas, produced in 1893. Unusually for them, it was a comparative failure. The title was revived for a review heading for Howard's book, the catchpenny phrase aptly evokes the perhaps unlikely combination of an ideal community with a development company. In later years, with Letchworth and subsequently Welwyn underway, Howard and his followers possibly recalled the operetta's subtitle *The Flowers of Progress*, an appropriate encapsulation of the movement's achievements which had won international acclaim. Overall, the press was fair, if critical. *The Times* grandly pronounced 'the details of administration, taxation etc. work out to perfection, the only difficulty is to create such a city, but that is a small matter to Utopians'. Perhaps the unkindest comments came from Fabian News which patronisingly concluded

> His [Howard's] plans would have been in time if they had been submitted to the Romans . . . we have got to make the best of our existing cities, and proposals for creating the new ones are about as useful as would be arrangements for protection against visits from Mr Wells' Martians.[1]

H. G. Wells (1866-1946), who had looked to the future through his vividly written science-fiction, was closely involved with the Fabian Society, and their secretary Edward Pease may have felt it incumbent on himself to make the gratuitous reference. Pease was scarcely complimentary about Howard's literary style. 'The author has read many learned and interesting writers and the extracts . . . are like plums in the unpalatable dough of his Utopian scheming', whilst his illustrations were 'pretty coloured plans, nicely designed with a ruler and compass'. Considering that the prominent Fabians, Sidney Webb and Bernard Shaw, had been close to Howard through the Zetetical Society, this was a patronising dismissal. However, Wells relented sufficiently to become a vice-president of the Garden City Association within two years, whilst Shaw was to remain affectionate, if unable to resist pushing the odd Shavian barb in Howard's direction.

Other reviewers were prepared to take Howard seriously, however. The *Manchester Guardian* felt that 'one or two model cities built under such auspices as to philanthropy and scientific modern ideas, as the Garden City . . . would be inspiring object lessons' whilst *Co-operative News* declared the concept 'a creative outlet for true co-operative enterprise', claiming that a 1d. levy per member per month for three years would purchase the freehold for the First Garden City.[2] Howard felt that its reception demonstrated that his scheme 'touches life at every point',[3] and that its broad potential appeal would stand it in good stead.

The Path Forward Shortly after publication, Howard began to lecture on 'an ideal city made practicable', first in December 1898 at Rectory Road Congregational Church, Stoke Newington, north London, then further afield to Glasgow and Manchester. By June 1899 sufficient interest had been generated to form the Garden City Association, with Fred Bishop of Tunbridge Wells as Chairman, and a barrister, F. W. Steere who was also Secretary of the Land Nationalization Society. The M.P. for Dundee, Sir John Leng, presided at the inaugural meeting held on 21 June 1899. Howard demonstrated an ability to attract public figures respected for their balanced views, which enhanced the credibility of the movement.

The Association's objects were

> To promote the discussion of the projects suggested by Mr Ebenezer Howard in *Tomorrow*, and ultimately to formulate a practicable scheme on the lines of that project . . .[4]

The minimum subscription was set at 1s. 0d. in order to attract a wide membership — perhaps Howard was appealing to the thousands of co-operators for their monthly pennies, whilst 2s. 6d. brought the Association's full literature. Lectures and publicity increased and Howard started the first of a series of thick press books, forming a valuable record of the movement's development, virtually its pre-Letchworth Old Testament. At a lecture in Hindhead, Surrey, Bernard Shaw was present and wrote of 'Ebenezer the Garden City Geyser' [*sic*], concluding that 'I [Shaw] was the man who really understood . . . the geyser being a mere spring of benevolent mud'.[5] Howard marked up a London street guide to aid his recruitment campaign and after three months claimed membership from professionals, industrialists, Members of the L.C.C., and all political parties. Sectional Committees were convened to discuss land tenure, manufacturers and trade, labour, housing and public health, taxation, liquor, traffic, education, smoke abatement, and art. In May 1900 the Association resolved to form a limited company with £50,000 capital to be called Garden City Limited,[6] although two years were to elapse before the Garden City Pioneer Company was floated to search for a suitable site.

Eminent Recruits In 1901 the Association's standing was assisted by the recruitment of two key, but different personalities, both of whom helped to promote the acceptance of Howard's ideas. Howard learned that Ralph Neville, K.C. (1865-1930) had given full support to the Garden City project in an article in *Labour Co-partnership*.[7] He enlisted Neville who was unanimously elected as Chairman within a short period. As a rising barrister his involvement provided tangible evidence that the Association was not lightly to be dismissed as a Utopian band of cranks. In April 1901, Thomas Adams (1870-1940), a young Scots surveyor with experience as a Liberal party agent and an interest in rural regeneration, was appointed Secretary of the Association.[8] His flair for publicity ensured regular reporting of the Association's activities, and he encouraged George Cadbury, one of the many Vice-Presidents of the Association, to host a National Conference, held in Birmingham, at the Y.M.C.A. Hall and in Bournville on 21-22 September 1901.[9] It was the first of many events which spread the propaganda value, both of the Garden City, and of model industrial communities such as Bournville. The Conference represented a benchmark, both for the Garden City movement and the evolution of British Town Planning.

The Bournville Conference and its Successors Neville and Earl Grey were joint Presidents of the Conference, whose objective was

> to consider the experiment of Mr Cadbury in moving their [sic] works to Bournville; the difficulties and advantages which attend the removal of works from large cities to new districts; how local districts . . . can co-operative with such movements . . . so that new towns may be established on land to be purchased for the community.[10]

Raymond Unwin moved the first resolution urging local authorities to make full use of the 1900 amendment to the Housing of the Working Classes Act 1890, and acquire outlying land for decentralised housing, to relieve inner city overcrowding. This would be, he declared, a preliminary step 'until we can realise something in the nature of the Garden City proposal'.[11] There was a pointed contribution from Shaw, in the unlikely role of a St Pancras Borough Councillor, castigating his authority for conniving at illegal overcrowding and underground housing. F. Lee Ackerman (1878-1950), subsequently the leading advocate of Garden Cities in the U.S.A., urged industrial decentralisation to 'areas . . . carefully planned so as to make adequate provision for the industrial and social needs of the people, especially with a view to securing for all time the advantages of town and country life'. Following an observation that the proposal appeared Utopian, Howard emphasised its practicability if a wide range of industries could be attracted. Whilst the problem was of national scale, it should not, he stressed, await a government solution, and he contended that there was, amongst the delegates present, 'sufficient power to start a Garden City'.

The next day there was a morning tour of Bournville and, at the concluding session, Neville emphasised his support on the basis of its financial soundness, and three essential pre-requisites.

1. The purchase, at agricultural prices, of land for a city.
2. The retention for the benefit of the community of the increased value of the land created by the community.
3. The permanent restriction of the area to be covered by buildings.[12]

The proceedings were enlivened by Shaw's imagining the discovery of a gold mine on the site, with the residents buying out the shareholders and retiring to Monte Carlo on the proceeds. Amidst laughter he provided the answer to his rhetorical question:

> The answer is perfectly inevitable: that you must keep the unearned increment in the hands of the trustees . . . . this notion that you are going to found a Garden City in order to make the inhabitants . . . the absolute proprietors would undoubtedly lead to this: if by an accident, owing to the development of industry, it became very valuable, you would enable the inhabitants to retire practically as landowners . . . sell their property . . . If you want to get this experiment through be prepared to meet that objective, and to show that your deed of trust does provide for that contingency.[13]

Shaw was not convinced by Neville's paper and corresponded with him at length after the Conference. As a committed Socialist, he felt that capitalists would circumvent any restrictions on their activities. They were indispensible to the creation of Howard's Garden City, but they could create their own, without his restrictions if they chose; they could afford to take a long view, and bind themselves through the five per cent limitations, but would repudiate it with alacrity once the potential return was worth fighting for. This proved to be the case during the take-over struggle almost sixty years later. Shaw had, almost casually, placed his finger on the flaw of the scheme, which was to prove almost fatal to the survival of Letchworth. For the present, however, doubts were silenced.

Other papers[14] included Howard's 'Garden cities: manufacturers and labour' which gave examples of industrial mobility and a thumbnail description of the project, and two on housing The first, by H Clapham Lander (1869-1954), extolled the merits of co-operative housing — he would later design 'Homesgarth' (Sollershott Hall) co-operative flats at Letchworth. Unwin's 'On the building of houses in the Garden City' will be discussed later for its significance as a design brief for the Letchworth Master Plan.

The Conference attracted extensive publicity — much no doubt in response to Adams's press releases. The December 1901 Annual General Meeting was widely reported under the eye-catching by-line 'a five per cent model township'. Even critical comments could be turned to advantage — in January 1902 John Burns M.P., stated that garden cities would not solve London's housing problems. Adams immediately reiterated the prime objective 'to secure the unearned increment of the land' as being almost more important than providing low rent, low density housing to relieve inner congestion.[15] Early in March 1902, Adams represented the Association at a Manchester Co-operative Housing Conference on the theme of 'Municipal Bournvilles'. W. H. Lever, evidently not to be upstaged by the Cadburys, offered to host a Garden City Association Conference at Port Sunlight the following July. Between December 1901 and July 1902, membership of the Association increased from 520 to 1300.[16] Howard revised his book for republication in a paper-covered shilling (5p) edition, under the title *Garden Cities of Tomorrow*, by which it would become universally known. This marked a change of emphasis from the 'real reform' of the original to the physical entity of the new community, symbolised by Walter Crane's Pre-Raphaelite drawing of a Medieval maiden holding aloft a model of a walled city. The drawing, used subsequently on the cover of the Association's journal *The Garden City*, almost unwittingly anticipated the takeover of the design image for the First Garden City by the Arts and Crafts movement.

The Garden City Pioneer Company   On 2 June 1902, the Association convened a major meeting in London, which resolved to establish the Garden City Pioneer Company, with a working capital of £20,000, duly registered on 6 July 1902.[17] Its Articles of Association required the acquisition of a site on which 'to lay out, construct, manage, and carry on any such Garden City'.

> The estate selected [is] to be carefully planned under the best expert advice, so that as the town grows, factories and workshops, the houses of the people, the parks and open spaces, schools, churches and other public buildings, may be placed in the most convenient position.

Furthermore 'a broad belt of agricultural land around the town' would be placed 'under such restrictive covenants as may secure to the inhabitants the enjoyment for all time the combined advantages of town and country life'. Town Planning in a readily identifiable form had virtually arrived.

   Not unnaturally, Neville became Chairman, Howard, Managing Director, and the Board included Edward Cadbury, T. H. W. Idris, a soft drinks manufacturer, and H. D. Pearsall, a London civil engineer who subsequently made Letchworth his permanent home. Amongst the principal shareholders were George Cadbury, Lever, and Alfred Harmsworth, proprietor of the *Daily Mail*. The £20,000 had been fully subscribed by December 1902. Adams and Howard masterminded the search for a site.

The Search Begins   The process was undertaken systematically. The Board formed a Site Sub-Committee who drew up assessment criteria:

   1. That the estate should consist of from 4,000 to 6,000 acres [1618 2428 ha.] of freehold land in a ring fence.
   2. That it should have on or adjacent to it a main line of railway.
   3. That there should if possible be means of water carriage.
   4. That the estate should be capable of an economical drainage scheme.
   5. That a completely satisfactory water supply should be available.
   6. That it should be near to London or some other large centre of labour.[18]

Lists of major landowners were drawn up by counties and estate agents were contacted.[19] Investigations were conducted on a confidential basis in order to inhibit premature speculation.

   By early October 1902 it was evident that Howard and Adams had favourable opinions of the 6,000-acre (2428 ha.) Chartley Castle estate in Staffordshire, which fulfilled many of the conditions. It was, however, remote from any large towns as Stafford, eight miles away, was still a modest County town. Howard began to investigate the potential for industrial development. By mid-November, the search area had widened and included Althorne on the River Crouch in Essex, Wytham Abbey near Oxford and Ribblesford near Bewdley, Worcestershire. Adams drew up a list for Howard to investigate on 18 November which included 'Letchford Manor, Nr. Hitchin [sic]'. He also contacted Lord Salisbury, through Herbert Warren, the Solicitor to the Association, about an 1800-acre estate at Wallington, Hertfordshire, a few miles east of Baldock.

   By the turn of the year there were conflicting reports. An army engineer, Captain W. Godsal had been severely critical of Chartley, claiming that it possessed no suitable town centre site and that the most convenient areas for industry occupied the best quality agricultural land. Idris had emphasised the importance of canals, and a major route ran close to the site. Howard telegraphed to Unwin, requesting him to meet Adams at Stafford on 11 January 1903. Unwin's report was enthusiastic. His detailed description of the geology reflected his training as a mining engineer and he noted the sources of building stone and brick earth, described a pattern of drainage and the possibilities for water supply. He confirmed that the obvious location for industry at Weston in the south west of the estate would bring environmental conflicts but found that the estate centre around Chartley Hall would make a splendid residential district and a good public park. Adams broadly agreed with him and engaged an estate agent, Evans and Evans of Stafford, with a view to negotiation for a purchase option. It looked as if Chartley might be the final choice.

The Board disagreed, industrialists declared their reluctance to move to Chartley and further sites were considered. Unwin visited Kirklington near Newark upon Trent, and Grendon, north west of Atherstone, Warwickshire. Both were eliminated, although Grendon possessed excellent transport facilities. Howard revisited Stafford at the end of April 1903 and unilaterally negotiated an option to purchase Chartley for £285,000, subject to a further valuation. Within two months, however, Howard tactfully withdrew, informing the agents that 'matters have so advanced with regard to another site that there is no longer any possibility of our re-opening negotiations with regard to Chartley'. The new site was none other than 'Letchford Manor Nr Hitchin'.

... It's Near Hitchin

In one of his less performed plays, *John Bull's Other Island*, Shaw speculates on the possibility of Garden Cities being built in Ireland. The following exchange occurs. 'Have you heard of the Garden City?' 'D'you mane [mean] Heaven?' 'No.' 'It's near Hitchin'. Indeed, the finally selected site was, and Hitchin has scarcely forgiven that fact. It was not until late Spring 1903 that 'Letchford Manor' was examined in detail. Whilst still pressing the case for Chartley, Howard travelled to Hitchin, inspected the site, and discussed matters with Reginald Hine (1883-1949), the well known local solicitor and historian, who was frankly sceptical about the whole exercise. Howard appeared as 'an insignificant little man who . . . did not appear to be worth many shillings'.[20] His cynical opinions were characteristic of the citizens of 'Sleepy Hollow', who led a tranquil and prosperous life in the historic town.

It fell to Herbert Warren, the Pioneer Company's solicitor, who had purchased a country practice at Baldock, an historic coaching settlement on the Great North Road in north Hertfordshire, to examine the potential of the Letchworth land.[21] The estate lay between Hitchin and Baldock, largely to the south of the Great Northern Railway, whose Cambridge branch left the main tracks at Hitchin. A mile south of the railway a connecting road ran between Hitchin and Baldock; centrally placed between the two. The existence of Letchworth was marked by a small Victorian estate cottage with a post office in a Tudor house opposite. The Letchworth Manor estate was only 1,014 acres (410 ha.), much too small by itself and, although Neville was favourably impressed with the site, it was essential to obtain additional land. A much larger area was pieced together by Warren's clerk, James Brown, who was also the Baldock Postmaster. The Roxley Court Estate at Willian, the Pryors' Willian and Baldock Estate, the Cotton-Brownes' Norton and Baldock Estate and the Pyms' Norton and Radwell Estate were the most important acquisitions, with several small inlying parcels, whose omission would seriously have impeded the rational development of the land. Altogether 15 owners were involved and most of the estates were acquired in the name of nominees, and with the assistance of the Hitchin solicitor, William Onslow Times.

Within a few weeks a site of 3,818 acres (1545 ha.) had been assembled at a total cost of £155,587, an average of £40 15s. 0d. per acre, with a few expensive acres near Baldock as

7. The original estates, 1903. Negotiation for the complex mosaic
of estates demanded astute work by Herbert Warren and his Clerk,
James Brown.

high as £101. The purchase was pressed through to enable notice to be given to any tenants
whose leases were to be terminated before Michaelmas. On 24 July, the Pioneer Company
convened its Engineering Committee to discuss obtaining a layout plan. The purchase of
the Letchworth land did not satisfy everybody. George Cadbury wrote to Howard that he
had supposed a site would be obtained at £20 an acre in one of the neglected areas of
England. He had not expected 'a suburb to a thriving town and important junction, such
as Hitchin'. The location was kept secret, although Adams wrote to inform Barry Parker
and Raymond Unwin.[22]

First Garden City Ltd   First Garden City Ltd was registered at Somerset House on
1 September 1903, with an authorised share capital of £300,000.[23] Membership of the Board

EDWARD CADBURY, Esq.

COLONEL F. S. BOWRING.

LORD BRASSEY, K.C.B.

REGINALD R. CORY, Esq.

HENRY B. HARRIS, Esq.

EBENEZER HOWARD, Esq.

FRANKLIN THOMASSON, Esq.

ANEURIN WILLIAMS, Esq.

T. H. W. IDRIS, Esq.

HOWARD D. PEARSALL, Esq.

BOARD OF DIRECTORS
FIRST GARDEN CITY LIMITED.

The Hon. Mr. Justice Neville, whose portrait occupies the central space, has been compelled, by reason of his appointment to be one of his Majesty's Judges, to retire from his position as a Director, and the Chairmanship of the Board of Directors of First Garden City Limited. He still retains his interest in the scheme and will continue to act as Chairman of the Council of the Garden City Association.

8. The Board of Directors of First Garden City Ltd. Ralph Neville, centre, is surrounded by his colleagues, including Ebenezer Howard, immediately to the right.

9a. & b. Old Letchworth. *Above*, Letchworth corner post office, the cottage in which Raymond Unwin and Robert Bennett made the first sketch plan for Letchworth. *Below*, Hall Farm Cottages. The handsome timber-framed and brick Tudor cottages survive but the tall elm trees have long since disappeared.

virtually remained unchanged from the pioneer Company, with the addition of W. H. Lever and H. B. Harris. The first £80,000 capital was sought, divided into £5 ordinary shares with a restricted dividend of five per cent. Investment was to be sporadic and slow: Directors and their friends undertook to find the first £40,000 and although £100,692 had been subscribed at the end of the first year's operation in September 1904, the total had only risen to £181,026 ten years later. With £93,934 mortgaged on the freehold of the land, development was inevitably piecemeal and cautious.

Nevertheless the prospectus confidently proclaimed that the Company would 'not only promote a great social improvement, but provide for those who could afford to wait an investment which will prove a sound one.' It was claimed that the Garden City represented the means of solving both urban overcrowding and rural depopulation. The location '35 miles out of London', was 'admirably adapted for the purpose of industrial and residential development . . . traversed not only by important highways, but . . . by the Great Northern Railway from London to Cambridge. . . [which is] prepared to give the Company facilities for starting the scheme and has consented to erect a temporary station at once.' The major part of the estate would be preserved from development, which would stimulate agriculture and provide a ready market for the existing farmers. The first issue of shares would finance part payment for the land and preliminary work including the layout plan. The Company hoped to issue the remainder of the shares within six months. Howard had not proved a very able Managing Director and, sensing that his uncommercial attitude might inhibit raising capital, the new Company restricted his role to publicity and promotion, lecturing and writing. He was, however, 'to give special attention to the work of the first designing of the town'.[24]

The Unveiling of the Estate 'I think Mr Ebenezer Howard is greatly to be congratulated upon the fact that within five short years his visionary hopes for tomorrow have become the almost fulfilled realisation of today . . . The fortunate community living on this estate will rejoice in the knowledge that the unearned increment which may result from the rents of a population of 30,000 souls will not go to enrich any individual landowner, but will be spent in such a way as will tend to refine the lives, enoble the characters and exalt the minds of all who reside on the estate'.[25] Thus spake Earl Grey, Lord Lieutenant of Northumberland, noble patron of the Garden City movement, as he declared the Letchworth estate open on Friday 9 October 1903. A marquee had been erected behind the fine Tudor farmhouse used as the Letchworth post office, south of the Hitchin-Baldock road. The ceremony took place in the pouring rain. C. B. Purdom (1883-1965), who had joined the association as assistant accountant in November 1902, wrote 'How it did rain! and how thick everyone was covered in mud! My recollection of that day is being soaked and muddy, for many visitors wanted to see as much of the estate as possible, which was very little'.[26] Purdom became seriously ill and spent several months convalescing. One thousand guests took lunch in the marquees and the hardiest later made forays into the undisturbed pastures of the estate. It had also rained two days previously when Ralph Neville, Ebenezer Howard and Thomas Adams had hosted a gathering of 250 representatives of the nation's press. Most appropriately the road leading to the site, now Letchworth cricket ground, was recently named 'Muddy Lane'. The mud was to be an essential part of the Garden City experience at both Letchworth and Welwyn. So little money was available for surfacing the roads that mud remained an abiding memory. F. W. Rogers, pioneer, printer and journalist, summed up the feeling of the earliest residents:

> When you've tramped the Garden City and shuffled round the globe,
> From China to the point where Howard stood.
> You will find, as he then found, that no other slice of ground,
> On this sphere has such a plenteous stock of mud.[27]

Chapter Four

Letchford Manor

A Sense of History   Any green field site in England is bound to have deep historical associations. After the opening of the Letchworth Museum in 1920, Reginald Hine, the Hitchin lawyer and local historian, wrote: 'A praiseworthy and laudable project to build a museum when as yet you have nothing to put in it but yourselves.'[1] Hine's tongue was firmly in cheek and he recognised that even the most liberated residents possessed a sense of history:

> . . . you can see the modernists in garden city, who at one time proposed to found a society for the complete obliteration of the past . . . satisfying their starving souls . . .. by digging for Roman and British remains in their own astonishingly prolific soil.[2]

There was indeed a great deal of history to be discovered, and this began with those hardy mortals who made muddy forays into the rain-soaked garden city site on 9 October 1903, following the map helpfully provided by the *Financial Standard*. The site was divided into three parishes, of which Letchworth, straggling along the sunken lane south of the Hitchin to Baldock road, was the smallest. In the extreme south was Willian, nestling in a hollow at the end of a minor lane leading westward from the Great North Road, whilst in the north Norton stood on a hillside looking eastwards towards Baldock a mile away. The land was subdivided into a dozen farmsteads. Letchworth Hall, the three historic churches, the vernacular cottages and yeoman farmsteads were a modest legacy of a long history of settlement which began with prehistoric encampments along the historic Icknield Way which curved into the site from Willbury Hill, an ancient encampment facing westwards over the Bedford plain.

Some visitors arrived at the Great Northern Railway's (GNR) temporary halt, built out of railway sleepers, located in the middle of nowhere in a cutting a few hundred yards west of the present Letchworth station. They picked their way across a muddy field to what is now Spring Road, which led southwards towards Letchworth corner on the Hitchin to Baldock road. Most preferred to leave the train at Hitchin and took a cab, or climbed briskly along the Cambridge Road. After the ceremonies, the recommended route led down into Old Letchworth, towards Willian, then back to the Baldock Road, eastwards to Pixmore Farm, north along Dunhams Lane, crossing the railway, and along what is now Green Lane to Norton. Here the adventurous pushed onwards to visit Norton Mill and Radwell. They returned along Wilbury Way, skirting the north flank of Norton Common, to Standalone Farm and Willbury Hill with its Roman camp, then back along Icknield Way to the station with its strategically located tea marquee. It was an eight-mile route march.

Topography and Geology   The site of Letchworth is comparatively level, between 200 and 300 ft. above sea level.[3] To the southeast of the estate the Weston Hills rise almost to 500ft., and are part of the Hertfordshire Downs, linking the Chiltern Scarp to the East Anglian heights. Extensive views are commanded by Jack's Hill on the old Great North Road and Lannock Hill on the Weston road. West of the estate the land drops away to Hitchin, 'sleepy hollow'. To the north-west of Letchworth the low lying Bedford Plain stretches away to the distant pine-clad greensand ridge, running from Woburn Park to

10. The route map for opening day. The recommended route took in all the existing tracks and lanes which were later incorporated into Unwin's layout.

Sandy. The outcropping of hard rock at the foot of the hills creates springs at Baldock, which forms the River Ivel, the north-east boundary of the Letchworth estate, with mills at Blackhorse Farm and Nortonbury. The Pix brook through the centre of Letchworth rises near Letchworth Gate and flows northwards, turning west through Norton Common, and north again through Standalone, to join the Hiz, and eventually the Ivel at Henlow Grange.

11. The historic setting; Dury and Andrews' map (1782). The regional setting of Letchworth included the historic market towns of Hitchin and Baldock whilst Willian village was shown as 'Welwin' on this fine 18th-century map.

It formed a marshy area along Rushby Mead, known as Pix Moor, the origin of Pixmore Way, and was later culverted through Howard Park.

Geologically, the local strata are the chalk, gault clay and greensand. The beds are part of the cretaceous system, laid down over a 40-million year period from 110 million years ago on the slowly sinking floor of a shallow sea. The earliest beds, the greensand, 150ft.-thick outcrop near Shefford, lie five miles north-west of Letchworth. The gault clay is 200ft. thick, containing an upper greensand bed with phosphate nodules known as copolite. The latter were dug for fertiliser in the 19th century, whilst the gault clay was extensively worked at Arlesey, three miles north-west of Letchworth, for making the distinctive yellow grey 'Arlesey White' bricks. The chalk marl outcrops near Arlesey and was used for cement manufacture. Above this the Toft lower chalk was worked at Arlesey pit for building stone similar to Totternhoe clunch from Dunstable.

The middle chalk underlies Letchworth and is a compact white rock, with a few flints, 300ft. thick, whilst the upper chalk outcrops at Jack's Hill. At the end of the cretaceous period, an uplift brought the strata above the surface, forming dry land. Later disturbances folded the rock into the gentle concave syncline of the London basin causing the chalk to outcrop as the Chiltern scarp. One million years ago, the Great Ice Age formed glaciers which moved slowly south, depositing accumulated detritus or earth and rock fragments — patches of gravel and boulder clay. There were four distinct periods of glaciation, with deposits from as far afield as the Pennines, Wales and Scandinavia.

Norton Common now forms the least disturbed habitat in the Garden City. Uncultivated and ungrazed areas soon became covered by hawthorn scrub, and larger trees developed to form a natural woodland. Ponds and streams silt as marshland. Near to Icknield Way are old oak, ash, maple trees, hawthorn, blackthorn and elder, with wild clematis and lesser celandines. The elms along Letchworth Lane and around Norton succumbed to Dutch Elm disease in 1974. A plantation of Scots pines at Willbury Hill forms a local landmark, as do the horse-chestnuts by Letchworth Hall. The three old oaks on the northern fringe of Town Square were a decisive factor in its location. The preservation of existing landscape features, the generous planting of new species and extensive gardens have fostered a rich wildlife presence. Moles, shrews and hedgehogs are common, with less frequent sightings of foxes and badgers. Although the black squirrel was native to Norton Common, it has virtually been ousted by its grey compatriot, which reached the district about 1940.

Early Settlement   The area had indeed a long record of settlement.[1] Mesolithic man may have settled beside Lake Hitchin at 7500 B.C., and the Neolithic inhabitants of the district made tracks across the chalk downlands bringing trade and supplies along what was to become Icknield Way, one of the principal pre-Roman routes, leading from the Norfolk coast to Salisbury Plain. Evidence of Neolithic occupation was found in Blackhorse Road when the extension to the industrial estate was laid out in 1960. Five pits, each dug ten feet deep for flint extraction, contained an antler pick, an ox shoulder plate and Neolithic flints including arrowheads and scrapers, with a radio carbon date of 1880 B.C. Late Neolithic beaker pottery of c.1640 B.C. has also been found. In the subsequent Bronze Age the Icknield Way maintained its importance. Willbury Hill was part of an Iron Age hill fort, with only its southern part remaining — two Iron Age brooches have been excavated, together with some pottery and many Roman remains.

According to Caesar, the inhabitants of southern England included the Belgae who had migrated from Belgian Gaul, first to plunder then to settle. Caesar's reconnaissance took place 55-54 B.C., and he brought Cassivellaunus, chief of the Catuvellauni to heel at his capital, Wheathampstead, 15 miles south of Letchworth. The main Roman invasion under Claudius in A.D. 43 had a major impact on Hertfordshire, and the Catuvellauni were a

major obstacle to Roman victory. Verulamium, on the outskirts of the more recent St
Albans, was the major regional city, with Baldock, a settlement of local importance on the
site of a native British community, and an important Roman cemetery was discovered at
Walls Field in 1925. Following the departure of the Romans the area went through turbulent
periods, but the expansion of Mercia brought more permanent settlement — Offa, best
known for his activities on the Welsh marches, built a house at Offley in 758, and consistent
rural settlement of the Letchworth area dates from that period. The Blackhorse Road
excavations of 1960 revealed a Saxon cemetery, with a skeleton buried with the remains of
the spear which killed him still embedded in his shoulder.[5] Further excavations west of
Green Lane in 1988-9 were to reveal more of the significance of the burial ground.

Lecha Weorthig   'Lecha Weorthig', the farm by the rivulet or 'Lecworde' or 'Lycce-
worth', probably began as a small settlement along a wooded track, which still remains
as Letchworth Lane.[6] The Manor, centred on Letchworth Hall, was in existence by the
time of the Domesday survey in 1086.

> William also holds LETCHWORTH from Robert. It answers for 10 hides. Land for 7 ploughs. In
> lordship 2. 9 villagers with a priest have 5 ploughs. 2 Freemen with 1½ hides; 4 cottagers; 1 slave.
> Meadow for ½ a plough; pasture for the livestock; woodland, 100 pigs. Total value £6; when acquired
> £7; before 1066 £8. Godwin of Souberie, a thane of King Edward's, held this manor; he could sell.
> 3 Freemen, his men, had 2 hides and 3 virgates; they could sell.

Robert Gernon, an Essex Baron had his major seat at Stanstead Mountfichet. He fortified
the Letchworth Manor and Church, and the arms of the Montfichets are in the east window.
It was c.1130-35 that St Mary's church was rebuilt; of flint, a two-cell structure with a
nave, the smallest in Hertfordshire, and a lower chancel, no tower, but only a small bell-
turret. Located off Letchworth Lane, its setting still serenely reflects its early remoteness.
   In the reign of Edward I the Manor passed into the possession of the Knights Templar,
received as a gift from Richard de Montfichet, one of the 25 Barons appointed to enforce
the Magna Carta of 1215. The Knights Templar refounded Baldock and prospered until
the dissolution of their Order in 1312, when Letchworth Manor passed to the Knights of St
John of Jerusalem, the Knights Hospitallers. In the reign of Henry VI it was acquired by
Thomas Barrington, Sheriff of Hertford and Essex who held it until the reign of Henry VIII.
The Hanchets bought the estate and the smaller Manor of Nevells, but quickly disposed
of them to Thomas Snagge in 1547. His 11-year-old grandson, also named Thomas, had a
distinguished career — Member of Parliament for Bedfordshire in 1571, Attorney General
for 1577, Speaker of the House of Commons in 1588. His eldest son was knighted by James
I in 1603 and later sold the Manor to Sir Roland Lytton of Knebworth. There is evidence
that Letchworth was neglected in the 16th century, both before and after the Reformation
and in 1552 the Church Commissioners reported of poverty, both in the vestments and plate
of the church, and in the maintenance of the chantry priest, by only 28s. 6d. in tithes.
   The Lyttons embarked upon a comprehensive remodelling of Letchworth Hall, the first
of many which resulted in an amalgam of building from the 15th to the late 20th centuries.
Some portions of 15th-century work remain, but the major surviving early fabric is of 17th-
century date, a notable example of Jacobean architecture, but modest compared with
Knebworth or North Mymms, let alone Hatfield. The porch and galleried great hall
survive, together with several fireplaces. The Lyttons retained the Manor through the
turbulent 17th and 18th centuries with Parliamentary leaders, including John Hampden,
being entertained at the Hall. The Hitchin to Cambridge Road became a turnpike, but
Letchworth remained a remote backwater.
   The Lyttons sold the Manor in 1796 to John Williamson, a Baldock baker. The Hall

12. St Mary's church, based on a drawing by William Ratcliffe, an artist who spent most of his working life in Letchworth.

13. *Letchworth Hall Hotel, c.1923.* Letchworth Hall was immediately converted to an hotel and its grounds were laid out as a golf course. It soon built up a fine reputation as the fleet of cars parked outside shows.

was downgraded to a farmhouse and after Williamson's death in 1830 remained empty until his grandson the Reverend John Alington came to live at the Hall. Alington had a long running feud with his rector and, after having been banned from taking services in the Church, held his own inimitable form of worship in the Hall with congregations of tramps, gypsies and 'all the whores of Hertfordshire', accompanied by music, dancing and with generous helpings of beer and brandy. Alington also embellished the Hall in an overscaled Victorian-Jacobean style, adding the west tower. He died in 1863, characteristically after tossing back a half tumbler of brandy. The estate returned to a quiet oblivion until its purchase by the Garden City Pioneer Company in 1903.

Weligas   Barely half a mile away lay Willian, 'Weligas' or 'Willen', the Manor of the Willows, partly owned by the Manor of Weston at the time of Domesday. After the Conquest it passed to Robert de Pontcardon, whose name is commemorated in the later constructed Punchardon Hall. There were prolonged disputes over the ownership of Willian during the 12th and 13th centuries, until in 1243 the Manor was granted by Henry III to Paul Peyvre for the rent of one sparrow hawk per year. All Saints church, Willian was an ambitious structure. Whilst a 12th-century doorway remains, much of the fabric dates from the 14th, and significantly, 15th centuries, the latter showing evidence of the work of Hitchin masons. The interior contains the remains of the 15th-century rood screen and the chancel seats have poppy head decoration of the same date. The patronage of the living remained with the Manor until 1384, and the first vicar was appointed in 1400. Near to the church was a small timber-framed cottage, the Old Vicarage, which, although much extended in the early 20th century, still gives the character of a medieval clergy house.

The last Peyvre died in 1429 and his daughter married into the Broughton family, who thus inherited the Willian estate. The village passed through a turbulent period during the Reformation and part of the Manor passed to the Crown. In the 17th century the village settled down to prosperity and in 1617 the rector, John Chapman, reported 'there is none in the Parish of Wilyen that be of requisite age, that have not received the Sacrament of the Lord's Supper at Easter last'. The Manor passed into the ownership of the Wilsons who reconstructed Punchardon Hall, a fine late Tudor house, notable for its clustered shafted chimneys. During the Civil War, in 1644, the vicar, Richard Way, a Royalist, was replaced by a Puritan, Isaac Bedford, who was to become a non-conformist minister in 1660. The village grew steadily and prospered. Towards the end of the 17th century, Brays Manor and half of Willian Manor were sold to Sir John Dimsdale, whose family retained ownership until 1867. In the 18th century, Thomas Dimsdale, who was ennobled by the Russian monarchy for the introduction of smallpox inoculation, reunited the two halves of the estate. By 1825 the population of Willian was 269.

After 1867 came Charles Frederick Hancock, a self-made businessman from London, who set about rebuilding Willian as a model estate village. His architect, Owen Jones (1809-74), was better known for his comprehensive analysis of decorative design and his display rooms of exotic decor at the 1851 Great Exhibition. For Hancock he designed distinctive white rendered cottages in short blocks set in generous gardens, with modern drainage. Their overall character anticipated the development of the Garden City 40 years later. Hancock also rebuilt the public house *The Willian Arms* (now *The Fox*) in a well-mannered Italianate style, which looks particularly well when seen across Willian Pond. In 1872 a school was built at a cost of £820 which also served Letchworth, and three years later a Free Library was started. Hancock considerably enlarged Roxley Court which, in 1903, was let to the Dowager Countess of Lindsey. By the time a fête was held in July 1903 to celebrate the marriage of her daughter, Captain Mortimer Hancock had sold a large part

14. Willian Pond. The pond with its views towards *Punchardon Hall* and the village centre remains one of the finest rural amenities on the estate.

of the estate to the Garden City Pioneer Company. In many respects Willian remained a model village within a Garden City after 1903.

Nortun Norton village dates from the Saxon era. In 795 Offa of Mercia granted it to the Monastery of St Alban. The ownership was reiterated in 1007 by Ethelred II defining its boundaries between Wiligbyrig (Wilbury), Stodfald (Stotfold) and Readanwylles

15. In 1908 Norton Common already served as an adventure playground for young explorers.

16. Little has changed in Norton Village except for the intrusion of modern traffic.

I. A group of smokeless, slumless cities. Ebenezer Howard's own cluster diagram for the Social City, pre-1989.

II. 'Harold Gilman's House, Letchworth', by Spencer Gore. No. 100 Wilbury Road was designed by Parker and Unwin.

III. 'Health of the Country — Comfort of the Town': poster issued by First Garden City Ltd., *c.*1925.

IV. First Garden City Heritage Museum, 296 Norton Way South, built in 1907 as Parker and Unwin's Letchworth Offices. *Above*, view of the west elevation. *Below*, the inglenook fireplace in Barry Parker's studio.

(Radwell). The Domesday survey recorded that Norton was 'terra ecclesia sancti albani' on the north edge of 'Heorotfordscir in Bradewatre hundred [Broadwater]'. Most of the land was under the plough with no woodland to support swine and worth £16 per year, 'A priest and a Frenchman with 14 villagers have 7 ploughs. 5 cottagers; 1 slave. 2 mills at 16s; meadow for 2 ploughs; pasture for the livestock.' The Church of St Nicholas was rebuilt in the late 11th century and dedicated in 1119. A Norman chancel arch survives but the church was greatly altered in the 15th century and in the early 19th century. The diocese of St Albans held the village until the dissolution of the monasteries — the monks may not have been just masters as records indicate that the men of Norton joined in the Peasants Revolt of 1381.

Henry VIII granted the Manor to Sir Richard Williams, alias Cromwell, ancestor of Oliver Cromwell. He disposed of it to his bailiff John Bowles of Wallington in 1542. The status of the church fell and in 1586 the examiner of the archdeacon of St Albans found the vicar, Thomas Longley 'ignorant in the Latin tongue and not able to decline a noun substantive or to discern parts of speech. And further to be unable to answer easy questions in the grounds of faith and religion, or to allege aptly any scripture for proof of any article of religion'. His successor, John Pratt, from Great St Bartholomew in London, certainly did not tolerate slackness, for he sent an order of penance to a local farmer George Clarke 'for appointing his servants to work in removing hay from a stack on a Tuesday in Easter week last'.

In the 17th century Norton became a prosperous farming community; Manor Farm, Norton Grange Farm, Paynes Farm, Norton Bury and Standalone Farm gave testimony to the growing wealth of farmers and landowners. In the Civil War, in 1643, a skirmish between Cavaliers and Roundheads near Wilberry Croft, and later in the decade, a case of witchcraft against John Palmer, who was found guilty of contracts with the devil, undoubtedly ruffled the rural calm of the community. In 1662 Norton Manor was acquired by William Pym and remained in his family until 1903. The Enclosure Act of 1796 changed matters. In 1798 Norton's enclosure award was made, and three broad fields were measured and divided up and planted with hedges. Pasture was allocated on the common in proportion to land held in the parish. In the mid-19th century there was a serious outbreak of cholera near to Baldock at Norton end. Many of the cottages in this area were demolished in 1850 when the railway connection was made through from Hitchin to Cambridge, via Royston. Public health matters again caused concern at the turn of the century and it was found that the drinking water in Norton End was 14 per cent sewage, only a few months before the estate was acquired by First Garden City Ltd.

'Rodenhanger' In May 1988 initial trenching for housing construction east of Green Lane, south of Norton, revealed archaeological features excavated between July and November.[7] The area had proved fruitful in 1960 when Blackhorse Road was constructed, and at that time an Anglo-Saxon burial ground had been found. This may have been related to the settlement unearthed in 1988, when traces of 23 cellars cut into the chalk strata were discovered, of which 16 appeared to be related to buildings, arranged in a linear pattern suggesting an east-west street. Few artefacts were found — sherds of pottery, fragments of bone and glass, and a piece of a decorated ring. The settlement was hitherto unknown. However, in a deed issued by Ethelred II in 1007, there was mention of 'Rodenhanger' next to Norton, and it was also mentioned in Domesday Book. The name means 'wooded slope by the road', possibly referring to the Icknield Way a few hundred yards south. Rodenhanger had been given to St Albans Abbey by Offa, along with Norton, but was repossessed by powerful nobles, before eventually being returned to the abbey by Leofric. The boundaries

17. This Saxon, whose skeleton was found in Blackhorse Road, had been speared to death.

18. 'Rodenhanger' excavations, 1988: rescue archaeology in advance of new housing development east of Green Lane.

were confirmed in Ethelred's Charter; only one dwelling seems to have existed in the settlement by that time.

The excavations were assisted by the developers, McLean Homes and Bryant Homes, English Heritage, Letchworth Garden City corporation and Hertfordshire County Council, and were carried out by G. R. Burleigh, K. J. Mathews and A. J. Platell of North Herts Museums Field Archaeology section. A successful public open day was organised before the developers began in earnest.

Museum pieces   Finds of prehistoric objects were a common occurrence from the inception of the Garden City. The Estate Forester, F. J. Cole, was an amateur archaeologist, but many remains were casually treated, and their location poorly recorded. The idea of a museum at Howard Hall was considered, but the first tangible action was the formation of the Garden City Naturalists' Society in April 1908. Its collection of cases of birds was exhibited at *The Skittles* until funds could be raised to start a permanent museum, aided by a legacy of £200. Barry Parker designed the Georgian-style building for a site flanking Town Square, and the ground floor was opened in October 1914. That July W. P. Westell was elected Secretary of the Society, and acted as curator of the Letchworth Museum until his death in 1943. In May 1920 Earl Lytton opened the completed museum, which was taken

19. W. P. Westell and museum visitors, *c*.1932. The curator explains about the Roman settlement nearby at Baldock.

over by the U.D.C. in 1926, with the collection transferred to the Council in 1939. Through Westell's formidable energy the museum was one of the pioneers of a schools' service, carried on to the present in a greatly expanded form. It was not until the postwar period that the Garden City movement was included, and a special exhibition was mounted for the Golden Jubilee of Letchworth in 1953. The creation of the First Garden City Heritage Museum 20 years later allowed the Letchworth Museum, which celebrated its 75th Anniversary in 1989, to concentrate upon the archaeology and natural history of the region, and to display collections of paintings by local artists such as William Ratcliffe, interspersed with travelling exhibitions. A North Herts Archaeological Society was formed in 1960, and its activities were encouraged by the curator of the museum, John Moss (Eccardt) who was responsible for the Blackhorse Road excavations.

What's in a name?   After dropping 'Rurisville' as a name for his ideal settlement, Howard had opted for the clear, but distinctly uncharismatic 'Garden City'. With the acquisition of the Letchworth estate the question of a name became pressing; early publicity emphasised the plain 'Garden City', but its location was often made synonymous with either Hitchin or Baldock. The movement would aspire to develop further 'Garden Cities', so the generic name was not entirely appropriate. A distinctive identity was required. In August 1904, a plebiscite was held amongst the shareholders and residents.[8] The alternatives offered included 'Garden City'; 'Letchworth', both with and without the appendage 'Garden City' in parenthesis; 'Wellworth', a truly awful combination of 'Willian', 'Willbury' and 'Letchworth'; 'Homesworth'; and 'Alseopolis'. This last attempted to rectify the mixed derivation of 'Rurisville' by using pure Ancient Greek. The concept of the Platonic Ideal of a democratic city appealed to supporters of the movement, but 'Alseopolis' had a distinctly mid-western American twang which would have been incongruous in Hertfordshire. Common sense, or at least a common denominator, prevailed and 'Letchworth (Garden City)' was chosen. The appendage quickly disappeared and Letchworth predominated; in 1919 when the second Garden City adopted the name Welwyn Garden City to distinguish it from the nearby historic town of Welwyn many forgot that Letchworth was the precursor.

The naming of streets and districts presented an opportunity to commemorate progress or literary achievement, following Howard's model. However, the visitor will look in vain for 'Boulevard Newton', 'Shakespeare Road', 'Edison Street', or even the prosaic but locationally precise 'Fifth Avenue'. In practice street names followed local historical features,[9] particularly field names from the tithe map, upon which the Hitchin historian Reginald Hine advised, or local worthies, including the lords of the three manors. Thus, the creators of the Garden City generally had to wait a long time for commemoration. Howard himself was the exception — during his lifetime, on 31 May 1905, representatives from the Worshipful Company of Gardeners named the open space east of Norton Way 'Howard Park' in his honour, and the small public hall nearby was named in memory of Howard's first wife Elizabeth, who had died in 1904. Howard Drive and Howard's Wood followed in the 1950s. As first Chairman of the Garden City Association, Ralph Neville Q.C. was commemorated in 1930, 12 years after his death, when the new bridge over the railway was named Neville's Bridge. Thomas Adams, secretary of the Association and subsequently Estate Manager at Letchworth, has not so far been honoured, but his successor, W. H. Gaunt lent his name to Gaunt's Way on the post-1945 Grange Estate. In 1982 two culs-de-sac on the new Fearnhill residential estate north of Sollershott West were named Parker Close and Unwin Close.

Several of the existing names were retained; Dunhams Lane and Green Lane, for example. Letchworth Lane was formalised as a name for the deep sunken historic track leading down from Letchworth corner to Letchworth Hall. Other names related to existing farms — Pixmore was widely used pre-1914, whilst the nearby Jackmans Plantation gave its name to Jackmans Place in 1919, and ultimately the much larger Jackmans Estate. Across Letchworth Gate, the connecting road to the Great North Road opened in 1931; the Lordship and Manor Farm Estates (1970-8) took their names from farms of the former Willian Manor. Field names were particularly popular; Birds Hill and Bowershott, for example; Campers Avenue, Field and Walk derived from Camps Piece, an 1839 field name. Croft Lane was named from a list of Norton land holders after the Enclosure Acts, and Glebe Road from the Glebe Fields. Leys Avenue also used a former field name and 'Leys', shown nearby on early plans, was renamed Gernon Road to avoid confusion. Rushby Mead was also a field name, and its line followed the gentle curve of the wandering bed of the Pix Brook.

The historic location of Letchworth in the Broadwater Hundred, the largest in the county, was marked by the designation of Broadwater Avenue in 1910, originally medievalised as Bradewatre, in succession to the distinctly suburban Acacia Road shown on a 1905 layout plan. Norton had later been hived off into the Cashio Hundred, which was commemorated by Cashio Lane. Icknield Way retained its historic name verbatim, but Wilbury Road to the north of Norton Common, named after Willbury Fort, was mispelled by the omission of the second 'l'. The same in reverse occurred, with the addition of a second 'l' to Allington Lane, named after the colourful Alingtons of Letchworth Hall, whilst in 1972, 'Chapmans' on the Manor Farm Estate, named after the founder of a Norton Charity, became 'Chaomans', through a typing error and the name stuck. Local worthies and families were extensively commemorated: Souberie Avenue after Godwin of Souberie, 11th-century holder of Letchworth Manor; Gernon Road after the Gernons, Norman holders of the Manor; Barrington Road after the lords of the Manor from 1400-1537; and Lytton Avenue, their 17th- and 18th-century successors. Nevells Road, a 1908 substitute for 'Exhibition Road', marked a smaller Manor, whilst Sir Richard Williams, alias Cromwell, who handled the disposal of Norton Manor for Henry VIII, was marked by Cromwell Green and Cromwell Road. The Dimsdales of Willian gave their name to Dimsdale Place off Ridge Avenue, built 1915, but the name disappeared when it was redeveloped as Holmdale barely 50 years later.

Some names were created with no apparent local connection. Eastholm and Westholm, with their Arts and Crafts overtones, were used for early cottage society housing groups, and the names were repeated, with the addition of Midholm, at Hampstead Garden Suburb. Eastcheap and the stillborn Westcheap were brought in to suggest the bustle of a central shopping area, with nearby Commerce Avenue, now Commerce Way, more overt in its mercantile imagery. Broadway was adopted for the main axial road in 1908, succeeding the more prosaic 'Main Avenue'. The first major road to be built, Norton Way with its link southwards along Willian Way, was shown as 'North Road' on some early plans, originating from a proposal to divert the Great North Road, through Baldock, and through the margins of Letchworth town centre. The Garden City had a merciful escape from the chaos which would have ensued had this suggestion been adopted.

Chapter Five

The Layout Plan

The First Designing of the Town   It was now imperative to obtain a layout for the new settlement without delay, and to begin development to convince sceptics that Howard's ideal city was being made practicable.[1] Whilst the land options were awaiting confirmation, little could be done. On 17 July 1903, in reply to Barry Parker, Adams guardedly wrote 'I think we owe it to you and to Mr Unwin to tell you where the First Garden City will be. We have decided on about 4,000 acres near Hitchin . . . please keep the matter absolutely private as there is still the possibility of an accident whilst the legal formalities are incomplete . . . we are not yet taking up the question of expert advice on architectural subjects, and note that when we do we shall have the benefit of your help'. A week later the Pioneer Company convened an Engineering Committee consisting of Howard, H. D. Pearsall and H. B. Harris. It was resolved that H. Howard Humphreys, a Westminster surveyor, should make a preliminary report,[2] with a map to indicate the position of main roads, site for the railway station and sidings to serve the industrial area. Humphreys later took spot levels and prepared a full contour survey. In August, G. R. Strachan was asked to report on sources of water supply: both he and Humphreys recommended the construction of a reservoir in the Weston Hills, three miles to the east. Humphreys advocated the construction of a station $1\frac{3}{4}$ miles west of Baldock, overlooking Norton Common and the shallow valley of the Pix brook, along which he envisaged that the main north-south connecting road, ultimately Norton Way, should run. The sector between the Pix and the railway, a rounded plateau, would provide an ideal site for the town centre and this subsequently influenced Unwin's layout plan. Humphreys felt that factory sites would best be placed to the leeward of the town, notwithstanding Howard's advocacy of improved technology and electricity. It was reported in August that Unwin had twice visited the estate and the Committee asked for his report. Regrettably this does not appear to have survived.

In any case, the Engineering Committee began to have other ideas about architectural advice. Although Unwin's name was discussed in October, no positive decision about his involvement was taken. The Committee consulted the architectural section of the Garden City Association,[3] led by H. Clapham Lander, who recommended Richard Norman Shaw, W. R. Lethaby and Halsey Ricardo. Shaw (1831-1912), the foremost architect of his generation, had in the 1870s popularised the eclectic 'Queen Anne' style through his involvement with the Bedford Park Garden Suburb. Lethaby (1857-1931) had trained in Shaw's office, and became a leader of the Arts and Crafts Movement and a founder of the Art Workers Guild. He was better known as a theorist and teacher than as a practitioner. Ricardo (1854-1928) had had a varied career ranging from Arts and Crafts houses to the Calcutta railway station. In October 1903, Herbert Warren was asked to consult Aston Webb (1849-1930), R.I.B.A. President and one of the leading architects of Edwardian Pomp and Circumstance, best known for the Baroque splendour of the Royal Naval College at Dartmouth and his proposals for The Mall and Victoria Memorial facing Buckingham Palace.[4] Both Webb and Shaw declined further involvement; had they not done so it is an intriguing matter for speculation as to what form the First Garden City might have taken.

On 20 October 1903, Pearsall, Howard and Lever interviewed prospective consultants.

Lethaby and Ricardo requested further clarification of the brief. Lever replied that the Board required the best plan with the least trouble. Pearsall asked them to participate in a limited competition, and also asked for advice on assessment! Parker was then called in and Howard queried him about Unwin's experience as an *engineer*. Pearsall asked how long it would take to prepare a plan: Parker replied that a week to ten days on site would be sufficient and a finished plan could be ready within five weeks. The Committee also suggested a £50 payment to each architect, with a premium of £200 for the best plan. The Board approved these arrangements on 29 October. A third plan, about which records were silent, was prepared by Geoffry Lucas (1872-1947), a Hitchin architect, who had worked for a prominent Arts and Crafts architect before commencing independent practice. His submission for the Garden City plan was prepared in collaboration with Sidney Cranfield. The press also tried to visualise development of the estate by hiring artists to give a bird's eye view of a slice through Howard's circular diagrams. At least one unsolicited entry was submitted to the Garden City Association, whilst A. R. Sennett, an engineer, prepared and published a massive two-volume work on Garden Cities,[5] which included his layout for the Letchworth site on a hexagonal grid resembling a giant honeycomb.

Barry Parker and Raymond Unwin: 'The Artistic . . . and the Practical'   Barry Parker (1867-1947) and Raymond Unwin (1863-1940) were acclaimed pioneers of both Garden City architecture and town planning.[6] Although they settled in the south-east they were born in northern England, which influenced their design philosophy. The Parker and Unwin families were related by marriage, and the ties became stronger when Unwin married Parker's sister in 1893.

Barry Parker was born in Chesterfield in 1867. His father, Robert Parker, prospered as manager of a local bank, and in the 1880s the family moved to Buxton, a fashionable spa, largely developed by the Dukes of Devonshire. In the mid-1880s Barry and his sister Ethel became close friends with their half-cousin Raymond Unwin, then working in Manchester. His enthusiasm for socialism elicited deep suspicion from the Parker *paterfamilias*. Barry Parker was educated at a private art school in Derby, taking examinations in decorative design at the South Kensington College. In 1889 he was articled to G. Faulkner Armitage (1849-1937), a northern Arts and Crafts architect whose richly eclectic designs for country houses included textiles, furniture and even wrought ironwork from the smithy at his Altrincham studio. Such a total approach was characteristic both of the Arts and Crafts Movement and, subsequently, of modernism, and was a technique whereby the realm of design ultimately extended from the individual object to the regional plan, largely through the efforts of Parker and Unwin themselves. Parker acted as Clerk of Works on several of Armitage's buildings. In 1891, however, Robert Parker purchased a large plot in the Park Ring, Buxton's fashionable suburb laid out by Sir Joseph Paxton. Barry Parker designed three houses for his father. The largest, 'Moorlands', completed in 1894, became the family home.

Although Raymond Unwin had been born near Rotherham his formative years were spent in Oxford. His father, a minor businessman, had sold up and took a degree at Balliol College, an unusual undertaking for a middle-aged family man in the 1870s. Unwin was educated at Magdalen College School, and was offered a scholarship to read for Holy Orders. He had become deeply concerned with social issues and consulted Canon Samuel Augustus Barnett (1844-1913), then recruiting students for Toynbee Hall, the first University settlement in East London. On learning that Unwin was more deeply concerned by man's unhappiness than his wickedness, Barnett advised against the Church as a vocation. Over twenty years later Barnett's wife, Henrietta, was to commission Unwin to prepare the layout for Hampstead Garden Suburb. Unwin became a secular evangelist, whose concern for

20. The Parker and Unwin families at Buxton, *c*.1898. Raymond Unwin stands in the back row at the extreme left, and Barry Parker at the extreme right. Parker's parents are seated in the wicker chairs, whilst in front, to the right, sits Ethel Unwin (née Parker) with the young Edward Unwin, already clad in flannel smock and sandals.

social questions drew him towards socialism. The physical entity of Oxford also exerted its influence and the collegiate quadrangles became a model for Unwin's earliest designs for cooperative housing. Lectures by Ruskin and Morris were the most potent formative experience. Many years later Unwin recalled

> One who was privileged to hear the beautiful voice of John Ruskin declaiming against the degradation of *laissez faire* theories of life, to know William Morris and his work . . . could hardly fail to follow after the ideals of a more ordered form of society, and a better planned environment for it, than that which he saw around him in the 'seventies and 'eighties.[7]

In 1884 he returned northwards and became an engineering apprentice at the Staveley Coal and Iron Company, a rapidly expanding combination of mining and iron founding interests based at Barrow Hill, near Chesterfield. In 1885 he moved to Manchester and, as Secretary of the local branch of Morris's Socialist League, wrote long polemical articles for the League's newspaper, *Commonweal*. He spoke on street corners for the League and the Labour

Church. He also became a close friend of the Socialist philosopher Edward Carpenter (1844-1929), who had formed a rural commune at Millthorpe near Sheffield, and whose prescription for the 'simple life' as '. . . healthy, democratic, vegetarian'[8] was taken up by Unwin and later by many of the Garden City pioneers. In 1887 Unwin returned to the Staveley Company as an engineer. His duties included the development of mining townships, and design of schools, chapels and churches. In 1894 he collaborated with Parker over St Andrew's church, Barrow Hill, their first joint work. The year previously, after a long and difficult courtship, with open hostility from Parker's father, he had married Ethel Parker. It was in the early 1890s that, in a letter to his bride-to-be, Unwin wrote that

> Barry seems to think that we might join up someday and set up as architects, he [Parker] doing the artistic part and me [Unwin] the practical . . .'[9]

In 1896, the Unwins moved to the Lodge by the Beeches, outside Chapel-en-le-Frith, Derbyshire, and Raymond Unwin travelled daily by train to Buxton to work with Barry Parker. The partnership lasted until 1914, shortly before Unwin joined the Local Government Board and began a distinguished Civil Service career.

'Concerning the coming revolution in domestic architecture'   The firm's first commissions were a sequence of middle-class houses, influenced by published designs by Voysey and Baillie Scott, and overlaid with the richly eclectic Northern Arts and Crafts style. 'The Shanty', Marple (1895-7); 'Woodcote', Church Stretton (1896-7); 'Greenmoor', Carlisle Road, Buxton (1898-1900); and 'Chetwynd', Northwood, Staffordshire (1899-1902), showed a distinct evolution in design, with progressive simplification of form, growing confidence in handling of interior spaces, and integration of fittings and furnishings into a total domestic environment. Such commissions did not satisfy Unwin's beliefs in the social purpose of the Arts and Crafts movement. In 1895, under Unwin's influence, Parker had sketched 'An Artisan's Living Room', later published in *The Art of Building a Home* (1901), a collection of essays and designs which impressed Ebenezer Howard.[10] In the late 1890s Unwin designed an urban quadrangle of co-operative housing, with shared common rooms and restaurant, anticipating 'Homesgarth' at Letchworth, a project promoted by Howard. He also sketched an idealised village green for a rural co-operative community, with informal groups of housing facing southwards over open countryside — a design which prophesied Westholm Green at Letchworth. Unwin also referred to the elimination of the 'festering suburb', interposed between town and country. He contrasted this with the self-contained organic nature of rural communities:

> The village was the expression of a small corporate life in which all the different units were personally in touch with each other, conscious of and frankly accepting their relations . . . it is this crystallisation of the elements in a village in accordance with a definitely organised life of mutual relations . . . which gives the appearance of being an organic whole, the home of a community, to what would otherwise be a mere conglomeration of buildings . . . We cannot of course put back the hands of time . . . the relationships of feudalism have gone, and democracy has yet to evolve some definite relationships of its own . . . we could, if we really desired it, even now so arrange a new building site . . . that it should have some little of the charm of the old village.[11]

The imagery of the Garden City was close, but theory had outstripped practice. By 1901 only three Parker and Unwin designed working-class cottages had been built. The most significant, a semi-detached pair in Cunnery Road, Church Stretton (1900-01), had roughcast walls, a hipped roof and a central gable, and served as a prototype for the first cottages at New Earswick and Letchworth. Unwin's commitment shone through and even his earliest writing on housing carried the tone of authority. He emerged from provincial obscurity in 1901-2, when his ability to be in the right place at the right time was noteworthy. Autumn 1901-Spring 1902 witnessed publication of *The Art of Building a Home* and *Cottage Plans and*

21. 'The Artisans' sitting room', Barry Parker, 1895. Parker's early sketch was revived, with a £200 price tag, for the *Daily Mail* interview of 18 September 1901, 'Concerning the coming revolution in domestic architecture'.

Common Sense, his appearance at the Garden City Association Conference, and several key lectures. In September 1901, the *Daily Mail* reported his advocacy of democracy and design under the by-line 'Concerning the coming revolution in domestic architecture'. The revolution was closer at hand than even Unwin supposed.

Towards Community Design Early on Unwin conceived the idea of a broad, overall framework to give a sense of form to urban development, and he described this with conviction in his Garden City Conference paper of September 1901. The title 'On the Building of Houses in the Garden City' was used as a peg upon which to hang a 'design brief' which strikingly anticipated the basis of the Letchworth layout. Acceptance of the village as a community ideal; notwithstanding, Unwin warned against over self conscious informality and advocated 'that beauty and orderly design for the creation of which alone power had been given to us', which suggested the formality of a renaissance plan. The layout was to be

> arranged in conformity with the land . . . sites for our civil, religious and recreative public buildings
> . . . have been determined, dominating the city. Wide avenues or roads must be planned to lead off
> from these sites in all directions, so that glimpses of the open country beyond shall be obtained from
> all parts . . . and vistas leading up to the finest buildings shall greet the visitor from every direction
> . . . In the arrangement of the space to be denoted to dwellings . . . a complete acceptance of natural

conditions must be combined with some definite design. No weak compound of town and country, composed of meandering suburban roads, lined with semi-detached villas, set each in a scrap of garden, will ever deserve the name of 'Garden City'.

Through promotion of co-operation the whole would attain still greater value than the sum of its parts:

> splendidly attractive as the Garden City scheme is . . . because it presents to us . . . a clean slate to work upon; it is yet more attractive . . . because it promises to call together a community inspired with some ideal of what their city should be . . . which will have in its life something more worthy to be expressed in its architecture than mere self-centred independence and churlish disregard of others, which have stamped their character on our modern towns.[12]

He was, however, persuaded of the necessity for bye-laws and regulations to control development, possibly through an advisory committee who would as a last resort possess 'an absolute veto on monstrosities'.

In his eight-page statement, Unwin sketched a series of elements — a broad development plan, detailed design standards, aesthetic control exercised by committees — which marked the transition from the Victorian reform tradition to a modern concept of environmental management which underlay town planning. He developed his ideas on detailed housing design more fully through lectures given to the Fabian Society and the workmen's National Housing Council in November 1901. The content was published as Fabian Tract 109, *Cottage Plans and Common Sense* (1902). It set out a rational approach to the housing and hinted at layout techniques which were soon to be used at new Earswick and Letchworth. Unwin balanced individual and communal aspects, and the latter had been tempered by pragmatism, over the utopian provision in earlier designs. He worked from first principles, stressing the necessity of 'shelter, comfort, privacy', defining general criteria and specific standards. Housing had to be freed from the bye-law straitjacket, and sunlight was a key agent, to be 'insisted upon as an absolute essential, second only to air space . . . every house should turn its face to the sun whence come light, sweetness and health'.[13] He defined accommodation standards, 930 sq. ft. for a three-bedroomed house of 18 ft. 9in. frontage. The living room, which included the stairs, was 195 sq. ft., with, in a few cases, a 126 sq. ft. parlour. The principal bedroom was 147 sq. ft., with two of 100 sq. ft. each, and a very small bathroom. These standards were adopted at New Earswick, Letchworth and Hampstead Garden Suburb, finally becoming national statutory requirements, largely through Unwin's advocacy. The plans showed built-in furniture to ensure space for all family activities. The exterior, for the moment, used a closed quadrangle form, whilst at New Earswick and Letchworth the housing was divided into short informal terraces, enlivened by gables and projections, derived from the Church Stretton cottages. In 1902 Parker and Unwin prepared a pilot study for development at Starbeck on the outskirts of Harrogate.[14] The layout included chequerboard siting of semi-detached cottages, with picturesque gables and dormers. Every attempt was made to break away from the unrelieved monotony of the bye-law terrace. The project, entitled 'Cottages near a town', was exhibited at the Northern Artworkers Guild in Manchester in 1903 — an indication of the fusion of the Arts and Crafts and Garden City movements in the emergent discipline of town planning.

At the 1901 Garden City Association Conference, one of the delegates was Benjamin Seebohm Rowntree (1871-1954), the younger son of Joseph Rowntree, the Quaker chocolate manufacturer who had recently moved his factory to the northern outskirts of York. Unwin's meeting with Rowntree resulted in the commission for New Earswick, a valuable testing ground for house layout and design. Unwin's initial layout of 1902 indicated the development of a flat, rather featureless 150-acre (61 ha.) tract a mile north of the Rowntree works, bisected by the Haxby road, running north and south, and bounded on the east by a sluggish meandering river. The layout utilised the Haxby road as a generator for an irregular street

22. Western Terrace, New Earswick. These cottages, developed from those designed for Church Stretton in Shropshire, represented the theme around which complex variant housing plans were woven.

grid. Western Terrace and Poplar Grove were underway in 1902-3, and about 26 cottages had been completed by December 1904 when the Joseph Rowntree Village Trust was formed. The designs were varied until rising building costs forced the adoption of similar forms. In May 1905 Unwin designed a small community hall which could also be used for religious services, which closely matched the (Mrs.) Howard (Memorial) Hall at Letchworth. Joseph Rowntree encouraged tenant participation and, on 30 October 1903, a residents' group met Seebohm Rowntree, Barry Parker and Raymond Unwin, which laid the foundations for the Village Council. Criticism of the cottages included the 'back to front' arrangement of the plans in Poplar Grove, which brought outside closet door into public view, an expedient adopted to enable the main living areas to receive the sunlight. This was generally avoided at Letchworth, but dislike of the open-plan living room with stairs rising directly out of it was to recur there. New Earswick was a valuable testing ground and although only a small part was under way before Unwin prepared the Letchworth layout, its influence was to be seen in the design of the housing neighbourhoods and of early housing groups.

'That the Plan be issued as the Company's Plan'   Preparation of the layout plan was divided between the Buxton Office and Letchworth. Parker and Unwin employed about six assistants and a secretary. Smooth running of the scattered domestic projects and the building of New Earswick required skilled management. Unwin, with his industrial experience, was more effective, but neither he nor Parker was a harsh task master. Robert Bennett (1878-1956), Wilson Bidwell (1877-1954) and Cecil Hignett (1879-1960) achieved successful independence at Letchworth. A more obscure assistant, Bowland Moffat (1880-1925) was clearly impressed by Unwin's 'quickness in grasping new ideas' as 'the Garden City scheme speedily took shape'. He found it

> A unique experience, . . . quite out of the general range of architectural knowledge . . . and valuable in helping one to regard architecture not as appertaining merely to isolated buildings, but as controlling whole towns and masses in one scheme.[16]

Unwin and Bennett set off for Letchworth, lodging in the post office at Letchworth corner, spending days tramping over the estate and their evenings sketching out overlays on Humphreys' survey. The position of the town centre was fixed and a natural feature helped Unwin to clinch matters.

> The three old Oak trees which stood out solitary in the central town area were very helpful in fixing exactly the main axis line . . . I often remember, with a feeling of gratitude to them, the day when . . . they suggested to me the exact position, and Mr Bennett and I were able to begin to lay the plan down on paper'.[17]

The final drawings were completed in Buxton in December 1903, with the Parkers' dining table commandeered for the preparation of a large scale layout.

The Board assembled on 7 January 1904. Ricardo and Unwin had explained their plans to the Engineering Committee shortly before. The final selection was left open until after a site meeting. On 28 January, the Engineering Committee met and compared the layouts with the requirement of the Great Northern Railway. They cautiously recommended acceptance of the Parker and Unwin plan. The Board concurred and instructed Adams

> To write to Mr Unwin for lithograph copies of his plan . . . and request . . . that he modify his plan in accordance with the Railway Company's plan . . . and also to inform him that his plan has been accepted, but only provisionally.[18]

On 11 February 1904 the waiting was over. The Board finally resolved 'that the plan be issued as the Company's Plan'.[19] There would be modifications and compromises, and Unwin would find that Adams had his own ideas on the layout. For the present, however, efforts were directed towards the public launch in April, at a *soiree* in London's Grafton Galleries, where printed copies of the plan were distributed to shareholders and guests.

The three alternative layouts all reflected a formality derived from the geometrical precision of Howard's original diagrams.[20] The Lucas and Cranfield plan was the least satisfactory, basically a grid layout imposed arbitrarily over the undulating landscape, emphasising the division of the site by the railway, with twin factory belts running through the centre of the estate on both sides of the tracks. Norton Common to the north was to be transformed into an elaborate, rather Victorian park with a grand boulevard running southwards to a vast *piazza* at the town centre. The quadrangle arrangement was shown for most of the housing. The Lethaby and Ricardo plan had several questionable elements. The industrial area was located to the north-west of the town, with sidings and a goods yard branching from the main tracks on the town edge. The first impression of the town from the railway approach via Hitchin and from the open terrain north of Willbury Camp would have been industrial, and difficult to screen with planting. The town area was compact, with a clear street grid overlaid with major diagonals. The report stressed that 'the city should not have the appearance of an overgrown village', the antithesis in some respects of Unwin's plan as implemented. A mile-long major axis led eastward from the station, towards the town centre, an impressive concept which would have been seriously weakened by undulating contours. The town centre was to be located on rising ground east of the Pix valley, close to the present location of the Hillshott School. The housing was shown as quadrangles with inner allotments as at Port Sunlight, and impersonal undivided strips of lawn and garden, planted and kept trim '[aiming] at efficiency, lastingness [sic]

23. 'The Company's Plan', April 1904. Although detail, particularly in the outlying housing areas, was modified, this plan endured as the overall layout for the First Garden City.

and ordinary pleasantness rather than . . . picturesqueness'. Adams was clearly impressed by the plan and later wrote that its compactness would have made early development more viable.

Unwin's plan contained a blend of formal and natural elements and fitted the character of the site better than its competitors. At a casual glance, it might seem to be an exercise in formal geometry, with its carefully regulated major and minor axes, but they fitted the contour base with effortless ease. The railway, the existing Wilbury to Norton road, the old Icknield Way and the Hitchin to Baldock road were given their due weight as east-west routes. Existing lanes such as Letchworth Lane, Spring Road and Dunhams Lane already provided fragmentary north-south communication. Unwin also followed Humphreys' recommendation for a north-south main route skirting Norton Common and running west of the Pix valley. This became Norton Way, one of the first major roads to be built. The main axis, now Broadway, ran at an angle from the Hitchin Road, through the area reserved for the Town Square (now J. F. Kennedy Gardens) to intersect the railway at the site reserved for the permanent station, and beyond through The Quadrant, and as a broad walk across Norton Common north of Icknield Way. Either side of Broadway, between Town Square and the station, were broadly parallel sweeping curved roads, recalling the line of Oxford High Street, one of Unwin's favourite historical examples. From Town Square itself minor axes radiated in all directions in a weblike pattern, providing open vistas of countryside from within, and glimpses of the intended group of public buildings in the centre, to visitors approaching the town, fulfilling Unwin's stated objectives from his Bournville paper. Minor roads created a modified grid layout which closely resembled the area surrounding the Exchange on Sir Christopher Wren's plan for rebuilding the City of London, prepared in 1666 after the Great Fire, one of the few major precedents for this type of layout.

Unwin took a justifiable pride in preserving most of the existing trees and hedgerows,[21] and this was highlighted by the more informal treatment of the outlying areas. The Pix valley represented a logical break on the east, although two of the minor axes, Hillshott and Pixmore Way, were thrust beyond. The upper slopes of Pixmore were to be developed for working-class housing, informally grouped as at New Earswick, with a defined neighbourhood centre. Detail was subsequently modified but guiding principles remained. The factory area was zoned as a broad belt north and south of the railway, but was concealed from the town centre by a bluff, for which Unwin designed the Birds Hill/Ridge Road housing scheme. North of Icknield Way the Norton Glebe lands were to be developed as a further neighbourhood, and the field boundaries and hedgerows were incorporated in the modified grid layout. During implementation Unwin reduced the number of roads, in accordance with his principle that the cost saved would justify better housing and larger gardens. This theme became the keynote of *Nothing Gained by Overcrowding*, published in 1912 by the Garden Cities and Town Planning Association. Norton Common was largely preserved in its natural state, but Unwin attempted to bring the major axis of the plan to its borders by a civic design sequence leading over the railway line, through a broad crescent and two interconnecting circuses. The name, The Quadrant, possibly recalling the terrace in Buxton where Parker and Unwin opened their offices, and the axial line are all that remain, for the area was radically replanned to accommodate the 1905 Cheap Cottages Exhibition. Adams felt that the axial line projected across the Common would make a convenient road. Unwin flatly disagreed stating :

> We do not need more than a wide handsome walk . . . A broad grass glade . . . with perhaps a narrow paved way . . . would carry forward the axial line of the town and provide . . . a short cut for pedestrians, the extra distance for vehicle traffic . . . would be very slight.[22]

The area north-west of the town centre contained another proposed neighbourhood centre, but in the early 1930s the plan was radically altered by Parker to create the bold line of the present Bedford Road. Likewise in the south-west there was little development beyond Spring Road until the early 1920s, with the exception of Sollershott West.

The individual elements were largely integrated by Unwin's strong geometrical framework, tempered by his regard for natural features. At a functional level, influenced by German practice, he developed the principles of land use and density zoning, with definition of town centre, commercial and industrial areas, varied residential districts forming the overall town area beyond which agricultural uses, corresponding to a modern green belt, would predominate. The plan thus provided the transition from Howard's diagramatic idealism to modern town planning of the 20th century.

Promoting and Controlling Development   On 23 March 1904 Parker and Unwin were appointed consulting architects to oversee building and to exercise design control. This role brought its frustrations from the beginning. 'Alpha Cottages', the first new houses, constructed by local builders, were of indifferent design, provoking Unwin to write to Howard stressing the importance of high standards. In July 1904 Adams advertised for the appointment of an independent consultant at £200 a year, which attracted 150 applications. Unwin passionately defended his position:

> People are expecting that the Garden City will be a more interesting and beautiful place than an ordinary new building suburb, . . . The general effect . . . may yet be made or marred by the way in which the plan is carried out in detail . . . [and] will depend not only on the detail of the roads, but on the planning of buildings, and their arrangement on the plots, and the treatment of corner sites; . . . it seems to me very important to make suggestions to builders . . .[23]

Although the Directors compiled a shortlist, the Board eventually confirmed the appointment of Parker and Unwin at £200 plus expenses. Subsequently Unwin dealt with matters relating to the layout until his partnership with Parker ended in May 1914. Parker undertook detailed design control, following Unwin's move to Hampstead in May 1906, and remained sole consultant architect to First Garden City Ltd from 1914 to 1943. The degree of control fluctuated according to the magnitude or urgency of the proposed development, and expediency often seemed to triumph. C. B. Purdom, as an accountant in the Estate Office, witnessed the conflicting opinions and the triumph of the 'practical men', anxious lest they deterred potential developers.[24]

Unwin also pressed for the adoption of building regulations. The Hitchin Rural District Council was generally permissive and, whilst experimental methods and materials were unlikely to be vetoed, thus permitting the Cheap Cottages Exhibition of 1905, there was no guarantee of sound construction. Unwin believed that construction and aesthetics were inseparable, as evident from his draft building regulations, dated June 1904.

> *General Suggestions and Instructions Regarding Buildings Other Than Factories on The Garden City Estate*
> The Directors of First Garden City Limited are convinced that the high standard of beauty, which they desire to attain in Garden City, can only result from simple, straightforward buildings and from the use of good and harmonious materials. They desire as far as possible to discourage useless ornamentation, and to secure that buildings shall be suitably designed for their purpose and position.[25]

Unwin included building area standards, building lines and grouping, aspect and prospect, the use of hedges to define boundaries and submission of materials for approval — many of the points earlier included in *Cottage Plans and Common Sense*. The building regulations, published in 1905, were largely successful in practice. Welsh slate, all too reminiscent of byelaw terraces, was vetoed in favour of tiles in all but a few cases. Bricks presented a problem, for Unwin found the local yellow-grey gault Arlesey whites drab, and insisted on their being pebble-dashed or colour washed over. However, the more expensive red facing bricks were permitted, and widely used in the town centre. The regulations included differential zoning of densities and land uses, following German practice. Residential density control was related to building cost, ranging from four per acre for houses costing above £500, to 12 per acre for those below £200. The smallest cottages had to include a living room of 144 sq. ft. Detailed constructional standards, ventilation and drainage were also covered by the regulations. Although most developers complied, Unwin was sometimes overruled. One of the earliest infringers was Halsey Ricardo who defiantly built Elm Tree Cottage, in Letchworth Lane, and an identical house on Hitchin Road, in Arlesey whites, not the red facings shown on the plans. The Building Committee, with Cadbury in the Chair, received Unwin's report but took no action. At the same meeting Unwin also lost out over his objections to a bungalow designed by a local builder, Mr Beckley. These

V. Houses designed by Parker and Unwin. *Above*, The White Cottage (The Den), Croft Lane, 1906, for the artist C. J. Fox. *Below*, 102 Wilbury Road (The Stanley Parker House), 1908-9, for Parker's craftsman brother.

VI. Garden in Common View. A typical garden of a working class cottage, with amenity and recreation area close to the house, vegetable plot and orchard beyond.

VII. 'Hallbarn', The Glade, 1923. Designed by Robert Bennett as his family home, this late example of a classic Garden City house is complemented by a garden layout influenced by Gertrude Jekyll.

VIII. Howard Cottage Society Rushby Mead Housing, 1911-12. Layout by Parker and Unwin with housing groups designed by Parker and Unwin, Bennett and Bidwell and C. M. Crickmer. The peak of achievement in Garden City housing. *Above*, Rushby Mead, north. *Below*, Rushby Mead, south.

skirmishes led Purdom to conclude that 'If the client was sufficiently determined he could put up much what he liked, as the buildings in the town bear witness'.[26] It was an overstatement, for the domestic architecture of Letchworth was one of its strengths, and attained a maturity and homogeneity, aided by good materials and generous tree planting and landscaping.

Garden City in the Making Development of Letchworth was heavily dependent upon infrastructure — public utility services, roads and transport facilities.[27] The estate had the advantage of the railway, but few made up roads apart from the Hitchin to Baldock road, and no public services. Well water and cess pits were unsuitable for town development. Provision of adequate services for a town with an ultimate population of 30,000 was an enormous task for a private company with little capital, the extension of whose borrowing power was dependent upon a rolling programme of development to enhance the value of its basic asset. The Garden City had, above all, emphasised a healthy form of development in contrast to the Victorian industrial city, and there could be no compromise over standards of public health.

In February 1904 G. R. Strachan prepared a water supply scheme. Springs outcropped at Norton Bury Farm on the north of the estate, where the Chiltern chalk gave way to gault and greensand. A 16-inch diameter bore hole was sunk 220 ft. below Baldock Road and tested up to 6,000 gallons per hour, and a 250,000-gallon reservoir was constructed in the Weston Hills above Baldock, which was also served. In 1907 the facilities were duplicated. Between 1905 and 1913 consumption rose from 10 million to 85 million gallons, and the length of water main from five miles in 1905 to 21 miles in 1913. Capacity was increased by a new 500,000-gallon reservoir. Up to September 1912, £26,183 had been spent on the water supply, with £7,000 towards a new bore hole to improve capacity. Strachan also designed the sewerage scheme. A temporary sewage farm, north of the railway in the Bedford Road area, provided a gravitation disposal system until 1923, when the newly created Letchworth Urban District Council built a new treatment plant allied to separate drainage system, off the Stotfold Road. Factories had to undertake to treat noxious waste before passing it into the sewers. Construction of the system proceeded with the roads at a pre-1913 cost of £18,000, providing $15\frac{3}{4}$ miles of sewers. 21 miles had been laid by the F.G.C. Ltd. by 1924.

Many roads on the layout plan were destined to exist only on paper for a long period.[28] In March 1904 the Board resolved to construct 'North Road' (Norton Way South) from the Baldock Road to the Great Northern Railway. Its width was to be 60ft. between fences, with a 16ft. carriageway, flanked by 12ft. greenswards and 10ft. paths.[29] The construction of Station Road, with a 45ft. reservation followed. Varied treatments of the highway reservation, with tree-lined greenswards and pathways, helped to create the Garden City character. In the winter of 1904-5 unemployed labourers from the East End of London dug out roads and sewer trenches. They were housed in a group of sheds erected north of the railway, subsequently used for the 1905 Cheap Cottages Exhibition, as the first primary school and as a temporary factory for Spirella.

'Main Avenue' (Broadway) was completed as far as the multiple junction with Spring Road and the Sollershotts, where one of the first purpose-built traffic roundabouts was constructed and named 'Sollershott Circus'.[30] This was opened with ceremony in 1910, and many of the waiting cars overheated in the summer sun. It was many years before Letchworth drivers became accustomed to the discipline of clockwise circulation. Broadway had a 100ft. reservation, with a 27ft. carriageway and broad but asymmetrical greenswards, the wider one originally intended to accommodate a tramway to Hitchin. The remainder of Broadway to Town Square was made up in the 1920s after long years as an informal

Norton

SMALL HOLDINGS

GARDEN CITY TENANTS LTD

COTTAGE EXHIBITION
SITES

SITE OF
CATTLE MARKET

SITE OF
GOODS YARD

STATION

Letchworth

FIRST · GARDEN · CITY · L^TD
PLAN · OF · PRESENT · DEVELOPMENT

This plan is subject to modification and
must not be taken as the basis of any
contract.

BARRY PARKER & RAYMOND · UNWIN
ARCHITECTS · BUXTON & BALDOCK

DRAWING N? 3654

24. Plan of Present Development, 1906. Many of the roads on the layout plan were destined to remain on paper for many years. The darker tone indicates roads built by Spring 1906, along which housing plots have been laid out.

25. The London unemployed outside 'The Sheds', 1905. Although the road builders departed after a single winter, 'The Sheds' endured to become the Cheap Cottage Exhibition Centre, the first infants' school, and the first factory for Spirella.

cinder path. In order to join the two sections of Norton Way, a major road bridge was constructed in 1913 beneath the railway embankment to join the two sections of Norton Way and supersede the old 'cattle creep', in the early years the only direct route between Norton Common and the town centre. The cost of the new bridge was shared between F.G.C. Ltd., the Great Northern Railway, the Hertfordshire County Council and the Hitchin Rural District Council. At the other end of the scale narrow lightly-paved roads and culs-de-sac were used in residential areas, and the subsequent widespread use of the motor car has caused problems. The length of new roads rose from $5\frac{1}{4}$ miles in 1905, to $11\frac{1}{2}$ in 1913, and 18 in 1924. F.G.C. Ltd constructed the major lengths, but Hitchin RDC made up Green Lane and part of Works Road in 1908. In 1911 the County Council took over substantial lengths for maintenance at public expense, and in 1919 the Letchworth UDC began building estate and other roads.

The Great Northern Railway branch line was an important asset, as indicated by the care to incorporate the railway company's requirements. The halt, provided for the estate opening in 1903, was replaced by a more imposing temporary station in April 1905, under Letchworth's first station master, Richard Thacker. The service included fast Cambridge

BROADWAY

NORTON WAY

SOLLERSHOTT E

BROADWAY NORTH END

LEYS AVENUE

HILLSHOTT

26. Typical road sections showing landscaping. The use of tree-planted grass margins helped to give the impression of *Rus in Urbe* on all Garden City roads.

27a. & b. The Great Northern Railway serves Letchworth. *Above*, the temporary wooden station, 1905-12, which soon became popular with commuters to London and daytrippers to the Garden City. *Below*, the booking hall, opened in 1912. The hall itself was produced to a fine Arts and Crafts design but the platforms in the cutting below used utilitarian standard G.N.R. designs.

to Kings Cross trains which took 50 minutes for the 34-mile journey from Letchworth.[31] A horse omnibus to Hitchin provided connections for the main line to and from the north, and the Midland Railway branch to Bedford. The G.N.R. acquired $24\frac{1}{2}$ acres for a permanent station site to the east, and for a goods yard beyond the Norton Way bridge. Purdom and others criticised the separation of the passenger and goods facilities, but this avoided major severance of the town centre. The permanent station was opened in 1912. The platforms, designed as islands to allow additional lines to be laid, were capped with traditional canopies and fretted valances of the standard G.N.R. pattern, but the Booking Hall, above the cutting, facing Station Place, entered into the spirit of the Arts and Crafts movement with its rich red brickwork, tiled roof and leaded bay windows.

Howard had stressed the necessity to capitalise on technological advance, but gas was given priority over electricity.[32] Construction of the gasworks, initially to produce six million cu. ft. coal gas annually, began early in 1905, south of the railway on Works Road, with sidings for delivery of coking coal. Gasholders and retort houses had to be increased in size almost immediately, with nine miles of mains laid, 1906-7, and an increase in demand from five million cu. ft. to 12 million. By 1912, the demand was 50 million cu. ft. The scattered form of development compared with industrial towns meant, however, that the consumption per mile of mains was much lower, and relatively less profitable. The Company was a subsidiary of F.G.C. Ltd. It initially provided metering and gas stoves free, which boosted domestic demand. Many cottages remained gas lit until the 1940s, and street lighting was by gas, with distinctive Parker and Unwin designed copper lanterns. The First World War boosted demand, which reached 118 million cu. ft. by 1924, with 22 miles of mains.

Electricity supply commenced in 1907,[33] a 500-volt direct current system supplied from a generator in Works Road. Initially, supply was restricted to the industrial area, with half-mile mains and a modest 44,017 units consumed in 1908. In 1909 a cable was run to serve the Picture Palace in Eastcheap, and mains gradually spread to the residential areas. Generating capacity was substantially increased in 1910 and again in 1912. Consumption reached 513,286 units in 1913 from five miles of mains. Expansion was rapid during the First World War and the generators were increased in 1915, 1916 and 1921. The peak wartime demand was reached in 1919 when 8,911,800 units were consumed; by 1924 this had dropped to 3,432,000 units, with 20 miles of mains.

The provision and rapid expansion of infrastructure was itself evidence of the successful implementation of the Garden City project. The plan and public services, however, were both to be regarded as a framework for others to develop. As Howard pragmatically stated

> The Company does not propose to build the town: its aim is to provide a well formed skeleton — and it asks others to clothe that skeleton — the ground plan which has been very carefully prepared, . . . with beautiful houses, churches, public buildings, well designed factories and convenient shops.

Chapter Six

Garden City Homes

'I am Alpha' On 26 November 1903 First Garden City Ltd. convened a Building Committee, concerned with the building of the Garden City, even before the layout plan had been resolved.[1] It made an inauspicious start: one of the directors, H. B. Harris, arranged to obtain details of four-roomed homes costing £135. In January 1904 the Committee agreed to build up to 20 cottages, based on Bournville plans, along Baldock Road adjoining New Farm. The local builders, Picton and Hope, took the lease, and submitted their plans for Unwin's scrutiny in April. Construction of 'Alpha Cottages', a semi-detached pair and a group of four (Nos 22-32 Baldock Road), was soon under way. On 7 July 1904, Miss Elizabeth H. Revill moved into No. 1 'Alpha Cottages', the first resident of a purpose-built house in Letchworth Garden City. Within a few weeks, the Collinses, Janeways, Furmstons, and Watts moved in. The latter family followed their furniture up Hitchin Hill on a railway

28. Alpha Cottages, 1904. Workmen building the first Garden City cottages pause from their labours for the cameraman.

29. 'Laneside' and 'Crabby Corner', 1904. Raymond Unwin lived in 'Laneside' from 1904 to 1906 when he left for Hampstead Garden Suburb. Newly married, Barry Parker moved into 'Crabby Corner' and he added the sleeping tower, at the right, in 1914.

30. Raymond Unwin's sitting room in 'Laneside'. The attributes of the simple life are here in abundance — bare limewashed brickwork and ceiling joists, an exposed brick inglenook fireplace with copper hood, bare boarded floors, a heavy settle, and elegantly proportioned rush-seated Clisset chairs.

dray only to find that the painters had downed tools leaving their new home incomplete. They dossed down on the floor to begin their new life in the Garden City.[2]

That summer a few more pioneers, including Howard, Parker and Unwin moved to the estate. Unwin lodged in Baldock, whilst building his house in Letchworth Lane, half of a semi-detached pair, a joint venture with the Howard Pearsalls. 'Laneside' and 'Crabby Corner' (both now 'Arunside') rejected conventional symmetery for an informal yet subtle composition in which differing internal arrangements were expressed externally. The building read almost as single storey, capped by a dominant roof punctuated by a variety of dormers, and surmounted by tall shafted Yeoman Tudor chimneys. The white roughcast walls received a lively pattern of shadows from the overhanging eaves and projecting bays. It was, in essence, an enlarged version of the grouped cottages of New Earswick, and in simplified form became a prototype for early grouped housing in Letchworth. The house became a centre for community life amongst the pioneers. A somewhat similar group of four houses was built on Norton Way South (now numbered 355-361), for Ebenezer Howard who lived at No. 359 until 1911. These were also designed by Parker and Unwin. Thomas Adams leased Punchardon Hall, Willian, a fine house of 16th-century origin. It was essential, however, to attract more extensive residential and industrial development.

The 1905 Cheap Cottages Exhibition   In the early 1900s the depressed agricultural wages, of 14s. 0d.-16s. 0d. per week, made the provision of sound dwellings on an economic basis virtually impossible. *The County Gentleman* took up the cause of the *£150 cottage*, and in October 1904 its editor, J. St Loe Strachey, wrote of the necessity to demonstrate new constructional techniques. In November 1904 Thomas Adams gained Board approval to provide a site at a peppercorn rent, to be developed for a Cheap Cottages Exhibition, to be opened the following summer.[3]

Although a high population of agricultural workers was never envisaged, Adams grasped the project's publicity value, and the fact that the permanent exhibits would subsequently be available for industrial workers. The chosen site, predominantly the area between Icknield Way and the railway, disrupted Unwin's objective of extending the axial line of the town centre. Norton Common, to the north, represented an appropriately rural setting, with one plot backing onto its eastern flank, and several more along Wilbury Road. A small estate of 22 houses was developed in Birds Hill, close to the industrial area, whilst First Garden City Ltd. entered their 'Ploughmen's Cottages' in Paddock Close, off Norton Way South. 119 dwellings were built, with the main emphasis on the detached cottage, rather than the group. A £100 prize was offered for the best £150 cottage with living room, scullery and three bedrooms. Other classes involved pairs of five-roomed cottages, groups of three or four, and the best cottage for £35 per room. Special prizes were also offered for the 'Cheapest Cottage', the 'Best Wooden Cottage' and the 'Best Concrete Cottage'. Unwin was warned against over-zealous control, for the Board ruled that 'Architects not to be interfered with as regards details or matters of taste by [the] consulting architect'.

The Exhibition was opened by the Duke of Devonshire on 25 July 1905. The event was a great public success with 60,000 visitors, many travelling by the 3s. 5d. cheap day returns from King's Cross. Near the station the sheds, built as a hostel for unemployed labourers and roadbuilders from London, were adapted as a restaurant and gallery. Many exhibits were furnished by London stores and incorporated novel kitchen gadgetry and patent folding baths. Press verdicts were mixed, with a suspicion that the cottages were better suited to middle-class 'week-enders' than to agricultural workers. Purdom, writing in 1913, was dismissive:

> there can be no question that the exhibition, while it gave the place a tremendous advertisement, did no little harm. It set a rage for cheapness from which Garden City has hardly yet recovered, it

gave the town the character of a village of tiny weekend cottages not very well built: its curiosities of planning, construction and material, which had nothing in common with the objects of the town, gave the place a name for cranky buildings . . . It will be a happy day for Letchworth when the exhibition is forgotten and all its consequences are destroyed.[4]

Although his interest in building technology was aroused, Unwin's verdict was also reserved:

Many a £150 cottage is an excessively dear cottage. It is necessary to emphasise this because it is one of the curses of our times that this idea of cheapness . . . acquires an artificial and altogether misleading meaning . . . we may be quite certain that we are on the wrong track . . . if we do not build them [cottages] well.[5]

Most of the exhibits have survived the major part of their 99-year span, some are 'listed' buildings, and all are located within the Letchworth Conservation Area. In several, traditional appearance concealed experimental construction, and a few were truly revolutionary. Exhibition Road (Nevells Road) was the centre of the Exhibition. Nos. 206/208,

31. Garden City in the making — market gardening near the Cheap Cottages Exhibition. This view emphasises the relative isolation of early groups of houses and the raw appearance of the streets before the newly-planted trees matured.

built by Bournville Village Trust, were inferior to the standard prevailing in that pioneer model village. No. 212 'The Stone House', built of concrete blocks, with a 'Canadian Style' projecting porch, was designed by Robert Bennett and Wilson Bidwell, former assistants of Parker and Unwin. No. 216, by the Barrow Construction Company, used a pre-fabricated system of grooved oak posts and concrete slabs, exposed externally but later rendered over to inhibit damp penetration. Nos. 218/220 Nevell's Road, set diagonally across the corner into Cross Street, and designed by Barrett and Driver, were economy versions of C. F. A. Voysey's design idiom, with their roughcast buttresses and chimneys. No. 4 Cross Street, designed by Gilbert Fraser for the Concrete Machinery Co. of Liverpool, won the prize for the Best Concrete Cottage. Its shell was built from blocks made on site by a

32. No. 4 Cross Street. The Concrete Machinery Company won first prize in 1905 for the best concrete cottage for this entry, built of concrete blocks manufactured on site.

33. No. 221 Icknield Way. Bennett and Bidwell, newly independent from Parker and Unwin, designed this charming black-boarded timber cottage which was awarded second prize in its class in 1905.

portable machine with a capacity of 150 per day. Nos. 13, 15/17, on the opposite side, were exhibited by Potter and Co. and won the First Prize in Class II. Although conventional in appearance, the walls were steel framed, with roughcast over expanded metal lathing.

The exhibits on Icknield Way ranged from rather basic structures such as No. 211, by John McManus, Iron Building Manufacturer, to No. 245, designed by Oswald Milne, a vernacular revival cottage with overhanging jettied front. No. 217, a solidly built roughcast cottage, won First Prize in Class I. It was designed by Percy Houfton, a Chesterfield architect responsible for progressive colliery villages in Derbyshire and Yorkshire. No. 221, at the junction with The Quadrant, won Second Prize; it was a timber framed cottage, designed by Bennett and Bidwell. The grouped cottage Prize was awarded to the 'Ploughmen's Cottages' at Paddock Close, designed by Geoffry Lucas.

Nos. 7/7A Norton Way North, 'Elmwood Cottages', were designed by M. H. Baillie Scott. Their cost of £420 eliminated them from serious consideration; Scott considered such materialism irrelevant and wrote in the Exhibition Catalogue that: 'the Cottage should be the dream come true, the result of infinite pains, and whether it pays five or six per cent is quite a secondary matter'. This design, 'new-old', consciously based on the revival of the medieval hall house, with genuine timber framed construction in part, received wide acclaim. The sophisticated open-plan interior had a single living space divided by a handsome elm staircase, and a recessed inglenook fireplace containing the kitchen range. The roof originally swept low over a scullery, set rather impractically a few steps below the main ground floor level, later raised, spoiling the exterior by flat-roofed extensions. Eastholm Green at the junction of Norton Road and

34. 'Elmwood Cottages', Nos. 7/7A Norton Way North, by M. H. Baillie Scott. This entry proved one of the most influential in creating the vernacular imagery of the Garden City cottage.

35a. & b. Prefabricated cottages, 1905. The Round House, No. 140 Wilbury Road (*above*), was possibly the most radical of the 1905 Cheap Cottages. It survived until 1987. No. 158 Wilbury Road (*below*) has survived for 85 years. It was built to an elegant and modern design by J. A. Brodie, with a hint of Art Nouveau in the detailing.

36. The panel system of No. 158 Wilbury Road. *Top*: withdrawing the panels from the moulds; *centre*: trial erection; *bottom*: loaded on railway wagons for the journey to Letchworth. J. M. Brodie's system does not appear to have been used for any other cottages apart from the Letchworth entry.

Wilbury Road was developed by Garden City Tenants, a branch of the Co-Partnership Tenants Housing Society. The plain grouped houses were designed by Parker and Unwin. Wilbury Road led westwards, marking the northern limits of the infant Garden City. Nos. 150-156, which used mansard roofs to cut down external walls, were designed by W. Clough of Ringwood, Hampshire, and supervised on site by his young nephew Clough Williams-Ellis. Further west, No. 126, an almost puritanically simple cottage designed by Randall Wells won First Prize in Class IV, and later became Purdom's home.

The two most revolutionary exhibits, Nos. 140 and 158 Wilbury Road, both pioneered prefabricated reinforced concrete technology. No. 140 'The Round House', designed by Hesketh and Stokes for Cubitts, the London contractors, was the most radical of the exhibits. It had a 16-sided plan, made up from heavy panels fixed to a prefabricated frame. Its form

37a. & b. Housing designs by C. M. Crickmer. *Above*, Nos. 7-17 Lytton Avenue, from the 1907 Exhibition. These neatly designed cottages with their tile-hung projecting gable ends became a prototype for local authority housing a few years later. *Below*, Nos. 34-6 South View, 1912. In order to produce this design, widely used in subsequent years, Crickmer ingeniously combined two of his prize-winning detached cottages from the Gidea Park housing exhibition of 1911.

was derived from a logical consideration of the material and methods of construction. It was claimed that work above foundation level could be completed in three days. The rooms were awkwardly shaped, like wedges of cheese. The cottage survived in an overgrown and deteriorated state, although still inhabited, until 1987 when, regrettably, the panels disintegrated whilst the building was being taken apart for re-erection at the Standalone Farm Centre.

No. 158 Wilbury Road was designed by John Brodie, City Engineer of Liverpool, who pioneered a prefabricated reinforced concrete system for model flats.[6] The panels were cast in a quarry near Liverpool, complete with joinery, with clinker ash from the city incinerator used in the mix. The constructional principle was that of a dovetailed box, and the 15 panels were dispatched to Letchworth on railway wagons. Visually the cottage still surprises with its smooth white walls and flat roof — the opposite of the Arts and Crafts picturesqueness of many of the exhibits. It appears remarkably modern, but the sinuous curve of the roof parapet, the boldly projecting cornice with its mildly classical brackets, a classical string course masking the joint between ground and first floor panels and the small paned windows, all confirm the early 20th-century date.

The novelty of the 1905 Cheap Cottages Exhibition was followed up at Letchworth and elsewhere. A second exhibition was held at Letchworth in 1907, under the auspices of the National Housing Reform Council.[7] The urban cottage area had a layout by Unwin, and included parts of Lytton Avenue, Gernon Road and Pixmore Way, and provided a demonstration of town planning. A site for rural homesteads to the south of the Baldock Road has long since been encroached upon by ribbon development. The overall design standard in 1907 was higher than in 1905, and the most awards were won by Courtenay Crickmer (1879-1971), a London architect who had moved to Letchworth. The Exhibition had become one amongst many and failed to attract large numbers of visitors. Shortly afterwards, the *Daily Mail* began to champion house design, and in 1910 sponsored the first Ideal Home Exhibition, and subsequently in 1921 a model village at Welwyn Garden City, Howard's second creation.

Co-Partnership Cottages   Housing Societies, registered under the Industrial and Provident Societies Act, 1893, carried on the tradition of 'five per cent philanthropy' and at the turn of the century began to develop suburban sites in London. Tenants were required to become investors which meant that they were skilled artisans rather than labourers. Ealing Tenants began development at Brentham in 1902, and contributed to the 1905 Cheap Cottages Exhibition. They were affiliated to a national body, the Co-Partnership Tenants Housing Society, chaired by Henry Vivian, M.P. (1886-1930), which, through Garden City Tenants Ltd. and Hampstead Tenants Ltd., played a key role in the housing development of both Letchworth and Hampstead Garden Suburb.[8]

Each of their Letchworth estates marked a distinct advance in the techniques of site layout and housing design. The first Eastholm Green (1905-6) was partly completed for the Cheap Cottages Exhibition, and showed little attempt to group the individual units into a corporate entity. Westholm Green, developed in 1906 on a site north of Wilbury Road, closely followed Unwin's idealised rural layout plan, published in *The Art of Building a Home* (1901),[9] which fitted the topography well, with an open-ended green commanding views of Norton Common, flanked on three sides by groups of two, four and five cottages, whose multiple gables and dormers and steeply pitched tiled roofs were similar to those in Station Road, New Earswick. Block ends were emphasised with projecting parlour cottages, with dominant gables derived from Unwin's early design for his own cottage at Chapel-en-le-Frith (1898-9). With 'Westholm'·and its successor, 'Birds Hill' (1906), there is an impression of a kit of parts, capable of almost infinite variety of assembly to fit particular site conditions

38a. & b. Garden City tenants' housing designed by Parker and Unwin. *Above*, 'Westholm', 1906. The village green layout was based on Unwin's 1899 diagram, published in *The Art of Building a Home* (1901). *Below*, Birds Hill, 1907. These designs with their multiple gables and dormers proved to be too expensive for rental to labourers.

39a. & b. The evolution of housing layout by Parker and Unwin. *Above*, Birds Hill, 1906. This estate layout incorporates a village green and a cul-de-sac, now very restricted for motor access, together with a communal playground and a planted buffer zone to separate housing from the adjoining factory estate. *Below*, 'Pixmore', 1907-9. This estate reached the scale of a self-contained neighbourhood, including a community institute, now the Hillshott School.

and orientation. 'Birds Hill' marked an important stage in the evolution of site planning, with a cul-de-sac to enable development in depth, in addition to a village green, a playground, and retention of a tree-planted 'buffer zone' to separate the housing from the adjoining industrial area. The commanding site above 'Birds Hill' and the rising curve of Ridge Road presented the opportunity to develop an effective sequence of street pictures, reflecting Unwin's enthusiasm for informal groupings advocated by the Austrian urban planner Camillo Sitte (1843-1903), whose book, *Town Planning According to Artistic Principles*, he had avidly read shortly after completing the Letchworth layout plan. Unwin was fast becoming accepted as an international authority on housing, and his Letchworth estates were featured in his 1906 R.I.B.A. International Congress Paper, 'The Planning of the Residential Districts of Towns'.[10]

The house plans were divided into parlour and non-parlour types, an important distinction in local authority housing for many years. Unwin generally favoured a large living room designed to eliminate the desire for aping social convention. Once the parlour had made its appearance, however, it remained an enduring status symbol distinguishing artisan from labourer. Rents ranged from 4s. 6d. ($22\frac{1}{2}$ p) per week for a two-bedroom non-parlour cottage to 8s. 5d. (42p) for three- and four-bedroom parlour cottages. These levels provoked a fierce controversy in *The Garden City* magazine, where it was claimed, with some justice, that the cottages were extravagantly constructed and excluded the poorer labourers, who rented rooms in the back streets of Hitchin and Baldock and walked to work. Unwin refuted his critics, both on the detailed costings, and by claiming that a wage rise of 9d. (4p) per week for the unskilled labourer would solve the difficulty:

> for if Garden City stands for anything surely it stands for this: a decent home and garden for every family that come here. That is the irreducible minimum. Let that go and we fail utterly. And if we succeed utterly what then? A beautiful home in a beautiful garden and a beautiful city for all.[11]

He was wise enough to prepare designs for simpler, cheaper cottages and to set out the pre-requisites for economy in design:

> If cottages are to be built cheaply they must be built in groups; thorough organisation of the building operations must be secured; a sufficient number must be built . . . to effect the great economies which arise . . . and a thoroughly economical plan . . . must be adopted. It is very important to standardise the various parts . . . Too much care cannot be taken in designing . . . doors . . . and windows, so that they may be pleasantly proportioned . . . Where groups of cottages must be kept absolutely simple, good results will depend largely on the arrangement of them. Here as in so many cases our forefathers have shown us the way . . . they knew full well that a degree of simplicity in design which would be wearisome if spread out in a long straight row may be extremely pleasant when the buildings are grouped round a square of green.[12]

A few of the simpler cottages were included in the ambitious Pixmore Estate, which Garden City Tenants built 1907-9, a pioneer neighbourhood unit complete with institute and recreational facilities. The site area was 16.35 acres (6.6 ha.), and the 164 houses, mainly in groups of four, gave an overall density of 10 per acre, 12 per acre net (30 per ha.), excluding roads, the institute and recreation space. The layout was intended to minimise road provision, a principle which Unwin took to its ultimate limits in *Nothing Gained by Overcrowding*, his brilliant critique of 'bye-law' development with its extravagant area of paved streets and back alleys.[13] At Pixmore, Unwin was almost too successful in serving the centre of the block by a single narrow access road, latterly chocked with parked cars, an unthinkable consideration in housing layout at the time of construction.

By 1907 Letchworth had begun to develop a significant industrial base, and there was a requirement for construction of a larger number of economical cottages. There was the possibility that industrialists might provide housing. For example, in 1907 J. M. Dent, the publishers, built 24 cottages for their key workers in Temple Gardens off Green Lane, but there was a notable absence of industrialists willing to provide housing as a matter of course, as had Cadbury and Lever at their own model communities. The time seemed ripe for First Garden City Limited to take a more direct role in housing provision. In 1907 Letchworth Cottages and Buildings Ltd. was formed as its subsidiary, and had constructed nearly 200 cottages by 1911, many costing under £150 each, with simple but visually excellent designs by Parker, following the principles for standardisation set out by Unwin. The Common View groups reduced brickwork to a minimum and brought the roof down to incorporate the bedroom windows in broad catslide dormers. A simple tiled porch identified the individual house within the block. The selfconscious picturesqueness of some of the early designs was avoided and the recreation of the vernacular cottage, advocated by the Arts and Crafts movement, was attained.

The original local authority for the Letchworth Estate, the Hitchin Rural District Council, possessed the power to raise loans from the Public Works Loan Board on the full cost of cottage building, with repayment spread over 60-80 years. This compared more than favourably with cottage societies, which could raise only two thirds of the building cost, with a maximum 40 years' repayment. Letchworth had little voice in local government, even after March 1908 when it became a Parish Council, a non-executive body, although through its urging in 1912 Hitchin R.D.C. at last built four cottages on Icknield Way. This was followed by more extensive construction under the wartime conditions of 1915-16.

The Howard Cottage Society   In August 1911 the Howard Cottage Society was formed to take advantage of more generous loan terms offered to housing societies under the 1909 Housing and Town Planning Act.[14] Among its shareholders was George Bernard Shaw, who assisted the work of several cottage societies. Ebenezer Howard, after whom the Society was named, was a Director, and the Chairman, Howard Pearsall, had long been interested in working-class housing. The office was in Pearsall's home, 'Glaed Hame', and in 1912 Frederic Osborn (1885-1978) was recruited as Executive Secretary.

Development of housing along Rushby Mead, facing Howard Park, began in 1911. The overall layout by Unwin was a masterpiece of informal design, through which he reworked his early admiration of village groupings in terms of his more recently acquired analytical approach. The road followed the old course of the Pix brook, and great care was taken to preserve existing hedges, and so to vary the siting of the housing to avoid monotony. Several architects undertook detailed design but their work blended together as a consistent whole without false individuality. Southwards from Birds Hill, the first two blocks were set back from the road behind long gardens, with a short return block at right angles followed by a frontage block. These were designed by Bennett and Bidwell who were subsequently responsible for many excellent Howard Cottage Society designs. Rushby Walk was a pioneer cul-de-sac, flanked by two blocks by Parker and Unwin and two by Crickmer. The southern section of Rushby Mead incorporated an 'L' form space, giving an effective focus to the view from Hillshott. Materials throughout were restricted to roughcast brick walls, with rich red tiled roofs punctuated by gables and dormers, occasionally with an infill of black weatherboarding or tilehanging. Features such as string courses, lightly curved dripmoulds or the boldly projecting timber cornices of the bay windows were indicative of the great care taken over detail. The original colour scheme of cream roughcast and green woodwork has been retained creating an overall effect of harmony, beauty, and an environmental quality not often subsequently achieved in mass housing.

The Society built further cottages in Ridge Road and Broughton Hill and by the outbreak of the First World War had completed 300 at costs ranging from £150 to £220, and rents from 5s. 6d. to 8s. 6d. There were two main types, both three bedroomed, but some incorporated a small parlour in addition to living room and scullery. All included a fixed

40. Rushby Mead, a landmark in housing design, 1911-12. This photograph shows housing groups by Bennett and Bidwell.

bath and were gaslit. Osborn became a man of all trades, consulting Howard, checking tenders and accounts for new cottages, allocating tenancies and collecting rents, becoming almost a social worker, sorting out complaints, and making suggestions for design improvements to the architects. Howard provided Osborn with detailed grumbles to sort out!

> Now one of the Ewarts men . . . who went into one in the Rushby Mead complains bitterly of his garden being overrun by dogs and I do hope something . . . will be done and done speedily to protect him. He and his son are very fond of gardening.

> Wood complains that his sitting room is draughty because of the stairs going straight out of it. He would very much like a door. Also he would like a dresser. Are they not absolutely reasonable complaints? I think they are.

The generous gardens were widely appreciated and Osborn organised a competition in which a week rent-free was offered as the prize for the best garden on each estate. Letchworth gardens soon became famous for their productivity.

The fame of the Howard Cottage Society spread, with correspondence from Canada and the U.S.A. and from Pavel Mizhuev, the Russian expert on Garden Cities. The outbreak of war in 1914, and the subsequent influx of Belgian refugees made it imperative to continue development. A new 100-cottage estate to the west of the town centre, around Campers Road, was soon nicknamed 'Little Belgium'. Osborn worked almost single-handed to supervise construction, using the pre-war designs, but at times he even designed new cottages himself when site conditions demanded.

Co-operative Living   What had become of the original vision of quadrangles of co-operative housing, advocated by Unwin and Howard?[15] With their emphasis on communal facilities these would have provided a radically different form of working-class housing. Howard remained loyal to the concept. In 1906 his 'suggestion' for co-operative housing was published both in *The Garden City* and the *Daily Mail*. He leased a four-acre site near the corner of Spring Road and Sollershott East, and raised finance by £10 mortgage debentures with 4 per cent interest. He had raised about £5,000 when the development, 'Homesgarth', was opened in a partly completed state in 1911. The scheme, designed by H. Clapham Lander, aimed at providing co-operative living for professional people. The 32 dwellings, set out around a generous quadrangle, were service flats with meals provided

41. 'Homesgarth' (Sollershott Hall), promoted by Howard in 1911. 'Homesgarth' originally provided communal facilities, including a residents' club, in the three-storey central block which served a partly-completed rear quadrangle of flats.

from a central kitchen, available either in the individual apartments or the communal dining room. The most prominent element was the three-storey front block containing the communal facilities, facing Sollershott Circus, dominated by a central gabled portion flanked by towers capped with copper roofs of a concave profile with elongated finials, an elegant detail, suggesting the influence of Voysey. The flats behind, linked by a glazed canopy, were of a more domestic scale. Regrettably the frontage was later cluttered by outbuildings and garages, and the quadrangle form was broken by new three-storey flat-roofed flats added in the 1960s. The communal facilities were gradually closed and converted into additional flats. In the 1920s the name was changed to 'Sollershott Hall'. Howard had remained resident until 1920 when he left for Welwyn Garden City. He had exactly fitted his own description of the kind of person for whom he had planned the project: 'One of those numerous folk of the middle-class who have a hard struggle for existence on a meagre income . . . those who require domestic help, but can very ill afford it'. In conjunction with the Howard Cottage Society, Miss Pym promoted the development of co-operative flats for single business women. Courtenay Crickmer designed the first phase of Meadow Way Green, set-back from Pixmore Way. Construction was initially delayed by discussions with the Public Works Loan Board as to whether the housing fell within the definition of 'working-class', with the Society insisting that the income limit should be £160 per annum, much higher than the prevailing average. The first phase opened in 1916, and a second block, south of Pixmore Way, was completed in 1925.

A Who's Who of Domestic Architecture   The residential areas of Letchworth represented a noteworthy achievement, widely recognised as a clear demonstration of the success of new density and layout standards.[16] The aesthetic control process worked well, curbing the exuberance of speculative builders, without imposing uniformity. Tree-lined roads such as Norton Way South attained a pleasant ensemble. Letchworth was notable for many progressively designed pre-1914 houses; after the First World War costs escalated and designs were simplified, with, in many instances, little difference between Garden City housing, and suburban development elsewhere.

The domestic work of Parker and Unwin was naturally extensive, with design themes already noted in their grouped housing developed in relation to requirements and budget, mirroring the range of domestic design illustrated in their *Daily Mail* article of 1901, 'Concerning the Coming Revolution in Domestic Architecture'. The following examples show a wide range of design motifs, indicating the degree to which Parker, in charge of the Letchworth office, was willing to give assistants an opportunity to develop as individual designers. Parker himself, newly married, moved into 'Crabby Corner' in 1906, shortly before Unwin's departure for Hampstead Garden Suburb. In 1914, with a growing family, Parker added a three-storey wing, with playroom, sitting room and sleeping porch beneath a tall hipped roof reminiscent of the towers of Bavarian hill towns.

The small middle-class house, costing £500-£750, gave scope for a wide range of designs. One of the most attractive, 'Briarside' (now 'Netherton'), Hitchin Road, 1905, belonged to a series based on a square plan form, with a number of 45-degree splays and diagonals giving the entrance hall, inglenook and corner bay; a spatial complexity, emphasised externally by the bold hips of a near pyramidal roof. Two pairs of semi-detached houses in Green Lane, Nos 14/16 and 22/24, designed in 1904-5, had ingenious cruciform plans set at 45 degrees to the road. A large square studio, originally open to the rafter roof, was the major element of 'The Den' (now 'The White Cottage'), built in Croft Lane in 1906, with interlocking squares defining the inglenook, kitchen and bathroom, with the generating module expressed in the recessed porch. The soft lines of the thatched roof, thrown casually like a blanket over the building, concealed the discipline of the plan. By contrast, houses built in 1908-10 were statements of elemental simplicity, a fulfilment of Parker's youthful manifesto for 'plain, simple and ungarnished homes'. They shared roughcast walls, with leaded casement windows set directly into concrete mullions. Internal finishes were puritanical; lime-washed brick walls, exposed joists and rafters, elm plank doors with wooden Norfolk latches and blacksmith made wrought-iron hinges, and boldly detailed fireplaces. No. 102 Wilbury Road was built in 1909 for Barry Parker's younger craftsman brother, Stanley, who designed and made his own furniture, complementing the ascetic interiors. All non-essentials were eliminated in the manner later advocated by reforming modernists, but on the basis of craft technology, and without losing the traditional image of the home. 'Treetops' No. 12 Cashio Lane, 1910, combined simplicity of detail with a sophisticated

42. 'Glaed Hame', 1906. This imposing house was built for Howard Pearsall, the Fabian Director of F.G.C. Ltd. The sleeping porch (now demolished) was added in 1920.

open plan based on an interlocking square grid. The living room projected outwards to gain views and aspect. Its square central area was defined by exposed posts and beams, with the inglenook balanced by a dining recess, and the bay projecting into the garden, corresponded to the entrance from the recessed front porch, flanked by larger squares containing den and kitchen. A richly concentrated spatial pattern was generated, and the linear emphasis of post and beam in counterpoint with the bare walls suggested Japanese influence. A square grid also underlay grouped housing at the junction of Field Lane and Sollershott East, built in 1910. Six houses, each with a square modular plan, formed twin blocks with low hipped roofs, and deep overhanging flared out eaves. Tall brick chimney stacks with angled tiled offsets framed the point where Field Lane sliced through the group.

The larger houses related to the earlier designs from Derbyshire: 'The Coppice', 1905, and 'Glaed Hame', 1906, both in Pasture Road, were developed from the plan of 'Greenmoor', in Buxton, 1898. Howard Pearsall commissioned 'Glaed Hame'. It was an unusually large house for Letchworth, with a garden front where three gables with exposed studwork, mullioned windows, and elaborate chimneys veered towards Stockbroker Tudor, but concealed a progressive plan with interconnecting hall, sitting and dining rooms, capable of use as one large space, or subdivision into separate rooms by sliding and folding doors. 'St Brighids', Sollershott West, 1908, was built for Edmund Hunter, the textile designer. The house was a variation on the popular Edwardian 'butterfly' plan, designed to attract maximum sunlight to the living rooms. The plan had complex 45-degree splays. Parker provided the initial sketches, and a gifted assistant, Samuel Pointon Taylor, worked up the details. The central hall, an irregular hexagon, led to the living room which had a half octagonal bay and angled fireplace, boldly detailed with a conical copper hood and an exposed concrete lintel.

Parker and Unwin worked in Baldock until 1907, when the Letchworth offices were opened in Norton Way South, backing onto the Pixmore valley with its attractive wooded glade. Parker designed the building and indicated a mirror image extension to house Unwin's drawing office and private suite, never built due to his remaining in Hampstead Garden Suburb after 1906. The choice of the most romantic of the vernacular forms, the thatched medieval hall house, emphasised the domestic quality of the building, but its planning was yet another example of a square grid. The open hall became the drawing office, lit by a range of concrete mullioned windows, open to the roof which was spanned by an enormous timber baulk, its outward thrust taken externally by a sloping buttress. The solar, at higher level, became Parker's private office, with a discreet squint, through which he could observe the goings-on in the drawing office. The centrepiece of the room

43. Parker and Unwin offices, No. 296 Norton Way South (now the First Garden City Heritage Museum), 1907. For the Norton Way offices, Parker chose the romantic model of a thatched hall house. The two-storey extension on the left was added in 1935 when the building became his home.

44. The Drawing Office, *c.*1910. Assistants, including Cecil Hignett and Samuel Pointon-Taylor, work hard to produce yet more designs for Garden City housing.

was an arched inglenook fireplace, with copper hood, comparable to many in the practice's houses. The large cruciform concrete mullioned north light window had stained glass inserts of 'The Four Seasons', by Hesman, a craftsman from Harpenden. Externally the building fitted unobtrusively into its bosky setting, whilst the garden was laid out following the design principles of Gertrude Jekyll. Parker added a two-storey south wing in 1937 when the building became his home, and it was further extended in 1973 to form the First Garden City Heritage Museum.

Several of Parker and Unwin's assistants achieved independent practice. This was encouraged: one of their assistants wrote, 'a new job was always given to one assistant entirely — he prepared the sketch plans and so on to the last detail and then settling up'.[17] Robert Bennett and Wilson Bidwell had joined the firm before 1900. Shortly after moving to Baldock, they set up an independent office. They were both excellent designers of individual and grouped housing. Examples of their cottage work have been noted above. Among the individual houses, 7 Willian Way was designed by Wilson Bidwell in 1909 as his family home. Bidwell was fond of the work of Baillie Scott, whose influence is notable in the handling of the bold gables facing Willian Way, and in the organisation of the open plan, with its interconnecting living spaces. The use of plain, high quality materials with natural finishes, the folding doors to subdivide or open up the living areas, and the judicious reworking of traditional features such as inglenook fireplaces created a practical and lasting home environment. 'Carfax', No. 501 Broadway, was built in 1909, a major house on the triangular site formed by the junction of Sollershott West and Broadway. The central gable with exposed timber work, between the two terminating principal wings of the plan, gave the appearance of a 'butterfly' plan. The major living hall was given extra height, pushing the bedroom above well into the roof. Robert Bennett built 'Hall Barn', The Glade, for himself in 1923, one of the last major Arts and Crafts houses to be designed with complete conviction. Bennett adapted the 'butterfly' plan but reversed it so that the house ran along the slope rather than embracing it. It was, unusually, built with an integral garage, with a loft above for Bennett's carpentry. The joinery details were of an excellent standard, the staircase balustrading being influenced by the work of Ernest Gimson and Sidney Barnsley. Smaller fireplaces were influenced by Lutyens's work at 'Daneshill', Old Basing but the living room inglenook was pure Letchworth, however, almost a room within a room, with a vast copper hood gleaming in the firelight and subdued artificial light of the room.

Cecil Hignett achieved independence about 1908. He had been one of the principal assistants since the firm moved to Baldock and had previously worked for Edgar Wood (1860-1935), one of the leaders of the Northern Arts and Crafts movement. Wood used progressive forms including flat roofs, and advanced materials such as concrete. Wood's only house in the south-east, 'Dalny Veed' near Royston, was built in 1907. Hignett appears to have been involved with the grid planning of several of Parker and Unwin's houses. His own house, 'The Three Gables', Croft Lane, was built in 1907, whilst he was working on the technical drawings for Parker's offices. Significantly, both buildings were thatched. The house was designed for open-air living and its central entrance hall led through into a recessed porch fitted with a settle. The thatched roof was brought down to the height of the ground floor window heads on the side facing the lane, and the building only appeared as two-storey scale from the garden, where a central gable with a half hip dominated the elevation. The other 'two gables' were little more than eyebrow dormers either side. Internally, the main living room turned towards the garden with only subsidiary windows towards the corners on the north side. This allowed Hignett to accommodate a handsome antique dresser which he had acquired prior to designing the building. All joinery was beautifully detailed, whilst the front door contained a delightful stained glass insert designed by Hignett, showing a pond and fish. 'Croft Corner', designed in 1911, was a larger

45. Designs by Bennett and Bidwell, and Hignett. *Above*, 'Carfax', No. 501 Broadway. This house, on an angled site at the junction of Broadway and Sollershott West, featured exposed timber studwork in the re-entrant between the main wings. *Below*, 'The Three Gables', No. 12 Croft Lane. Hignett's own cottage used thatch to complement its rural setting on the north of the Garden City estate.

version of 'The Three Gables', diagonally set across the corner of Croft Lane and Cashio Lane.

Courtenay Crickmer (1879-1971) was the most important Letchworth architect outside the Parker and Unwin circle. He built a pair of modest, competent houses on Baldock Road in 1904-5, Nos. 15/17, and moved into one of them. 'Crossways', Hitchin Road, 1906, was one of his best early houses, dominated by an 'M' gable with exposed vertical studding above the windows. This design was simplified for 'Arana', built in 1908, a short distance away on the north side of Hitchin Road. The brick ground floor contrasted effectively with the rendered first floor, and the studwork of the earlier house was eliminated, making the dominance of the 'M' gable the more effective. The plan ranged the principal rooms along the south front with interconnecting drawing and dining rooms, an arrangement elaborated in 'Dean Row', a substantial brick and stone house built in 1910 in Pasture Road. Crickmer's best work included grouped houses and cottages. At the junction of Sollershott East and South View a dominant block was built in 1911 by Town Planning and Garden City Estates Ltd, Nos. 32-38 Sollershott East and No. 47 South View. The centre of the block was dominated by a gatehouse with a brick gable incorporating traditional tumbled-in brick-work, and flanked by twin octagonal shafted chimneys. The long gardens in front of the block have, regrettably, been spoiled by the recent introduction of car parking spaces. Nevertheless, the group as a whole remains one of the finest in Letchworth. A short distance away in South View, Nos. 34-36 were a semi-detached assembly of two of Crickmer's First Prize cottages in the 1911 Gidea Park Competition. Externally the stairs occupied distinctive narrow gabled turrets forming a transition between the single and two storey parts. Crickmer repeated this design on many sites in Letchworth and elsewhere. Nos. 41-43 South View and three similar groups in Spring Road, built 1922-6, show a post-1919 economy version of the same basic design, with simplified detailing and metal casement windows substituted for the original leaded lights.

H. Clapham Lander (1869-1954) designed 35/37 Baldock Road in 1905. These wide frontage, semi-detached houses, with roughcast walls and prominent gabled tiled roofs, were among the best of the early Letchworth houses, clearly modelled on Voysey's work. In 1911 Lander designed 'Abendheim', 302 Norton Way South, one of the most endearingly eccentric houses, modelled on a Bavarian chalet, but executed so well as to disarm criticism. The building formed an effective townscape element at the junction of Pixmore Way and Norton Way South. On the first floor corner balconies with dark stained slatted balustrades nestled beneath the overhanging eaves and all windows were fitted with shutters. Allen Foxley (1869-1955) was more restrained. Nos. 3/5 Norton Way North had a rectangular plan, and wide frontage. The rear elevation was divided by an irregular sequence of brick pilasters containing the windows within a grid, a visually effective design. No. 508 Broadway, built in 1912, was the best of Foxley's Letchworth houses, a design which reflected his classical inclinations. The pilaster treatment was emphasised by the use of contrasting grey and red brickwork, whilst the gables of the roof were designed as pediments. The south elevation was prominently visible from Broadway, and Foxley ran a central chimney picking up flues from the drawing room and principal bedroom through the pediment, with an arched window for an attic bedroom in the centre of the chimney breast. Above the ridge of the roof the twin flues were connected by an arch. Foxley must surely have known of the games played with such details by Lutyens. At the rear of the house was an impressive two-storey verandah, which on the first floor served as a sleeping balcony.

M. H. Baillie Scott (1865-1944) was the most distinguished of the outsiders. He had commenced practice in the 1890s in the Isle of Man and sprang to prominence with his articles on the 'lower middle class house', published in *The Studio*, and his competition winning scheme for 'An art lover's house', sponsored by Alexander Koch, a German publisher. Scott had moved to Bedford in 1901, and was thus close at hand when the development of Letchworth began. Apart from his influential entry in the 1905 Cheap Cottages Exhibition, 'Elmwood Cottages', Nos.7/7A Norton Way North, he received four more Letchworth commissions, each of which showed his characteristic emphasis on picturesque massing, sometimes bordering on idiosyncracy, as with 29 Norton Way North, 1906, where he brought the eaves of the almost pyramidal hipped roof to within two feet of ground level to the right of the studwork entrance feature. Such a capricious feature could only be achieved by sinking the scullery floor, almost a ship's galley of a room, 18 inches below the level of the remainder of the ground floor. 'Springwood', Spring Road, 1906, was built for a local artist, Edward Docker, and incorporated a two-storey studio within an open plan

46. 'Tanglewood', No. 17 Sollershott West, 1907, by M. H. Baillie Scott. This house, with its open-plan interior including a 50 ft. living-dining room, is one of Scott's finest designs for 'the smaller middle-class house'.

ground floor. The house faced southwards over a generous garden, and was placed at right angles to the road. 'Tanglewood' No. 17 Sollershott West, built in 1907, was one of Scott's best small houses. The studio and sitting room formed a single space 36 feet long. The fireplace and bay window were defined by exposed principal beams, effectively breaking the overall room down into functionally distinct areas. The exterior was clearly derived from the medieval vernacular, especially the immaculately detailed central section with its structural timber studwork, within which were placed ranges of leaded casement windows and the front door. The garden elevation was different, incorporating an 'M' gable. Scott repeated the design at Biddenham, north west of Bedford. 'Corrie Wood', Hitchin Road, 1908, was the last and most sophisticated of Scott's Letchworth houses. The principal living rooms were ranged across the south front, with a large living area, incorporating a slightly raised dining recess, parlour and garden room, with a total length of 42 feet. Externally the house originally had an overall pyramidal form, emphasised by the sweeping hips of the roof, in places with eaves only two feet above ground level, and an 'M' gable dominating the garden front. The bedrooms were broken up by the irregularities of the roof, and the building was lengthened in 1923, and subsequently further extended, losing some of the original compactness of form. C. H. Townsend (1851-1928) was acclaimed for his distinctive Whitechapel Art Gallery, 1897-1901. He also designed many small houses and 'The Glade', 1906, is a sound example of an Edwardian house, if without any special flair. Randall Wells (1877-1942) was one of the fundamentalists of the Arts and Crafts movement, and modelled his work on vernacular architecture, especially evident in his Cheap Cottages entry, No. 126 Wilbury Road. A larger, and more self-conscious version was built at No.1 Norton Road in 1906-7. Curtis Green (1875-1960) began as a designer of small houses, but ultimately branched out into commercial practice. No. 109 Wilbury Road, 1909, a good example of his early work, incorporated a variant on the popular 'butterfly' plan to turn its major living areas southwards towards Norton Common.

Reputation Building Although the architect had been brought into much greater prominence, most houses in Letchworth were designed by their builders, under the control of Parker and Unwin as consultants.[19] Within a few years many building firms were active.[20] Picton and Hope have already been noted as the contractors for 'Alpha Cottages', a fact which featured for many years in their trade advertisements. They also built the 'sheds' in Exhibition Road, and several of the 1905 Cheap cottages. Beckley and Turpie were a somewhat similar firm, and built some of the smallholdings cottages for the 1907 Exhibition. J. F. Bentley was both a contractor and an entrepreneur, involved with the Picture Palace, and extensively constructing his 'Palace Gem' bungalow, remarkable value at £175, in the Meads and Common View. Some builders became prominent local figures.

J. T. Openshaw founded his firm in 1905, and built many of the best known Letchworth public buildings, including the Post Office, the

47. The Palace Gem Bungalow. This bungalow was built extensively in Common View and, after the First World War, The Meads. Its builder also constructed the Picture Palace in Eastcheap.

Girls Club and the Free Church. Amongst his housing, the three blocks of 'Silver Birch Cottages' in Station Road were commissioned from Parker and Unwin in 1905 and were closely related in design to the Westholm groups, whilst their layout at a slight angle gave interest to an otherwise rather monotonous street. Openshaw also constructed much of the Birds Hill Estate. He became a member of the Parish Council and later of the U.D.C. Charles Ball, another firm of high repute, operated principally as civil engineering contractors, constructing many of the highways in Letchworth.

With the rapid development of housing both for sale and private rental, estate agents flourished. Before professional standards were rigidly codified, they sometimes doubled as architects. Edgar John Simmons (1874-1938) was an auctioneer, estate agent and man of all work. He designed one of the earliest shop and office developments in the town centre, 'The Colonnade', and later remodelled three tudor cottages on Baldock Road to become 'Scudamore', notable for its elaborate shafted chimney stacks and exposed timber studwork. The house featured on posters issued by F.G.C. Ltd., and was Simmons' home. His local rivals, Underwood and Kent, were only in business for a few years. Like Simmons, Underwood designed one of the town's best known houses — 'Melverley', Pixmore Way, basically a 'butterfly' plan set diagonally against the road frontage, with an infill between the wings containing an irregular polygonal hall and gallery. Gables and dormers proliferated, with rich exposed studwork, a stone entrance porch and red brickwork, looking like a stray piece of Victorian Cheshire revival architecture which had found its way to Letchworth.

Nothing Gained by Overcrowding   The reform of domestic architecture promoted by the Arts and Crafts movement was internationally publicised from the 1890s. Such was its acclaim that the Prussian government appointed an ambassador, Hermann Muthesius, to prepare a comprehensive report, *Das Englische Haus (The English House)*, published in 1904. Although Muthesius did not include any Garden City examples, this was rectified by his successors Bernard Kampffmeyer and Berlepsch Valendas who visited Letchworth and Hampstead Garden Suburb in the first decade of the century. Georges Benoit-Lévy was an early French visitor who systematically described early development. The influences of Letchworth and the Garden City movement were soon reflected throughout Europe, and further afield.[21]

Unwin and others began to press for legislation to bring the new residential standards into more general use. The Housing and Town Planning Act, 1909, enabled local authorities to regulate suburban development to garden city layout and density standards.[22] Amongst the first schemes to be prepared, the Ruislip Northwood scheme, involved Thomas Adams as the first Principal Planning Inspector at the Local Government Board, and Unwin acting as consultant to the principal land owner, King's College, Cambridge. Hampstead Garden Suburb, developed from 1907 onwards with a master plan by Unwin and much excellent copartnership housing in the 'Artizans' Quarter', was widely emulated, although C. B. Purdom, and other fundamentalists of the movement, felt that suburban town planning 'weakened the good wine of the Garden City'. In 1909, Unwin put together a textbook which became a classic. *Town Planning in Practice* contained a comprehensive review of historic towns, and also analysed the design of residential development, the basis of most early town planning schemes. Unwin drew lessons from Letchworth and Hampstead, claiming that the famous '12 to the acre' standard literally sprang from grass roots level:

> Twelve houses to the net acre of building land, excluding all roads, has been proved to be about the right number to give gardens of sufficient size of commercial value to the tenants — large enough that is, to be worth cultivating seriously for the sake of the profits, and not too large to be worked

The By-Law Method of Development.

ORDINARY SUBURBAN VILLAS, SHOWING AMOUNT OF SPACE FOR FRONT GARDEN.

48a. & b. The Garden City and Bye-Law housing compared: from *Nothing Gained by Overcrowding* (1912). The verdant front gardens in Hampstead Garden Suburb (*above*) are contrasted with the hard urban character of North London Bye-Law housing (*below*). Unwin and the Garden City movement relied heavily on such propaganda to create the political climate for the acceptance of new housing standards in 1919.

The Garden City Method of Development.

FRONT GARDENS TO HOUSES UNDER TOWN PLANNING.

49. The two systems of development contrasted: from *Nothing Gained by Overcrowding* (1912). The contrast between the harsh urban terraces and hard paved streets and alleys, and the looseknit Garden City development with its communal facilities underlined the desirability of the new standards but underplayed the fact that, unless land could be obtained at agricultural rates, the more widely-spread development was inevitably much more expensive.

by an ordinary labourer and his family. This figure ... has now been fairly well tested ... at Bournville, at Earswick, at the Garden City at Letchworth, at Hampstead and many other places.[23]

Unwin argued that the value of food produced in the gardens helped to offset higher rent levels for the lower density housing. He extended this argument, albeit at times with some dubious reasoning, to a general theory of site design, published by the Garden Cities and Town Planning Association in 1912 as *Nothing Gained by Overcrowding*.[24] Here he contrasted alternative plans of development showing the urban terraces with their compulsory 'bye-law' hard paved streets and alleys, with the lower density Garden City development with much cheaper roads, and cheaper suburban land, benefits which could be returned to the community through larger gardens, and allotments and play grounds at the rear of the housing blocks. The concept was clearly developed from the housing quadrangles of Port Sunlight and Unwin's own early theoretical schemes. Contrasting pairs of photographs juxtaposing the gloom of terraced development with the verdure of Hampstead Garden Suburb underlined the message.

A public career for Unwin was, perhaps, inevitable and in December 1914 he became Principal Inspector for Town Planning at the Local Government Board, following Adams's departure for Canada. Initially he held planning inquiries into schemes prepared under the 1909 legislation. However, in 1915, he was seconded to the Ministry of Munitions to advise on the development of housing for munition workers in remote areas. An ambitious plan for development at Gretna and Eastriggs north of the Solway Firth was prepared, and Crickmer acted as the site architect. The Gretna development has claims to have been the first state-assisted new town. In addition, the Ministry of Reconstruction was giving careful consideration to housing standards after the war. It was already evident that rising construction costs would seriously inhibit the private sector, and even housing societies, from providing adequate working class housing. Unwin worked closely as an unofficial colleague of Seebohm Rowntree who sat on the housing panel. The panel's recommendations were that an ambitious programme for state-aided housing would need to be put in hand immediately after the war. To develop the detail of the programme, a major housing committee of investigation was convened under the chairmanship of Sir John Tudor Walters. Evidence was taken from a full cross section of spokesmen for progressive housing design and town planning, including Crickmer, fresh from his experience at Gretna, W. J. Swain, the Clerk of Works from New Earswick, and representatives of bodies such as the National Housing and Town Planning Council. The Tudor Walters *Report*, published in 1918, bears hallmarks of being largely written by Unwin. It pressed for a massive state-subsidised housing programme, with standards clearly based on the Garden City precedent of 12 houses to the acre. They represented the post-Armistice commitment by David Lloyd George to 'Homes for Heroes', and were enacted through the Housing Act 1919, which also established the Ministry of Health as the new body responsible for housing and public health. Christopher Addison became the first Minister, and Unwin was appointed Chief Housing Architect. The initial generous subsidy restricted the local authority loss on housing to 1d. (0.4p) rate; an inducement to fulfil the statutory duty to provide working class housing. There was an unpromising start as construction costs soared in the period of post war scarcity — the cost of a three-bedroomed house rose from £350 in 1914 to £900 in 1920, reaching a peak of £1,050 early the following year. The generous subsidies were soon terminated and housing became a sensitive political issue. Nevertheless, an important principle had been accepted and, with it, the Garden City as the physical model. Unwin must have been pleased to see the newly created Letchworth Urban District Council amongst the first to comply with the new legislation, and their housing role will be examined in a later chapter.

Chapter Seven

The Spirit of the Place

The Arcadians The years 1904-14 were a Golden Age of Garden City life, perhaps already fading as war broke out and shattered illusions. Whilst the community was little larger than a village, all pioneer residents shared a common experience, exciting if beset by minor hardships. Accounts by A. W. Brunt, C. B. Purdom, Charles Lee and Ethel Henderson all attest to the feeling of a new beginning and of a community spirit binding individuals together.[1] The lapse of 85 years since the inception of Letchworth has removed virtually all who experienced the pioneer decade, but the tangible relics of the buildings and circumstantial, personal accounts form a starting point from which to discover the quality of life. Buildings alone are imperfect landmarks. Reginald Hine, the Hitchin lawyer and historian, posed the rhetorical questions:

> But what shall it profit a city to gain all these adjuncts of town planning and fail to acquire a soul? And what city can possess a soul unless it be inhabited by honorable men?[2]

This chapter will be concerned with the soul of Letchworth, personified as the *genius loci*, the 'spirit of the place' in the Garden City pantomimes, and with the personalities that shaped the distinctive pioneer lifestyle. A note of caution must be sounded, however. The most articulate of the pioneers were almost universally middle class, the successors of the Utopianists of earlier centuries.

Despite attempts to break down class barriers with receptions for newcomers, distinctions remained. Mabel Barry Parker, who actively promoted social harmony, unwittingly referred to divisions between residents north and south of the railway tracks as *The Left Bank* and *Champs Elysées* respectively.[3] This division ran through many aspects of Garden City life, particularly the 'improving' lectures and the temperance question. Description of the Arcadian lifestyle therefore needs to be tempered by a realisation that it was enjoyed by a minority. Nevertheless the tangible environmental benefits accrued to all, reflected in the dry vital statistics of public health, and generally in a sense of community well being. The *camaraderie* was enduring, too. In February 1934, a pioneer meeting was held in Icknield Halls, Eastcheap, attended by those who had been resident in Letchworth before December 1908. Group photographs were taken and signatures were recorded in a Pioneers Book, and later worked into a circular cloth radiating from Howard's.

The Simple Life Pre-1914 Letchworth gained a reputation for smocks, sandals and, in the context of highly conventional moral standards of the day, scandals. Though rational dress, associated with late 19th-century free thinking, was a minority cult, it was identified with plain living and a high moral tone. Raymond Unwin's daughter, Peggy, recalled the discomfort of Ruskin flannel, hand woven in the Isle of Man, and the use of horn handled cutlery at the family table to consume the vegetarian fare.[4] The Socialist philosopher Edward Carpenter (1844-1929), a close friend of Unwin's, had spread the vogue for the simple life,[5] assisted by George Adams (1857-1910), craftsman and sandal maker at Carpenter's Derbyshire commune at Millthorpe, who moved to Letchworth. Smocks were worn by few, but widely publicised, not least in Letchworth itself which appears to have relished its cranky reputation. Hats and gloves were also generally discarded by Garden City folk. The Cheap Cottages Exhibitions attracted mass visits to Letchworth, and therein lay the persistent theme of 'scandalising' the bourgeoisie.

50a. & b. The Arcadians. a) Through a Garden City window: Mrs. Wilson Bidwell. The photograph was taken by her architect husband, at 7 Willian Way, the family home which he also designed. b) Smock and Sandals: Andrew Muir. Rational dress was adopted by the followers of Edward Carpenter of Millthorpe, Derbyshire, and his sandal maker, George Adams, moved to Letchworth.

Louis Weirter, brother-in-law of Thomas Adams, published many cartoons in *The Citizen*. His targets included F.G.C. Ltd., and the new Letchworth Parish Council. One of the best, 'What some people think of us', published 1908, took the theme of shocking the outsiders. The cartoon showed day trippers, in their Sunday-best, bemused as if in a human zoo. 'Daddy! I want to see them feed!' shouted a child in front of a table spread with 'nuts for the bald headed nut-peckers'. The family was directed to the 'non-tox-pub' (*The Skittles*), the 'Single Life Hotel' (Simple Life). In the foreground were three prominent local figures, described in the doggerel caption:

> 'Our architect is harmless quite,
> *Un'win*some too at present
> Our di-rector Ap-*Pears all* smiles,
> Our agent, *Gaunt* — but pleasant'

CARTOON No. 3.—WHAT SOME PEOPLE THINK OF US.

Two German ladies, who visited Letchworth last week, said on leaving :—" We are awfully disappointed in one thing : we were assured before coming that the people at Garden City were only half clothed, and that they all went bare-headed and wore sandals, and we have not seen one person of that sort ! "

51. 'What some people think of us', Louis Weirter, 1909. The Garden City soon earned a reputation for the eccentric behaviour of its middle-class 'simple lifers' with their cult religions, vegetarianism, Esperanto, smocks and sandals. Raymond Unwin, Walter Gaunt and Howard Pearsall are all the subject of gentle satire in this cartoon published in *The Citizen*.

Raymond Unwin sat clothed in smock and sandals at his drawing board, photographed by Clutterbuck clad in 'flat 'at' and leopard skin. To the right, Howard Pearsall dug his luxuriant cabbage patch, fed through Dr Poore's patent drainage system with the effluent of his own home, whilst Walter Gaunt, Estate Manager, hopefully hawked 'Garden City

52. 'The Garden Citizens of Tomorrow', Horace Taylor, c.1910. Aesthetic poses, back-to-the-land principles, and free expression amongst children, shock visitors from London.

plots to let'. A 1909 painting by Horace Taylor, 'The Garden Citizens of the future', showed an immaculately dressed couple — she with a huge broad brimmed hat, and he resplendent in top hat and morning dress confronted with naked children, a bearded man digging a manure heap, a poet reciting to an 'earth mother' figure, and two women striking 'aesthetic' poses. 'Are you intense?' ran the catchphrase from one of George du Maurier's most famous *Punch* cartoons from the aesthetic '80s. That cult lingered on in the First Garden City. With the roseate hue of hindsight exaggeration crept in. Could Charles Lee, co-author of the Garden City pantomimes, really have known 'Fredric Farmer — typical Garden Citizen', who wore knickerbockers and sandals, dabbled in art, and was a vegetarian Theosophist? Could he have kept two tortoises, polished with the best Lucca oil, and burned joss sticks beneath Madame Blavatsky's portrait?[26]

George Orwell, who later moved to Wallington, a few miles beyond Baldock, included Letchworth amongst his targets in *The Road to Wigan Pier* (1937), equating the presence there of 'every fruit juice drinker, nudist, sandal wearer, sex-maniac, Quaker, nature cure quack, pacifist and feminist in England' with the popular failure of Socialism.[7] It undoubtedly made good copy. The vegetarians founded 'The Simple Life Hotel' in Leys Avenue, which included a food reform restaurant and health food store. Vegetarian banquets became regular social events into the 1930s and beyond. Open-air living became popular, and sleeping porches were added to several homes. Possibly the best known was Barry Parker's three-storey extension to his home, 'Crabby Corner' in Letchworth Lane. Esperanto, the universal language, quickly found favour. Howard, with his inventive turn of mind, commended its study, and was almost detained in Paris shortly after the outbreak of the First World War, where he was attending an international Esperanto conference.

Temperance: a local option   Howard had described Temperance Reform as a 'local option', and suggested regulation rather than abolition of alcohol.[8] F.G.C. Ltd. acquired

53. *The Skittles Inn* (*The Settlement*), built 1907. A fine Parker and Unwin design, the exposed studwork also shows the influence of Baillie Scott. The fitted settles under the covered porch were a pleasant meeting area on summer nights.

THE SKITTLES INN

━ *NEVELLS ROAD, LETCHWORTH* ━

is A PUBLIC HOUSE (Unlicensed) conducted on the lines of the Old-fashioned Inns

The *Liberty Hall* of the Letchworth worker

Fellowship; Rest; & Recreation

Good Meals and an extensive variety of Beverages

PROPRIETORS: ANEURIN WILLIAMS & EDWARD CADBURY
MANAGER: W. G. FURMSTON

54. 'Temperance — a local option'. *Above*, advertisement for *The Skittles*, *c*.1910. The Cadbury sponsorship perhaps coincidentally resulted in a brisk demand for Bournville chocolate. *Below*, W. G. Furmston ('Friar Boniface'), 1935. 'Old Bill' acquired his nickname as a result of Fitzwater-Wray's 1923 'Sir Gadabout' saga. Despite his emphasis on healthy eating he was a heavy smoker! *Left*, The Drunkard's Map, 1935. The granting of a licence to Letchworth Hall saddened many of the teetotallers and the map reproduced in the 1935 Civic Week Programme predicted dire consequences.

THE PEOPLE'S HOUSE **BEER IS BEST** GINGER

SHTREET PLAN OF LETCHWUSS GARNCITY. GOING FROM LETCHWUSS HALL (2 a.m. apsox).

Friar Boniface weeps over Licence in High Places

The Three Horseshoes at Norton and *The Fox* at Willian, leased them to the Peoples Refreshment House Association, and continued to permit them to sell alcohol. *The Three Horseshoes* at Willian belonged to a local brewery. All were over a mile from the town centre.

Demand for a town centre public house increased as the population rose to 4,300 in 1907. A poll was taken in June 1907 on the question of opening a licensed public house, near the station. There were 631 noes, 544 ayes, majority against 87. Further polls were taken in 1908 — 89 against, and 1912 — 596 against.[9] The latter poll was organised by the Letchworth Parish Council. Edward Cadbury and Aneurin Williams founded *The Skittles Inn (The Settlement)*, in Exhibition Road (Nevell's Road), which opened on 8 March 1908. 'The Liberty Hall of the Letchworth Worker', it offered 'fellowship, rest and recreation, good meals and an extensive variety of beverages all non-alcoholic.' The building was one of the most successful Parker and Unwin designs, a series of gabled roofs, some with exposed timber studwork, and an open porch or 'stoep' with fitted settles, facing westwards to the track from the 'cattle creep' to Station Road. A long low offshoot housed the skittle alley. The interior with its inglenooks and exposed roof trusses lent itself to congenial pastimes. Tantalisingly prominent was a green-tiled bar counter, over which Cadbury's drinking chocolate and 'Cydrax', a non-alcoholic apple wine, were dispensed. *The Skittles* became notorious as 'The pub with no beer', a 'Blackcurrant Julep kind of pub' indeed, renowned for its affable host, W. G. 'Bill' Furmston (1869-1950), who claimed a varied clientele from tramps to millionaires. Many were spectators, however. One hundred and fifty sightseers once spent 2d. between them. *The Skittles* became a meeting place for trade unions, local clubs, and housed the nucleus of the Letchworth Museum, with cases of stuffed birds ranged round the principal room. In 1923, *The Skittles* was reconstituted as *The Settlement*, an adult education centre. It had been hoped to build new premises designed by Barry Parker on the north side of Leys Avenue, opposite Howard Park. However, in 1924 commercial premises north of Station Place were leased and *The People's House* was opened. Bill Furmston, caricatured as 'Friar Boniface' in Fitzwater-Wray's *Sir Gadabout*, continued to run a somewhat barn-like restaurant.

In 1920 a further poll showed a narrow 65 majority against a public house. Sensing capitulation, the opponents countered with a vigorous campaign. It was calculated that the Letchworth residents spent £20,000 a year on alcohol, compared with £90,000 in a town of similar population with public houses, so there were rich pickings at stake. The result of the second poll was: 1,532 for, 2,149 against, majority against 617. In 1930 another poll produced a close result. Meanwhile licences had been granted to the Conservative and Unionist clubs, and to the golf club; in 1935 *Letchworth Hall Hotel* received a licence. Friar Boniface was not amused! *Hullabaloo*, the Civic Week programme, helpfully published a 'drunkards map' upon which all roads led inexorably back to 'Letchwuss Hall'.

Churches and Creeds   Acquisition of the Garden City Estate marked a watershed in the religious life of the area.[11] The Rev. W. Walls retired from St Mary Letchworth in 1905, and long incumbencies drew to a close in Willian and Norton. The new Rector of Letchworth, Rev F. N. Heazell, was acutely conscious of the remoteness of his church from the town, and founded the Mission Church of St Michael and All Angels, Norton Way South, dedicated on 22 February 1908, a small red brick basilica designed by Crickmer. It was envisaged that the Established Church would eventually find a permanent home in the central buildings of Town Square, and St Michael's was rebuilt there in 1968. Heazell was succeeded by Rev. G. K. Olivier, father of Laurence Olivier, the eminent actor, who grew up in the Garden City. All Saints, Willian, built a Mission Hall in 1917, on the acute angled site between Pixmore Way and Baldock Road, and construction of a 'Victory' church,

55. The Free Church's first building, 1905. Looking like a colonial mission room, the Free Church was first extended in 1908-9, by Parker and Unwin, before being replaced by Parker's excellent classical design of 1923.

56. 'Howgills', Friends Meeting House, 1908, designed by Bennett and Bidwell. With its stone mullioned windows, and excellently crafted interior, 'Howgills' was one of the most successful of the early Garden City buildings.

St Paul's began in 1919. Designed by A. H. Ryan-Tenison, in Gothic style, an imposing fragment was consecrated in 1924. In 1915 Norton parish opened a church hall on Norton Way North to serve the Glebe housing area, and the site frontage was developed for the modern St George's church in 1963.

Many pioneers were agnostic. Unwin's home, 'Laneside', became an early focus for community life, beginning on Whit Monday 1905 with a 'United Religious Meeting'. Services were conducted by Joseph Wicksteed, and later by Rev. J. Bruce Wallace, a charismatic Ulster Scots Congregational Minister, who had served at the Canning Town settlement.[12] Wallace later formed the 'Alpha Union', a fundamentalist group with Christian Socialist sympathies, to develop an international non-sectarian federation which recognised a spiritual basis for universal harmony. The Sunday Evening Meeting at Howard Hall, in which Wicksteed, Purdom and A. W. Brunt were involved, also became a regular feature of spiritual life. Purdom conducted the first non-conformist meeting at Abbis Collins's home in 'Alpha Cottages' in December 1904. Later meetings were held at Letchworth Hall. A committee was formed, chaired by Thomas Adams, with A. E. Stark as Secretary, and including the local builder J. T. Openshaw. £49 3s. 9d. was raised to begin construction of a hall which cost £300. On 17 October 1905, the Free Church, Gernon Road, opened a simple building with buttressed roughcast walls and a tiled roof, twice extended by Parker and Unwin. The first permanent pastor, Rev R. W. Jackson was appointed on 18 September 1907, and remained for 10 years. In 1923-4 a new church was built alongside, a classical design on a cross plan, by Parker, built by Openshaw.

The Methodists built two Letchworth churches. The Primitive Methodists with James Brown, who had negotiated the options of the Letchworth land, as secretary, built their handsome red brick classical style church on Broadway, and it opened in August 1914. The Wesleyans chose a site on the south-west corner of Pixmore Way and Norton Way South and built a Gothic style church, designed by George T. Baines, which also opened in 1914. The Roman Catholics began worship in 'Astley Cottage' on Baldock Road, home of Bernard Newdigate, manager of the Arden Press. The Rev. Adrian Fortescue (1874-1923) administered the Sacrament in the 'sheds' on 30 November 1907, and shortly afterwards Charles Spooner designed the church of St Hugh of Lincoln, Pixmore Way.[13] A simple brick structure, it was embellished with Arts and Crafts fittings. Fortescue was a well-loved priest, a linguist and a respected figure in the social life of the town. Purdom, a convert to Catholicism, was the first to be married at St Hugh's, in 1912. Quakerism flourished. There had been a Quaker meeting at Norton in 1669. In 1908, Juliet Reckitt, daughter of a Hull industrialist, sponsored the building of 'Howgills', the Friends Meeting House in South View. Designed by Bennett and Bidwell, it was an excellent example of their work, carefully detailed throughout, with a Meeting Room itself based on 'Briggflatts' in North Yorkshire, a sober and beautiful interior with much excellent joinery.

Of the more unorthodox religions, Theosophy was perhaps the most pervasive. With its emphasis on spiritual ecstasy, its belief in the coming of the World Teacher, and its worship of a new Messiah, Krishnamurti, a Holy Boy from India as the new Supreme Lord, Maitreya, the cult attracted a wide following. Miss Hope Rea became the first President of the Letchworth Theosophical Society, and assisted the building of 'Vasanta Hall', Gernon Walk, an odd little building with a flat concrete roof, designed by W. H. Cowlishaw. The Christian Scientists opened a hall and schoolroom almost opposite. Dotted throughout Letchworth more small churches — Baptist, Liberal Catholic, Elim Tabernacle, Salvation Army, and Spiritualist — were testimony to the broad religious tastes of the early residents. It is small wonder that John Buchan noted in his thinly disguised parody of Letchworth, 'twenty seven varieties of religious conviction including three Buddhists, a Celestial Hierarch, five latter-day Saints and about ten varieties of mystic whose names I never could remember'.[14]

A Liberal Education   Education was greatly prized by the pioneers.[15] Amongst the earliest advisers was John Russell, headmaster of the liberal King Alfred School, Hampstead. In 1905 the 'Garden City Education Council' held a public meeting to press the County Council to provide permanent school premises without delay. They also approved educational principles based on equality of opportunity for all, far-reaching at the time.

The elementary schools in Norton and Willian were inadequate, and the need for central facilities was urgent. The County Council decided to go no further than the opening of a 'non-provided school', opened in November 1905 in the versatile Exhibition Road sheds. The Education Council levied a voluntary rate of 1s. 4d. in the £, subsequently reduced to 6d. Cyril Arthington Pease, brother of the secretary of the Fabian Society, was the first headmaster, transferring to the Norton School in 1909 but remaining in Letchworth until 1917, after accomplishing much pioneering work. Miss Edith Booth, a cousin of Raymond Unwin's, was the infant mistress. The County Council built the Norton School in 1909, on a courtyard plan, influenced by Unwin's advocacy of open-air schools. In April 1913, the Pixmore Elementary School, on School Walk, was opened. There was then a long interval before the Westbury Elementary School opened in June 1925.

Private schools flourished early on. The Letchworth School was run by J. H. M. Stephenson, on advanced lines, with co-education, running from kindergarten to university preparation. It soon built purpose-designed premises by Crickmer, in Barrington Road. In 1912, Miss Cartwright opened the Letchworth Modern School for Girls in Norton Way South and there were several private preparatory schools on a domestic scale. In January 1915 a group influenced by the educational theories of Dr. Arundale took over the Letchworth School buildings, and in 1919 Mrs. Annie Besant, a Theosophist leader, laid the foundation stone for a Theosophical Trust school located site between Spring Road and Broadway. Mrs. Besant herself chose the name The Saint Christopher School. Lyn Harris joined the staff in 1923, became headmaster in 1925, and in 1953 was succeeded by his son, Nicholas King Harris. It became one of the most progressive private schools in the country, consolidating its premises in Barrington Road after selling its Broadway buildings which became the St Francis College for Girls after 1934.

Evening and adult education began with gardening classes in the winter of 1904-5 at Letchworth Hall, expanding into machine construction, building construction, arts and crafts, poultry and bee keeping, singing, and sociology. In 1907, the *Letchworth Magazine* looked towards 'a Lawrence College, a Howard College and a Gorst College, sending out their men and women graduates to do champion service in science and art and commerce and industry'. The Letchworth Academy did not materialise, although efforts were made in 1914 to commemorate the first decade of the Garden City. In July 1914, a week before the outbreak of the First World War, a conference on further education was attended by the Teachers Guild, the Workers Education Association and the Letchworth 1914 Celebration Committee, under the presidency of Lord Salisbury. It was many years before Letchworth acquired its college.

Recreation and Amenities   A wide range of sports was catered for in the pioneer years.[16] Thomas Adams the Estate Manager was an outdoor man and promoted the layout of a golf course in the parklands of Letchworth Hall in 1905. Initially a modest nine-hole course, it was extended in 1911 to 18 holes. Harry Vardon, a well known professional, designed a 6,000-yard course to utilise every club in the golfer's bag and every stroke in his repertoire. Although the course length has been adjusted, it still retains its character. F.G.C. Ltd. reserved the field south of Baldock Road, where the estate had been opened, for cricket. The Letchworth Cricket Club was formed in 1907, and its earliest players included Harry Burr, F.G.C. surveyor, Harold Craske, F.G.C. secretary, H. G. Griffiths, H. Blay,

57. Infants' class, Norton School, c.1911. The infants' teacher, Miss Edith Booth, to the right of the picture, was a cousin of Raymond Unwin.

58. The Letchworth School, 1909, now the premises of the St Christopher School. C. M. Crickmer designed the first buildings for the campus, which has been greatly extended over the years.

H. Hankin and W. H. Sumsion. W. P. Westell, the naturalist, was a mainstay of the team, whilst A. W. Brunt was umpire. The club took the championship of the North Herts League in 1914.

Letchworth Town Football Club was also founded in 1907, with a ground south of the Baldock Road. Local rivalries, particularly with Hitchin, Biggleswade, Baldock and Stevenage, were acute. The team won the North Herts Charity Cup in 1912, beating Hitchin 3-2, and in the same season carried off the Hitchin Hospital Cup. The Rugby Union Football Club was formed in 1925. Hockey was popular in the early years, with Edgar Simmons, the estate agent, and Allen Foxley, the architect, being particularly enthusiastic. Mabel

59. The open-air swimming bath, c.1912. Despite its lack of heating, it was always a popular spot especially in the school holidays.

Barry Parker was a keen defender on the ladies team. Tennis flourished, and many of the larger houses included tennis courts in their grounds. Thomas Adams and his wife were keen players. Bowls was played on private greens until a public facility was provided in Howard Park in the 1920s. An open-air swimming bath, south of Howard Park adjoining Pixmore Way, was opened on 27 June 1908. Although unheated, and with primitive dressing cubicles, it quickly became popular, although the 'pea soup' constitution of the water shortly before the weekly flushing was long remembered, as was the day when a man rushed out of his cubicle to the aid of a lady in distress, oblivious of the fact that he had removed his bathing drawers![17] The bath served the town until 1935.

Many factories provided their own sports facilities, and contributed to an inter-works league with Spirella a notable leader. Separate boys and girls clubs were founded. The Girls Club, funded by Miss Juliet Reckitt, was opened by Mrs Bertrand Russell on 12 July 1908, in a wing added at the rear of the Howard Hall. 'Swedish Drill' gymnastics and hockey became popular. The Boys Club began in a shed at the corner of Pixmore Avenue and Works Road, but eventually in 1914 was accommodated in a neat Georgian building fronting Broadway, designed by Parker and Unwin. Formal gymnastics were popular amongst boys' groups as photographs of 'human pyramids' testify!

Literature and Music   The (Mrs.) Howard (Memorial) Hall was the focus of literary and musical life in the developing Garden City. Funded by public subscriptions in memory

60. The Mrs. Howard Memorial Hall, 1906. The first public building in Letchworth, designed by Parker and Unwin, the Howard Hall was similar to the Folk Hall at New Earswick and a number of similar community buildings.

of Lizzie Howard who had died shortly before she was due to move to the Garden City, the hall was designed by Parker and Unwin. Boldly set at an angle, near the junction of Norton Way South and Hillshott, the hipped roof, punctuated by picturesque dormers, was offset by a large inglenook on the north-west side, a recess off the plain hall with its exposed queen post roof. Stage and dressing facilities were very restricted. The management committee, headed by Miss M. E. Nicholson, had lofty cultural aspirations.

> You will stroll into the Howard Hall one wintry day and find an artist . . . busy with decorating it . . . You will learn that there is to be a *conversazione* that night . . . or a gathering of new residents, or what not besides . . . There will be a scene from one of Tolstoy's plays or an impressive recitation . . . discussions upon the Liquor Question, the Unemployed, Methods of Education. Political Organisations, Arts and Crafts, Science and Civilisation and so forth.[18]

A Library opened at the hall on Whit Monday 1906, assisted by a £5 donation from Howard

Pearsall.[19] By 1912 it was evident that the library, run by volunteers, was inadequate, but moves to make the Parish Council a library authority were blocked. Dr Mervyn Gilbart-Smith, the opposer, organised a book exchange scheme, with a central catalogue and collection point at the Howard Hall. Amateur music-making was extensively supported. The First Garden City Band was formed in 1905, but was soon superseded by the Letchworth Philharmonic Society which gave Haydn's *Creation* at the Free Church Hall on 27 April 1906, the first of many choral works under the direction of H. Gomersall. Miss Margaret Fowles formed an orchestra which performed at the opening of the Howard Hall and, after her death, her nephew, Dr Leonard Fowles, conducted concerts in the Pixmore Institute in 1908. Subsequently, musical life was centred on The Cloisters for many years.

Miss Lawrence and The Cloisters   Annie Jane Lawrence (1863-1953) became a dominant force in the social life of Letchworth. One of five children — her younger brother Frederic William (1871-1961), Baron Pethick-Lawrence later helped to promote the Letchworth Garden City Corporation legislation — Miss Lawrence settled in Letchworth in 1906. She leased an isolated three-acre plot a half mile south of the Baldock Road, and built 'The Cloisters', with a house for herself, 'Cloisters Lodge' ('Ladybarn') alongside.[20]

   She chose William Harrison Cowlishaw (1869-1957) as her architect. He had a craftsman's view of architecture, and numbered church needlework and pottery amongst his interests. 'The Cloisters' was unique amongst his designs and faithfully reflected the requirements of his patron, who spent £20,000 upon the project. Intended as an open-air school, building stopped in November 1907. A vast shell had been constructed, consisting of the 'cloister garth', a half oval, with large glazed bays to the north and an open colonnade to the south. There were two wings: one for kitchen and store rooms, the other with cubicles and dressing rooms leading to an oval open-air swimming bath. The outward expression of these functions was remarkable, with myriad symbolic overtones. It was rumoured that the building had appeared to Miss Lawrence in her dreams.

   Approaching from Cloisters Road, built up south of the Baldock Road in the 1960s, the observer is confronted with a towering mass; the overwhelming impression must have been even more remarkable when the building stood in glorious isolation. The rich palette of materials — grey Suffolk bricks, Purbeck stone, flintwork, and vivid orange Suffolk tiles — allied to the romantic massing which culminated in a soaring octagonal tower compounded the effect. The flat roof of the cloister garth had a brick balustraded walkway. Although bare blocks of stone inside and out and the gaunt brickwork and unfaced mass concrete vaults of the interior bear witness to the sudden termination of the work, enough of the symbolic artefacts were installed to indicate the overall intentions. Cowlishaw was a gifted sculptor and modelled designs for the rainwater heads — doves represented guilelessness, bats were about to start their dusk patrols, bees built up honeycomb to provide food for the gods, and 'butterflies dancing in the empyrean'. The casement windows were to have received stained glass showing the rising of the sun; the interior walls were to have been clothed in mosaic, but sheet glass and Hall's washable distemper had to suffice.

   The Cloister Garth arcade had columns of green veined Swedish marble, suggesting upward growth. Residents slept there in hammocks let down from the vaults, with men and women strictly segregated by the central hall. The arcade was provided with canvas screens to close off nocturnal breezes, but the problem of heating in winter was not solved by a series of fireplaces. In the central hall a fountain was installed around the central support to the tower, pure Art Nouveau in design. Water flowed from the dedication stone in the springing of the twin arches above, dripped into twin basins, the lower of which was divided into eight small receptacles for ceremonial hand washing, and overflowed around the cloisters in open channels — no doubt representing the dissemination of worldy wisdom.

61. 'The Cloisters', Barrington Road, designed in 1907 by W. H. Cowlishaw. Seen from Barrington Road, the soaring tower with its conical roof and tall chimney is a landmark in this eccentric complex of buildings.

A blue-vein marble 'stream' laid at the foot of the fountain emphasised this. Communal meals were taken at a marble faced dining table, on a raised altar-like dais, which stretched across the great bay window. The swimming bath, installed on Miss Lawrence's insistence of *mens sana in corpore sano*, was used at dawn.

Miss Lawrence dedicated the building on 27 January 1907, placing an illuminated vellum scroll, inscribed by Cowlishaw, in a glass casket which was sealed into the springer stone above the fountain. Her dedication 'To the unity, eternal reality' sought to promote the ascent 'to a full harmonious and joyful expression of life, in soul, body and social organisation'. She was inspired by J. Bruce Wallace, founder of the Alpha Union, who

62. Miss Lawrence at the Alpha Union Summer School, 1907. Miss Lawrence sits right of centre in a group which includes, left of centre, Ebenezer Howard.

63. Miss Lawrence at the Iceni Pottery, with Andrew Muir. In addition to education and music, Miss Lawrence was also interested in the promotion of local craft industries.

became her protégé for some years. Although deaf, Miss Lawrence had a four manual electric organ installed, with the console in the entrance hall, and the sound percolated downwards from the pipe chamber through louvres above the fountain. Bruce Wallace organised residential summer schools, and holidays for Board school teachers, leaving an indelible impression for many participants. More than 50 years later, R. W. Sorenson, Labour M.P. for Leyton, included his reminiscences of life at 'The Cloisters' in the Commons debate on the Letchworth Garden City Corporation Bill.

The first Alpha Summer School had been held at 'Cloisters Lodge'; in 1907 the second took place at the partly completed 'Cloisters', in 1908 the first residential school was held, which became an annual event until 1911. Wallace provided a syllabus ranging from English Literature to Psychology and Progressive Religious Thought. In 1908 Georgia Pearce, an American journalist, described Miss Lawrence, at 45 already 'white haired and elderly with a strong keen intellectual face', presiding over the activities, although hampered by growing deafness. Apart from the mid-day meal, eating was alfresco and, intriguingly, housework was a male province. Miss Pearce was clearly impressed by 'this 20th century temple . . . erected to the hallowing of humanity'.[21] The utopian delights were palpable; berobed and sandaled acolytes essaying their daily tasks, engaged in earnest discussion or simply observing the sunset or stars from the rooftop promenade, with soft organ music wafting upwards. The dream faded rather suddenly, however. Bruce Wallace married Miss Mary Tudor Pole in 1912, and 'The Cloisters' was not available for the Alpha Union Summer School, which was hosted by the town.

Frank Merry, the organist, became warden and encouraged courses including one at Easter 1913 on the 'Garden City Philosophy of Life'. After the First World War, the Letchworth Adult Educational Settlement arranged academic courses, which ceased in 1926. Miss Lawrence promoted the concept of a 'Dual Day' with morning work, a two-hour period for rest and food and a re-assembly for communal recreation, and she circulated tracts on the subject for many years. Music was an indispensible accompaniment, and she organised public concerts in the Cloister Garth with audiences of 1,000. Organ recitals, band and choral concerts became part of the town's cultural life. In the 1920s a band shell improved acoustic projection and the organ was enlarged. A highlight was the appearance of the London Concert Orchestra, 40 unemployed musicians brought in at Miss Lawrence's expense. The last concert was given by the Brotherhood Orchestra on the fatal Sunday, 3 September 1939, when the Second World War broke out. Craft classes and folk dancing were organised and swimming lessons for children. For many years the reward for swimming the length of the murky pool was a 'Blackbird' fountain pen, personally presented.

Miss Lawrence became deeply concerned about the future of the building. In February 1932 she offered it free to the County Council, with an annuity of £1,000 and income from £20,000 after her death. The offer was refused. The building was commandeered and damaged during the Second World War. In 1948, aged 85, Miss Lawrence moved to *St Catherine's Nursing Home*. She made over 'The Cloisters' to be adapted as the North Herts Masonic Lodge, and died aged 90 on 3 August 1953. The £17,500 residue of her estate formed the Lawrence Cloisters Trust. Regrettably, extensions by the Freemasons were visually insensitive, whilst structural problems related to the deterioration of the iron reinforcement of the concrete structure developed. Yet 'The Cloisters' was listed as a Grade II* building in 1979, and surely deserves to survive as a tangible link with Letchworth's golden age.

Artists in Residence Letchworth produced its own crop of literary and artistic talent, and played host to several distinguished authors and artists. The *Letchworth Magazine* appeared in August 1906 under Purdom's editorship. In January 1909, Henry Bryan Binns founded *The City*, a high quality and short lived production printed by J. M. Dent.[22] The tone was set by Binns's poem, 'The City', which appeared in the first issue:

I see a City being wrought
Upon the rock of Living Thought

The opening of the fourth stanza, 'Foursquare our City' was worked into a handsome processional banner, by Edmund Hunter. A. W. Brunt, editor of 'The Citizen', portrayed the Garden City prolifically in verse, whilst Canon H. D. Rawnsley, a founder of the National Trust, John Drinkwater, and local author William Loftus Hare were diverse contributors to the poetic genre. Hare's charming 'Garden City Alphabet' was published in *The City* in 1909, and his naive sketches and quatrains featured local scenes and

A for the **A**rchitects buried in thought, Arranging the houses to go where they ought.

O for the **O**ffice; how charming it looks! Who would not wish to get on to its Books?

B for a **B**uilder, computing the cost; & the bitter remarks when a contract is lost.

D for **D**irectors who sat down to dine; We tasted their wit and they tasted our wine.

64. Garden City Alphabet, by Harold E. Hare, 1909. In this charming primer, Parker and Unwin lay out houses on a chess board under 'A'; J. T. Openshaw calculates his profit margins under 'B'; the Directors, including Howard at left, toast themselves in non-alcoholic wine; and the young C. B. Purdom walks to the estate office under 'O'.

personalities. Raymond Unwin appeared under 'A' for architect, the Directors of First Garden City Limited paused for non-alcoholic refreshment under 'D', and Purdom strolled casually to the Estate Office under 'O'. Local rivalries were also remembered:

'H' is for Hitchin which likes a good laugh, and gets it by walking four miles and a half.

The tone of parody was rekindled by John Betjeman in two poems.[23] 'Group life Letchworth' dwelt on the rampant individualism of a breed of children supposedly devoted to work 'each for weal of all'. 'Huxley Hall' was set in 'The Garden City cafe with its murals on the wall', actually Nott's *Icknield Halls*, Eastcheap. The narrator dwelt on 'the deep depression of this bright hygienic hell', and wondered whether the uninhibited behaviour of the children, and adults plotting each others downfall 'in the interests of the state', were after all a confirmation that man was born in sin. Although perhaps not quite so irredeemable as Slough, Letchworth's idiosyncrasies made a natural target for Betjeman's cynicism.

A few artists settled for long periods. Edward Docker and Charles Fox commissioned houses from Baillie Scott ('Springwood') and Parker and Unwin ('The Den' now 'The

White Cottage'). Harold Gilman (1876-1919), one of the leaders of the Camden Town group of British post-impressionist artists, came to Letchworth in 1907,[24] and in 1909 commissioned a house and studio, 100 Wilbury Road, from Parker and Unwin. Shortly after his American wife, Grace, left him, Gilman let the house to Spencer Gore (1878-1914),[25] who recorded its newness in vibrant colours, with the red tiles of the roof set against an electric blue sky, and the garden a riot of golden irises. Gore painted several Letchworth scenes including 'The Road' and 'Letchworth Station', the latter showing waiting passengers set against a vivid landscape with, in the middle distance, a single white house as a token of the advancing development. A lesser known member of the Camden Town group, William Ratcliffe (1870-1955), moved to Letchworth in 1906, settling first on Westholm Green, then at No. 102 Wilbury Road with Stanley Parker.[26] He spent virtually his whole working life in Letchworth. His water colours and oil paintings included many characteristic Letchworth scenes, painted with charm and freshness. In the 1940s Francis King, art master at the St Christopher School, painted a number of Garden City scenes in a style modelled on Thomas Rowlandson, the 19th-century social caricaturist. 'Garden City revels' shows a group of garden citizens paying homage to the great God Pan, tweedy and tubby men, brandishing a rake and a cornucopia of nuts, women bearing a laurel wreath and a floral garland. It was a fitting tribute to the simple life. His 'The Hitchin Bus, Station Place' was a souvenir of the war years when, under the admonition 'Is your journey really necessary?', even a trip to 'Sleepy Hollow' acquired exotic overtones.

Pageants and Plays   Pageants, masques and folk dancing were frequent events.[27] May day was celebrated with the crowning of the May Queen, and processions in which representatives of the schools, F.G.C. Ltd., the Parish Council, estate workers and Trades Unions, clubs and institutes, participated with banners held aloft. 'Arbor Days' were begun on 29 February 1908, imported from America via the 'beautiful Oldham Society'. Certificates were issued to all tree planters including Howard. The following year, H. Rider Haggard (1856-1925), novelist and enthusiast for progressive agriculture, was Guest of Honour, followed in 1910 by Walter Crane (1845-1915), the Socialist artist. After 1911 the ceremony lapsed altogether, with a passing revival to mark the Coronation of George VI in 1937. The Coronation of George V in 1911 was marked with due ceremony, with Howard speaking against a backdrop of banners. In July 1913, Miss Lawrence held a 'Battle of the Flowers' at The Cloisters, whilst in July 1914, a few days before the outbreak of war, a *Masque of Letchworth* brought the curtain down on such events after three performances given by a cast of two hundred.

C. B. Purdom was the mainspring of early theatrical life in Letchworth and a founder of the dramatic society in October 1906.[28] Tolstoy's *Ivan the Fool* and Hardy's *The Three Strangers* were presented at Howard Hall on 30/31 January 1907. The players included Harold Hare, James Henderson, Alice Hoffman, Jack Dent, Mr and Mrs Murray Hennell, C. F. Townsend, Mr and Mrs R. P. Gossop, and W. G. Taylor. Shakespeare: *The Merchant of Venice, Two Gentlemen of Verona, Much Ado About Nothing*; and Shaw: *Candida, Arms and the Man*, and *You Never can Tell*, were soon staples, though plays by John Galsworthy, J. M. Synge and W. B. Yeats were also given. Purdom aimed to encourage the establishment of a Letchworth theatre, with a permanent company. He set high standards, and was not afraid of controversy. Shaw's *The Shewing-Up of Blanco Posnet* was still censored and its performance at the Pixmore Barn in August 1912 was its first by an English company. The venture folded with the outbreak of war, but Purdom revived his theatrical ambitions at Welwyn.

The Garden City Pantomimes, co-written by Purdom and Charles Lee, were long remembered.[29] The first was presented in January 1909 in Howard Hall — a local satire on politicians, poets, food reformers, a Lady Bountiful and suffragettes. The second was a

65a. & b. Ebenezer Howard in public life. *Above*, in May Day costume, 1912. Howard entered into the spirit of Garden City life but sometimes looked rather self-conscious and uncomfortable. *Below*, speaking on Coronation Day, 1911. Howard speaks in front of Edmund Hunter's banner 'Four square our city' as part of the Coronation commemoration on the Market Place facing Leys Avenue.

comic operetta — music was credited to Charles Lee, but the metre of Purdom's rhymes suggested the rhythm of Gilbert and Sullivan. The plot involved children taking over the management of the Garden City, Company and the Parish Council. The innocent sixth form fun can be gauged from the chorus of the Councillors of Norton.

> Sleep parishioners sleep,
> Sleep deep, innocent sheep,
> Round the fold the gaunt wolf prowls;
> Never heed his threatening howls,
> We your Council watch we'll keep,
> Sleep sleep parishioners sleep.'

The 'gaunt wolf' was of course, W. H. Gaunt, the estate manager. The spirit of the place or *genius loci* was a benevolent *djinn*, played by Percy Gossop in a get-up resembling a Burne-Jones madonna. His song, modelled on the Lord Chancellor's 'Nightmare' from *Iolanthe*, poked fun at the simple life, and took architects to task.

66. Percy Gossop as 'The Spirit of the Place', 1910. Got up like a Burne Jones madonna, Percy Gossop not only starred in but also co-wrote the Garden City pantomimes.

> When the lamps are lit and the shadows flit and a balmy breeze from Norway
> Is dodging the screen you've erected between the fireplace and the doorway
> And the rain and the sleet and the hailstones beat through every chink in the casement,
> And the plaster fails from the mouldy walls, and the damp wells up from the basement
> Perhaps you reflect that your architect was a bit too art-and-crafty,
> And you wish that your lot had been cast in a cott that wasn't quite so draughty.
> Ah, then is the hour when you need my power to brace and fortify you;
> For draughts and chills bring exquisite thrills when I am hovering by you.

The third pantomime, and the last, was a mild skit on Aristophanes' *Lysistrata*. With the women on strike, the men of Norton undertook domestic duties. The militant suffragette leader, Miss Bunting M.P., proved to be a man in drag. Perhaps it went a little too far even for the liberal free-thinkers.

Construction of the Picture Palace in Eastcheap heralded mass entertainment.[30] The fire station was

67. The Picture Palace, Eastcheap, as built in 1909 — a simple domestic building fronting a bald fletton brick hall marked the first utilitarian structure of one of the earliest cinemas in the county.

next door in case of conflagration of the highly inflammable nitrate film. A domestic-style frontage masked the single level auditorium. The opening programme on 6 December 1909 six shorts including *Joan of Arc*, *Princess Nicotine* and *Foolshead Married*, was very different from the Hollywood epics which would soon fill the house. In November 1916, Miss Lawrence and the naturalist, W. P. Westell, organised Saturday afternoon shows for children — a lantern lecture on nature, and educational and travel films.

The Village Named Morality   It might have been expected that there would be mixed feelings about the First World War. The night war was declared there was an angry debate and resounding defeat of the Socialist party's protest against Britain's entry into the fray. Later an influential minority resented the 'jingoism' of a 'great patriotic meeting' addressed by the Divisional M.P., Lord Robert Cecil, held in the Spirella Hall on 28 January 1916. The Letchworth Fellowship of International Goodwill held meetings at *The Skittles*, with speakers from the British 'Stop The War' Campaign. Some supported moves towards international reconciliation, later codified in the League of Nations. Raymond Unwin published a booklet on the subject, *The War and What After?*, in 1915. Controversy broke out when the Howard Hall Committee refused bookings to individuals or organisations who would not undertake to desist from criticising the government's war policy.[31] Matters came to a head in November 1916 when the national *Daily Mail* and *Daily Sketch* attacked the Garden City as a haven for communists, with 200 jailed conscientious objectors. Harold Armitage, editor of *The Citizen*, branded the reports as lies, and succeeded in obtaining their unreserved withdrawal.

68a. & b. The First World War in Letchworth. *Above*, the Territorials depart: crowding the 'up' platform, the trainee soldiers await departure for Hertford. *Below*, the Belgian refugees arrive: the first nine families arrived as early as 25 September 1914 after the fall of Antwerp.

All this provided striking raw material for the novelist John Buchan (1875-1940), famed for the derring-do yarns of his hero, and alter-ego, Richard Hannay. Buchan was invalided out of the war, and convalesced with Captain Trotter at 'Derenda Cottage' ('Rest Harrow'), Willian Way in 1915. His observations on Garden City life appeared in 1919 in *Mr Standfast*, the third Richard Hannay novel.[32] Hannay, alias 'Cornelius Brand', lodged with Mr Tancred Jimson, whose 'badly built and oddly furnished' cottage overlooked 'a pleasant Midland common' in 'Biggleswick' Garden City. The Jimsons, who studiously followed the simple life, were the expected caricatures. He, a shipping clerk in London, wore grey flannels, soft collar, orange tie and a soft black hat. His wife, Ursula, 'a large red woman with hair bleached by constant exposure to weather', was habitually clad in a 'gown, modelled on a chintz curtain'. Biggleswick itself was 'one great laboratory of thought'. Buchan-Hannay, on the look out for fifth-columnists, described the citizens with ill-disguised contempt at jokes about the war, and longed to make a man of Letchford, 'celebrated leader-writer of *The Critic*' and 'a double-engined high-speed pacifist', by enlisting him in his battalion. The 'League of Democrats against Aggression' met in the Moot Hall, and the range of issues provided Hannay with diverse targets including Russian unrest, alternative medicine, and latent African nationalism. The climax was a meeting, addressed by John Blenkiron 'in stark defiance of the Defence of the Realm Act', which exceeded the tolerance of the audience who did not mind proving Britain wrong, but stopped short of rejoicing in the enemy. Blenkiron was an *agent provocateur* who had come to give Hannay marching orders for further exploits of patriotic espionage. Thus ended the 'Biggleswick' interlude.

Actual events were more diverse and complex than Buchan's highly selective account. Early in the war, the army arrived for exercises and were annoyed to find the Garden City on a site that, on their outdated maps, appeared ideally suited. Many citizens volunteered or were called up, and the Garden City territorials left for Hertford. The volunteer training corps drilled preparatory to forming Four Company First Batallion, Hertfordshire Volunteer Regiment. Altogether 600 enlisted in the services. Against his better judgement, Purdom enlisted,[33] trained at Ampthill, was graded E3, but insisted on serving in France, and narrowly missed Passchendale. He was invalided out in January 1918, but took no further direct role in Letchworth affairs. Frederic Osborn was non-combatant.[34] He undertook sterling wartime work for the Howard Cottage Society, then avoided call-up by lying low in London, working daily in the British Library. Conscientious objectors working the land in Letchworth included Herbert Morrison (1888-1965), subsequently L.C.C. leader and a Labour Minister. Blinded in his right eye, Morrison would have been turned down, but insisted on proclaiming his pacifist principles to the Wandsworth tribunal. Employed by J. J. Kidd, a socialist market gardener who admired his principles, Morrison was digging for winter planting as the Armistice of 11 November 1918 was proclaimed by church bells and sirens. Morrison remained a good friend of the Garden City. In humanitarian terms, Letchworth's most positive contribution lay in its hospitality for Belgian refugees, the first of whom arrived on 25 September 1914. The newly developing housing area to the west of the town centre — Burnell Rise, Campers Square and Campers Road — became known as 'Little Antwerp', whilst their compatriots Georges Kryn and Raoul Lahy began munitions manufacture. Their story belongs in the following chapter.

Chapter Eight

Industry and Commerce

'Factory Sites to Let'   Without a roster of manufacturers willing to throw in their lot with the Garden City, the overall objective of social reform was hopelessly impractical, and the concept would have remained a minority Utopia. Industrial location was universally *laissez faire*, with no regulation of factory sites within towns, still less any attempts to direct decentralisation of population and industry. Consequently Howard had to convince industrialists of the soundness of his ideas, hoping that a few key participants would attract others through economies of association. The Pioneer Company had found that in the London area 50 per cent of a sample of 80 industrialists expressed a willingness to consider moving to a Garden City; in the Midlands, however, only 16 out of 82 were in favour, which evidently played a decisive factor in the decision to reject Chartley.[1]

H. Howard Humphreys's appraisal of the Letchworth Estate also considered its industrial potential.[2] He found it was 'admirably suited . . . just within what I may call a commercial distance of London, and the growth of self-propelled traffic [motor vehicles] will be a powerful factor in the development of your town . . . if a maker of automobiles can be induced to place his works upon the estate, I am certain that others would quickly follow suit'. The location of the industrial estate to the leeward of the town was also recommended and crystallised in Unwin's layout, with 135 acres south of the railway, served by Works Road, connecting via the Green Lane railway bridge to Icknield Way north of the tracks. The G.N.R. built a goods yard, and individual private sidings could be taken from the main line. The grouping of factories was in its infancy, but was also being pursued at Trafford Park, Manchester, alongside the ship canal. Attraction of industry to Letchworth depended upon land, labour, and infrastructure being available at competitive rates. Utilities provided by First Garden City Ltd. were first made available to the industrial estate. The ability to expand was important as cramped town centre sites were beginning to inhibit technological advances, notably the introduction of production-line processes which worked most efficiently with an uninterrupted horizontal sequence of operations. Manufacturing, with a high value-added content, small raw material inputs, and a high skill content, to produce goods with a high ratio of value to weight, was gaining in importance. Letchworth lacked basic raw materials and was better suited to skilled manufacturing than to heavy industry. This would minimise the impact of transport costs of raw materials. However, its comparatively remote location away from a pool of skilled labour and distant from markets, was also critical. Humphreys' perceptive remarks about links with London, and the potential for skilled engineering or automotive industries, were to prove substantially correct.

Had the Company possessed adequate working capital, advance factories might have been constructed and leased out. With over £200,000 invested in infrastructure by the end of 1906, against the estate purchase price of £155,000, and share capital of £148,000, there was no room for manoeuvre.[3] However, efforts were made to attract industry, based upon the low ground rent and rates, provision of services, availability of housing and good transport facilities. Ground rents began at £25 a half acre (0.2 ha.), with 999-year leases subject to revision every 99 years. In 1915, the annual rates were 5s. 9d. in the £ including County, District, Parish and Poor Rates, with 4d. in the £ added for sewage disposal. Construction of standard steel-framed factories of 10,000 sq. ft. was considered, for a £400

112

initial payment, and the balance of £3,600 repayable over 15 years. In 1914 a six-unit tenement factory was constructed on Works Road. Land cost and rates weighed most heavily with industrialists. Benoit-Lévy, the French garden city expert, compared a 2.2 acre (0.91 ha.) London site with an annual cost of £1,740, with a 5.45 acre (2.2ha.) Letchworth site leased by the same company for only £175.[4]

Ewart and Son, manufacturers of hot water geysers, were the first lessees in 1905, but did not build their factory for five years. T. H. W. Idris, a Director of F.G.C. Ltd., opened an offshoot of his mineral water plant, and Vickers and Field, asphalt paving manufacturers, were both early recruits but did not remain long. Printing and engineering were the most notable early successes. Thomas Adams added industrial promotion to duties as Company Secretary and Estate Manager. In the hectic period from October 1903 he became over-committed, and was replaced as Estate Manager in August 1905, notwithstanding his recent success in attracting Dent's, the publishers.[5] His successor, Walter Gaunt (1874-1951), came from Trafford Park. Purdom, in an outburst of snobbery, castigated Gaunt's 'Manchester mind and accent. His ideals were within the terms of business and common sense, and he said so in an unmistakable way'.[6] Purdom evidently had old scores to settle. He melodramatically evoked Gaunt as the philistine, bent on destruction of idealism, as he pursued factual materialism with the single-mindedness of Mr Gradgrind in *Hard Times*. Gaunt remained Estate Manager until 1917, and whilst some of his actions were controversial, he undoubtedly consolidated a significant industrial base. It was not a little unfair that he was palpably guyed and parodied in the *Citizen* cartoons by Louis Weirter, who as Adams's brother-in-law continued to grind the family axe.

Printing and publishing   In 1904 a co-operative group of printers from Leicester learned of Howard's Garden City project. Initially they had intended to rent smallholdings land, but were critical of the terms both for agricultural and industrial land. In November 1905, however, they were established as Garden City Press Ltd.,[7] the first printers and publishers to locate in the Garden City. Bert Williams, the manager, was an idealist: all the employees received a proportion of the profits, through retention of 1s. 8d. (8p) wages weekly, and 10 per cent interest was paid out of the trading surplus. One employee had 'invested' £16 in this way, which by 1911 had accrued to £86, of which £70 represented 'interest' and 'dividend'. The Press produced many brochures published by F.G.C. Ltd. Wages were no higher than average: 35s. (£1.75p) for men for a 48-hour week, 16s. (£0.80p) for women and 7s. (£0.35p) for boy and girl employees. The company was exceptional in granting one week's paid holiday, and organised a Works Council and Education Committee. It also guaranteed the Co-partnership tenants occupancy of a number of cottages for employees. Notwithstanding its democratic organisation, there was early industrial trouble, following which three employees left to found the first successful Garden City newspaper. In 1911 the Company was reorganised on a conventional limited liability basis.

The attraction of Dent's was proof positive of the industrial viability of Letchworth. J. M. Dent and Sons were nationally renowned publishers whose cramped printing and binding works was near Bishopsgate in the East End of London.[8] They had recently produced their attractive 'classic' reprint *Everyman* Edition and it became essential for them to find new premises to increase production. Joseph Malaby Dent (1849-1926) was an employer in the tradition of Victorian altruism, concerned with the social conditions of his workforce. He met Adams at a lecture, and subsequently leased five acres (2.02 ha.) at £2,550 compared with £17,500 for a similar site in central London. Construction of the single storey factory with its basement warehouse was begun in August 1906, and it opened a year later. It was soon in full production, with 150 employees. The workforce was critical of Garden City housing, and the firm built Temple Gardens, off Green Lane, for senior employees and

69a. & b. Letchworth at work. *Above*, Dent's printing shop, *c*.1910: trimming edges of books and binding the *Everyman* Edition. *Below*, Phoenix Motor Co., *c*.1912. A range of hand-finished cars, each with a phoenix radiator mascot, awaits delivery.

their families. Social welfare included a works library and gardening club. The lack of social life, particularly music halls, also prompted some employees to return to London, though most adapted to the change. Dent's elder son, Hugh, built 'Dents' Cottage' in Letchworth Lane, whilst his younger son Jack played a leading role in many early theatrical events in the town. Firm and family remained mainstays of the Garden City for many years.

W. H. Smith and Son were expanding rapidly as national retail newsagents and book-sellers.[9] They were also involved in high quality printing and bookbinding and were attracted to Letchworth by the potential for expansion. They and their associate company, recently acquired, the Arden Press of Leamington Spa, were housed in an impressive single storey factory at the corner of Works Road and Pixmore Avenue, one of the few early industrial buildings in Letchworth with architectural distinction. The bindery, under the control of Douglas Cockerell (1870-1945), one of the most skilled craftsmen in the field, was involved in presentation binding for parish registers and historial documents. The Arden Press was distinguished for the work of Bernard Newdigate (1869-1944), best known for his restrained type style evolved in conjunction with the sculptor, Eric Gill (1882-1940). In 1911 the Arden Press employed 80 men, 12 boys and 100 girls. The firm was an early user of road transport for distribution to its London headquarters. Smiths ceased work during the First World War, but Douglas Cockerell subsequently started a small hand bindery in Norton Way, notable for high quality tooled bindings, and hand marbled endpapers. In 1935 he bound the *Codex Sinaiaticus* for the British Museum. Other pre-1914 printers in operation included Letchworth Printers Ltd., who published *The Citizen* newspaper, and the Hayes Printing Machinery Company Ltd., pioneers of colour lith-ography.

Engineering Heatly Gresham moved from Bassingbourn near Royston, about 12 miles distant. The firm made bodies for London taxi cabs. Other motor manufacturers located in Letchworth over the next few years. The estate was most suited to the industry whilst its products were virtually hand-built; it was an unlikely centre for mass production. Con-versely, had a major company located in the town, it would have attained dominance; indeed, the Vauxhall Company nearby, at Luton and Bedford, developed into a mass manufacturer as the English branch of the American General Motors concern.

The Lacre Motor Co. moved from Long Acre near Covent Garden, London.[10] The firm built an impressive factory on Works Road in 1909 (architect Albert Dawkins), with a two-storey office block fronting the large production hall. The firm concentrated on chassis building, manufacturing neither bodywork nor engines. Labour was recruited from Bedford and Luton and an average weekly wage of 32s. (£1.60p) was paid, compared to London levels of 48-50s. (£2.40-£2.50). The discrepancy brought about an industrial dispute in 1912, and a trades-unionist employee was dismissed, allegedly for breach of conduct. The union executive requested an immediate wage rise of 4s. (20p) per week to match Luton levels, which the company rebutted by sacking the branch secretary, declaring that only non-union labour would be employed in future. The subsequent walk-out was joined by 26 non-unionists.[11] A meeting was held in Howard Park; there were allegations of police brutality, with pickets brought before the Hitchin Magistrates. A national paper, *The Evening News*, publicised working conditions in Letchworth. The dispute consolidated local union activity: E. K. Simmons, secretary of the Letchworth branch of the British Socialist Party, wrote to F.G.C. Ltd.[12] urging their best endeavours 'to persuade the Lacre Company to give up an ignoble and hopeless struggle ... the publicity given to the strike has already damaged the name of Letchworth. F.G.C. ought to refuse leases to firms who do not undertake to pay the standard rate of wages ... The conditions of labour here are in many instances a disgrace to our town whose high aspirations as regards the general conditions of life have World wide renown ... The F.G.C. cannot ignore its responsibility in the matter'.

The Phoenix Motor Company moved from Finchley in 1910, and built premises on Pixmore Avenue. Its Dutch owner, Joseph van Hooydonk, took an active role in the town's life. Other motor companies established after the First World War will be mentioned in a later chapter. Other specialist engineering firms were also established. The Foster Instrument Company Limited, manufacturer of industrial pyrometers for furnaces, opened in Pixmore Way in 1913.[13] In response to Purdom's surveys, the founder, C. E. Foster, stressed that Garden City conditions, with the closeness of factory and home, contributed to increasing productivity. Foster's paid London wages. The only serious disadvantage lay in the need for personal contact with customers, entailing lengthy telephone calls on the infant trunk network, and additional travel time.

Consumer Goods   The emergence of a consumer manufacturing sector was a 20th-century phenomenon. It expanded rapidly in south-east England in the inter-war period, but a number of firms in this sector were established in Letchworth before 1914. Dent's *Everyman* Edition fell into this category. The Herz and Falk Embroidery Company was a Swiss firm which opened in Letchworth in 1907.[14] Their labour force was largely female, but key male workers had been brought in from St Gall, and Letchworth housing conditions were stated to be a revelation, even to the Swiss. Few companies employed married women pre-1914, and the Herz and Falk employees were mainly girls, who received only 10s. (50p) for a $52\frac{1}{2}$ hour week. Lloyds Ltd. began manufacture of lawn mowers in 1913. The same year D. Meredrew Ltd., cabinet makers, moved out of the East End of London. Fred Hard, the proprietor, later recalled:

> My method was to move the families lock stock and barrel, by means of a small motor van ... we moved 192 men women and children ... ask any one of them his opinion of the move: 'finest thing you ever did guv'nor'.[15]

A wide range of furniture was soon produced, expanding in the 1920s into wireless cabinets.

The Arts and Crafts movement encouraged the growth of craft workshops. A firm which allied handcraft to volume production was the St Edmundsbury Weavers.[16] Edmund Hunter (1866-1937) from Bury St Edmunds had studied art against his father's wishes. He was a skilled designer, reflecting the influence of Morris, and his personal interest in Theosophy and Astrology, and Persian art. The firm was founded in Haslemere, Surrey, and moved to Letchworth in 1908. Hunter employed Spitalfields handloom weavers. His fabrics were supplied to churches and cathedrals, country houses, and even for lavish stage productions such as Beerbohm Tree's *Anthony and Cleopatra*. His Letchworth home , 'St Brighids', Sollershott West, and his factory in Birds Hill were both designed by Parker and Unwin. The factory featured concrete mullioned studio windows, a gabled tiled roof, and a domestic inglenook fireplace: Benoit-Lévy commented upon its charming aspect. The availability of electricity enabled a combination of hand and power weaving. Hunter employed four men, who earned 39s.-47s. 6d. a week (£1.95-£2.37) and five apprentices who received 5s.-15s. (25p-75p), depending upon experience. He was exceptional in paying for two weeks holiday and Bank holidays. The firm remained in Letchworth until the 1920s. The Iceni pottery was formed by Miss Lawrence and the architect W. H. Cowlishaw. A 'leadless' glaze was used, and the firm's products were characterised by deep green or blue colourings, simple form, and ornamented by pierced rims.

Castle Corset   The Spirella Company represented a consumer industry related to skilful marketing of female fashions in the early 20th century. It was an American concern, founded by William Wallace Kincaid (1868-1946), who used a spiral wound spring, invented by Marcus Merritt Beeman, as a substitute for whalebone in corsets. The firm opened temporary premises in the old 'sheds' in Nevells Road in 1910.[17] They demanded, and received, at a cost more than double that of an industrial site, a town centre site in Bridge Road, which was developed for the most imposing factory in Letchworth. Their first corsetière, Frances Wright of Hitchin, began work on 30 March 1910. Benoit-Lévy surveyed the infant company with 12 men and 48 women[18] — in contrast to other employers Spirella preferred married women as more expert than younger girls, who required greater training. Already the most progressive features of American social welfare were being considered. Kincaid claimed enlightened self-interest as the prime motivation for bringing the company to the Garden City.

> Letchworth . . . is built according to a pre-arranged plan . . . not more than 12 houses built upon an acre, giving every cottage a good garden . . . These conditions make for efficient contented progressive workmen and women. A principle of Spirella's policy has been to instill into its employees right thoughts, right methods of living, right methods of work, an appreciation of the vital needs of

70. 'Castle Corset' (Spirella), Fitzwater-Wray's 1923 cartoon. Cecil Hignett's imposing building (1912-20) towers above early Garden City buildings including 'The Cloisters', the Estate Offices, 'Homesgarth', *The Skittles*, and a host of 'Bentley' bungalows.

sunlight, of wholesome food for health, and of congenial employment for happiness. The Spirella found itself in sympathy with every detail of the Garden City Movement which has found its best expression in Letchworth.[19]

The new factory was built in three phases between 1912-20. The architect, Cecil Hignett, used the commission to branch out from Parker and Unwin, and the contractor was Howard Hurst. A remarkable building resulted, dominating views northwards across the railway from the town centre, subsequently nicknamed 'Castle Corset', by Fitzwater Wray in his satirical *Sir Gadabout* saga. The three blocks enclosed a courtyard, open to Bridge Road and facing axially down Nevells Road. The workshop block nearest the railway was the first phase, built in 1912, with the central block in 1913-4, and the third block in 1919-20. The composition of the workshop blocks was dominated by four pavilions capped with Arts and Crafts hipped roofs with small upstand gables, somewhat at odds with the boldly functional treatment of the workrooms between. The pavilion windows were enormous mullioned and transomed bays, complete with leaded lights, cast in concrete. The building structure was

71. Spirella Gardens opening, *c*.1930. The founder of Spirella, William Kincaid, looks somewhat bemused as A. W. Brunt declares the gardens open, whilst C. F. Ball looks on rather sternly.

largely reinforced concrete, exposed in beams and string courses. The structural grid wasreflected in the workroom elevations, which were totally glazed between the columns. There was a reinforced concrete mezzanine gallery running the length of the workrooms. These were flat roofed, with deep exposed concrete edge beams, which acted as parapets, protecting sitting out and sun bathing areas, like the top decks of a great ocean liner. The central block was more classically treated, with the top floor containing a large social hall, complete with stage and fly tower. Spirella not only dominated visually, but provided a natural focus for the town's social life during the inter-war period.

The company provided remarkable staff facilities.[20] The large workroom windows enabled every bench to obtain direct sunlight. Free optical testing was provided, with spectacles at wholesale prices. Bathrooms were available, and it was claimed that over 75 per cent of the workforce used them (one wonders what the other 25 per cent did!). There was a large canteen, fitness was encouraged through gymnastic classes, whilst a choral and orchestral society and a library catered for quieter tastes. An enclosed shed to store 350 bicycles undercover was built, and the firm even issued capes on wet evenings to employees travelling homewards without a coat. The Company recruited an army of 4,500 corsetières. The house journal, *Spirella Monthly*, urged greater and greater conquests!

> Attention! Comrades, veterans and recruits upon the firing line. The old adage advises to aim high, set a mark, point at it, shoot straight for the centre ... Get on to the firing line, never mind if you miss at first for practice makes perfect. All ready, aim, fire![21]

The salesladies covered the length and breadth of the land, quietly selling Spirella in the intimacy of customers' homes, and achieving ever higher sales targets until the 1950s. The company transferred most of its operations to Harlow New Town in the 1960s, but maintained a presence in Letchworth until the 1980s. Although not quite extinct, following the sharp decline in demand for firm foundations, the Spirella army seems headed towards the same fate as the dinosaur and the dodo. 'Castle Corset' remains the most tangible legacy of this once enormous enterprise.

K. & L. and the Munitions of War

The beginnings of the K. & L. factory contrasted with the popular image of Letchworth as the 'Village named Morality'.[22] In October 1914, with the German army rapidly closing

72. The millionth K. and L. shell in the war effort. David Lloyd George, the Minister of Munitions to whom the shell was presented, would soon become famous for his 'Homes for Heroes' pledge of November 1918.

in on Antwerp, Jacques Kryn, a prominent diamond merchant, fled to England with his younger brother, an engineer and car manufacturer from Liège, and his works manager, Raoul Lahy. They arrived, according to legend, with rags on their backs, and pockets full of diamonds. Thousands of their countrymen had taken refuge in England, and a flourishing Belgian colony in Letchworth celebrated their National Day on 21 June 1915. Kryn suggested to an English associate, Sir Bernard Oppenheimer, that they should build a steel foundry to utilise the skills of the refugees. Two cupolas, and a one-ton converter were erected before Hitchin R.D.C. even received the plans! With an increasing demand for shells, tank parts, and portable bridges, the firm rapidly expanded on their Dunhams Lane site. Machine shops were enlarged and at the height of the war effort almost 3,000 Belgian refugees found employment. Munitions manufacturing was as far as possible kept secret to discourage Zeppelin raids; however, one did make its way to Hertfordshire, but discharged its bombs short of Letchworth and was eventually brought down at Cuffley. The 'village named morality' had more nearly assumed the role of Andrew Undershaft's garden city, financed from munitions profits, in Shaw's *Major Barbara*.

Co-operative Commerce   Howard had envisaged company shopping to ensure wider availability of goods during the earliest years of development, a system subsequently adopted at Welwyn Garden City. Lack of capital prevented this at Letchworth. Initially, there were no shops on the estate. Hitchin traders, in particular, offered a delivery service for middle-class customers, but this was of no use to industrial workers. Consequently Bert Williams, manager of the Garden City Press, formed the Garden City Co-operative Society.[23] In 1905, with a share capital of £50 16s. 11d. (£50.84) and 95 members, he opened a single-room shop at Letchworth corner in an estate cottage. A house in Cross Street was used to serve the Cheap Cottages area. Purdom had endeavoured to interest the Co-operative Wholesale Society, but to no avail. Garden City Co-operators and Garden City Tenants built premises in Leys Avenue in 1907, a handsome Tudor-style building designed by Parker and Unwin. Business prospered under the manager, T. L. Pearce, and in 1913 the first phase of more extensive premises in Eastcheap was opened.

The first shops were opened in Station Road, strategically located between the Birds Hill housing area and the future town centre, with access from the 'cattle creep' for shoppers from north of the tracks.[24] A general store was opened by H. Cullip, followed by Ansell's butchers, Bradshaw's ironmongery, Beddoe's confectionery and newsagents, Snowden's drapery, Smith's grocery, Martin's Garden City Dairy and Housden's cafe and druggists. All were modest buildings, with little attempt to make a visually co-ordinated shopping parade. In 1907 construction began on the south side of Leys Avenue, between the Eastcheap corner and Commerce Avenue. This block was designed by Bennett and Bidwell as a varied but unified parade, with a skilfully handled roofscape. The corner was initially occupied by the Joint City and Midland Bank, with the architects' offices above. *The Simple Life Hotel*, J. L. Wells outfitter and tailor, J. H. Green furnishers, W. B. Moss, a branch of the Hitchin grocers, and W. H. Smith followed down the hill to Commerce Avenue. Unlike Station Road, which was laid out following the straight line on Unwin's first plan, the line of Leys Avenue was subtly curved, which created a more interesting townscape. A further parade on the south side of Commerce Avenue followed in 1908/9, together with shops between the Wynd and Norton Way South, on the north side. Boot's the chemists occupied one of these, whilst further down towards Norton Way a distinctive block designed by Allen Foxley with triple projecting gables and ornamental plasterwork was partly occupied by Spinks' Drapers, a firm which remained for many years in the town.

73a. & b. Town centre shops. *Above*, opening of Garden City Co-operators Ltd., Leys Avenue, 1907. Now one of the principal shopping streets, Leys Avenue had not been properly made up when the store opened. *Below*, F. Nott, Bakers, Eastcheap, *c.*1911. Fred Nott proudly displays his local delivery vehicles in front of his Eastcheap shop, built in 1909.

74. Leys Avenue, 1909. Two dog lovers pose in the middle of the thoroughfare whilst the soon-to-be-abandoned flower beds can be seen between pavement and carriageway. Otherwise the buildings remain the same today.

75. Station Place, 1925, with passengers crowding around the open-top bus to Hitchin. All the buildings survive to the present.

At the head of Station Road and Leys Avenue, a projecting gabled block, 'The Colonnades', was built in 1909. A rather coarse design by Edgar Simmons, the estate agent who occupied one of the ground floor shops, provided a distinctive accent, and illustrated Unwin's technique of using articulated building lines to achieve a varied townscape. Beyond this lay the site of the Estate Office, a somewhat utilitarian structure looking like a colonial outpost, set well back from Broadway to allow the construction of more permanent offices. Eastcheap was intended to be one of the principal shopping streets, but the development of the cottage estates east of Norton Way made Station Road and Leys Avenue more attractive for early letting. This lack of balance in the town-centre development remained for many years and is still evident in Broadway. Development in Eastcheap proceeded slowly. Shortly before the war Nott's, the bakers and confectioners, moved from Leys Avenue to an elegant building fronting Eastcheap, which had a distinctive series of projecting oriel windows beneath a gable. Nott's became a Letchworth institution and extended along Eastcheap in the 1920s with the 'Icknield Halls'. Opposite on the west side, was the first phase of the Co-operative stores. The rest of the road remained undeveloped until the 1920s, save for the Picture Palace and adjoining Fire Station at the south end. Broadway, too, received little development. The corner running around Station Place towards Bridge Road was developed in 1908 for Barclays Bank, an excellent Georgian-style building designed by Hugh Seebohm, with a projecting tower which linked the single-storey banking hall to the two-storey bank house. This was intended to be a symmetrical development turning from Broadway across the bridge road axis to Westcheap, a second shopping street equivalent to Eastcheap, which was never developed. The bank building did, however, establish a precedent for Georgian-style architecture along Broadway, broken in the early years only by the free Tudor-mullioned frontage of the Post Office, designed by Bennett and Bidwell in 1910.

Many of the early stores required workshops and even stables which were provided on rear frontages facing Commerce Avenue and The Wynd. Both of these streets developed in a more or less unplanned fashion which defied reorganisation for many years. By the early 1920s Parker prepared plans for redevelopment of The Wynd but it was more than 60 years before any significant reorganisation was achieved. The growth of shopping was marked by the existence of 30 shops by July 1907. At the same date the town had a 33-line telephone exchange.[25] By 1924 there were 162 shops.[26] The acute-angled site between Leys Avenue and Eastcheap was originally allocated as an open market, but the experiment was unsuccessful, and the vacant plot was developed in the early 1920s when much of the town centre was consolidated.

Newspapers and Publicity   The growth of the social, commercial and industrial life of the town brought the need for newspapers and publicity. The Garden City Press brought out a *Garden City News and Advertiser* in January 1905, with F. W. Rogers as Editor and Advertisement Manager. It did not survive for long. However, L. A. Wheeler, W. Odell and Arthur William Brunt, who left the Press after industrial trouble, formed a newspaper with the encouragement of W. H. Knight who became its first, unpaid, Editor. *The Citizen (Garden City Record and Advertising Journal)* first appeared on 22 September 1906, and its unbroken run of publication since that date has left a valuable record of the town's development and personalities.[27] The first issues were printed in Wheeler's Green Lane house. Brunt was Advertisement Manager, and he and a colleague delivered the paper free every Friday. 'Guaranteed weekly circulation 1,000' proclaimed the first issue, with the Latin tag *floreat urbs hortorum*. Local stores and builders advertised their services, whilst a Residents' Council public meeting about a licensed public house was announced at the Howard Hall.

Brunt soon became Editor and 'trebled' as compositor and reporter for 32s. (£1.60). He conducted a lively paper, and his encyclopedic knowledge of Letchworth formed the basis for his *Pageant of Letchworth*. His tenure was not without controversy. In 1912 he wrote to the *Daily Herald* about the Lacre strike and industrial conditions, and local employers felt he had used his position to aggravate the situation. He was discharged from the paper early in 1913, to be succeeded by Harold Armitage, who skirmished with the national *Daily Sketch* and *Daily Mail* over their reporting of Letchworth as a town of cranks and cowards during the First World War. He was forced to resign in 1928 over his support of a critical theatrical review by Harold Hare.

The first *Letchworth Directory* appeared in 1907, published by Garden City Press, and F.G.C. Ltd. sponsored a pocket sized *Borough Guide* in 1908, both of which indicated the variety of businesses already trading in the town. First Garden City Limited brought out its own guides to spread knowledge of Letchworth beyond its boundaries — *Garden City in the Making* (1905), *Guide to the Garden City* (1906), and *Where shall I live?* (1907) — the latter acting as an illustrated catalogue of the Urban Cottages Exhibition; they were attractively produced, with artwork covers. Pictorial guides such as *Letchworth Garden City in Pictures* (c.1912), contained high quality photography, whilst colour lithograph posters extolling the 'Health of the Country — the Comforts of the Town' were issued before and after the First World War. Several excellent books recorded the development of the town. C. B. Purdom's *The Garden City* was published in 1913, a beautiful example of Dent's skills, with a cover illustration from an attractive view by T. Friedenson, with the gabled fronts of Silver Birch Cottages in Station Road gold blocked on the spine. Purdom provided a comprehensive account of the Garden City movement, the development of Letchworth, and with appendices contributed by Howard, Unwin, Aneurin Williams, Harold Craske, Howard Pearsall and others. Europeans were frequent visitors and *La Cité Jardin* by Georges Benoit-Lévy of the French Garden City Association appeared in 1908 with a revised edition in 1911. German interest was considerable and Berlepsch Valendas's *Die Gartenstadt Bewegung in England* of 1912 contained a thorough account of Letchworth and the Garden City movement. By the outbreak of the First World War, the Letchworth experiment was internationally renowned in town planning and housing circles.

Chapter Nine

Company, Council and Community

Residents Union Howard's proposed integration of the functions of landlord, development company and local authority, possibly influenced by the Fabians' municipalisation of utility services, was the weakest part of his concept, and uneasily reconciled with local democratic control through the local government structure. Local government in the 1890s was settling down to the use of the powers conferred by the 1888 legislation, and whilst urban boroughs and city councils had built up valuable experience, there was little indication of the potential effectiveness of county councils, let alone the rural district and parish councils who had acquired limited responsibilities in rural areas. The Garden City was located in Hitchin Rural District, split between the parishes of Letchworth (67 inhabitants), Willian (176) and Norton (248). The newcomers had neither a voice in local government nor in the Company unless they were shareholders. Electoral registration had enrolled less than 200 voters out of a possible 1,000 by 1905. That June residents resolved to 'form a Council to watch over the interests of the residents during the development of the estate'.[1] The Residents Union was formally created at the 'sheds' on 14 July 1905 to assist in carrying out Garden City ideals. Mrs. Ebenezer Howard, Mrs. MacFadyen, Miss M. E. Nicholson, Miss F. Bates, the Rev. H. Janner, Mr. E. Docker, Raymond Unwin and Mr. R. W. Tabor were members of the first committee. The Union acted primarily as a sounding board.

As population rose, the Union generated local political interest — in January 1907 there were 144 candidates for 16 places. Residents' enfranchisement was universal at a time when women's suffrage was still controversial. Prominent local figures such as Norman MacFadyen, Henry Bryan Binns, Joseph Wicksteed, H. Clapham Lander, John T. Openshaw, T. Clarence Howard and Cyril Arthington Pease were elected. Wicksteed became Chairman, Pease and Howard secretaries. The unsatisfactory railway service, education, provision of a public library and museum, regulation of alcohol and poor relief were key concerns. The Union's influence diminished after the formation of the amalgamated Civil Parish of Letchworth in April 1908. The Poor Law was notorious for its Dickensian approach and the workhouse still represented a threat to the elderly and destitute. Consequently, 'The Guild of Help' was formed in 1906 by Edgar Wing, with the Rev. F. N. Heazell and Miss Nicholson.[2] The scheme worked through a central committee of 12, 5 district heads, and 45 helpers, on a voluntary basis. The income for August 1907-June 1908 was £54 2s. 5d., and rose to £144 7s. 2d. the next year. Only through unstinting voluntary work could such small sums be put to good use. In 1911 there were the following disbursements: Temporary loans £19; Provision of groceries £16; Clothing £15; Medicines £7; Meals for school children £6; Domestic help £8; Pensions for elderly women £1. 10s; Expenses of convalescent homes £6; Subscription to National Guild of Help £1.

The Guild strove to avoid the 'Lady Bountiful' approach and was also involved in rent collecting for the Howard Cottage Society and in counselling tenants in difficulty. Medical assistance was also necessary in an era long before universal health care. Mrs. H. Craske, wife of the estate accountant, founded the Letchworth Provident Dispensary, based in a house on Cross Street, and supported through weekly subscriptions. Drs. Leward and MacFadyen were members of the Committee. It was also intended to appoint a district nurse, and ultimately to provide a cottage hospital. Nurse Webb (1881-1962) came to Letchworth in 1905. She trained at Queen Charlotte's Hospital in London before returning to serve the Garden City in 1910. In 1919 she became Staff Nurse at Spirella, retiring in 1941. In October 1914, Pixmore Farmhouse was opened as a temporary hospital, which developed into the town hospital in 1921. The Letchworth Civic Trust, formed in 1914 to promote the welfare of the town, rounds off this account of early community organisations. Through subscriptions and bequests it built up a shareholding in F.G.C. Ltd. which was later to prove a valuable lever for promoting the formation of the Garden City Corporation.

The Parish Council   The Local Government Board approved the creation of a unified Letchworth Civil Parish, amalgamating Letchworth, Norton and Willian.[3] On 6 April 1908 the first elections were held. The following were elected: C. F. Ball, C. Brown, D. B. Cockerell, G. Cramp, F. J. Godbehear, Sir J. E. Gorst, H. Hall, H. Heatly,

76. The Letchworth Parish Council, 1908. Sir John Gorst, front centre, poses with the Council outside the Howard Hall. Left to right: front row, C. F. Ball, E. Heatley, Sir John Gorst, D. B. Cockerell, George Brown; second row, J. S. Lander, C. Brown, R. J. E. Underwood, H. Hurst, H. C. Lander, T. Hudson, J. T. Openshaw; back row, N. MacFadyen, T. C. Howard, H. Hall, T. J. Godbehear.

T. C. Howard, T. W. Hudson, H. E. Hurst, J. S. Lander, J. T. Openshaw, H. D. Pearsall, and R. J. E. Underwood. Sir John Gorst, K.C., a London barrister, was elected Chairman; George Brown became Clerk. The Council existed until the formation of the Urban District Council in 1919. In 1910, 43 candidates contested the 15 seats. Well known local figures including A. W. Brunt, H. R. Dent, Norman McFadyen, Edgar Simmons and John H. Wicksteed took seats. The Chairmen were successively Sir John Gorst (1908-9); H. Bond Holding (1909-12); Douglas B. Cockerell (1912-13); Dr. Norman MacFadyen (1914-16); Charles F. Ball (1916-19).

Parish Councils had little power, although they were able to raise finance through rates. Friction between F.G.C. Ltd., Council and community built up, with the Company cast in a 'big brother' role, and the Council well-intentioned but lacking financial and decision-making expertise. The Garden City pantomimes and the cartoons of Louis Weirter reflected local disdain for institutions. Street lighting provoked one of the most heated arguments. The Company had installed a few gas lanterns, designed by Parker and Unwin, mainly near road junctions, and had, of course, laid the mains. They were anxious that the Parish Council provide more general lighting. Wary of expense, the Parish Council rejected the proposition. A public meeting was called at which it was suggested that the cost of street lighting should be borne by an increase in the Company's water rate! As one of the Garden City pantomimes proclaimed, the Council was powerless 'to implore the naughty gas-man not to leave us in the dark' for after all they were 'nobodies by Act of Parliament'.

The Council reluctantly spent £2,000 making up Green Lane and Dunhams Lane, and in 1911 the County Council took over $4\frac{1}{2}$ miles of roads. The R.D.C. took over refuse collection in 1909, and in 1911, at a cost of £850, the Fire Station was erected in Eastcheap, and through special donations raised by A. W. E. Bullmore, the Chief Officer (who became the U.D.C. Engineer), a fire engine was bought. Even this had been queried as some Councillors thought that ladders were unnecessary, as most houses were low enough for the residents to jump from the roofs! As for Police, Benoit-Lévy reported in 1911 that the two policemen truly had a sinecure since it would be impossible to envisage less crime than in this model settlement.[4] In 1918, however, a Magistrates Court and Police Station were built on Broadway, prompting *Punch* to state that it was up to the garden citizens to make sure that the new facilities were well used! Rates were undeniably low: for the years ending March 1909 and March 1910, only the Poor Rate was levied and this amounted only to 2s. 8d. and 4s. 8d. (14 and 24p) respectively. From 1910-16 this varied from 4s. 6d. to 5s. 6d. ($22\frac{1}{2}$-$27\frac{1}{2}$p) with a street lighting rate from 1d. to $3\frac{1}{2}$d. (0.4-$1\frac{1}{2}$p) in the pound.

Political Life 'Garden City revealed a peculiar situation politically — it had neither liberal nor conservative traditions . . . quite different from the usual country town . . . Garden City was to some extent the outcome of socialism, and for that reason I have myself invested in the scheme'. George Bernard Shaw thus revealed his own political disposition which he expected to be strongly reflected in Letchworth. In the early 20th century the notion of Socialism gaining control was revolutionary, and national governments alternated between Liberals and Conservatives. Keir Hardie and the Independent Labour Party held a handful of seats, although the 'progressive' Fabians of the London County Council had spearheaded the advance of local authorities into housing and public utilities. In Letchworth the Fabians were led by the Howard Pearsalls and Raymond Unwin, prior to his departure for Hampstead. Further left were Mr. and Mrs. J. Kidd, whilst the Christian Socialists looked to J. Bruce Wallace. There were early arguments over whether the Socialist Society should include all shades of Socialist thought. George Bates, H. Clapham Lander and Arthur Brunt were local leaders of the Labour Party.[6]

Letchworth was located in the Hitchin Constituency, traditionally a Conservative seat, but the 1906 General Election brought the Liberals to power, with T. T. Gregg as the local member. Local Liberals included W. H. Knight, editor of *The Citizen* and Dr. MacFadyen. Barry Parker was a Liberal supporter, whilst Thomas Adams had acted as a local party agent in the Scottish Borders.

The Conservatives organised the first political club in 1908, located between the Birds Hill housing and the town centre, with a licence which denoted it as the 'Pub Club'. The local leader, Charles Ball the contractor, was subsequently a member of the Parish, Urban District and County Councils. Howard Hurst, another contractor, J. H. W. Stephenson and J. van Hooydonk were also prominent. Miss M. A. Nicholson, public spirited and sympathetic, was the Conservative women's leader. For many years, however, party politics held a low profile in local government, with 'independents' or 'all parties' dominant, irrespective of their personal allegiance.

'Our Mutual Friend' — the Company   F.G.C. Ltd. inevitably attained primacy. In 1909, *The City* referred to the Company as 'Our mutual friend' but stressed the importance of local shareholders to ensure the fulfilment of the Trustee role. Greater demands were being made on F.G.C. Ltd., but subscription of capital was slow, impeding development. The period 1903-15 was, with good reason, characterised by Purdom as 'The years of struggle'.[7] Purdom and Harold Craske had control over the Company's accounts. Purdom later claimed that the 1907 valuation, by Drivers Jonas and Trustram Eve, of £379,500 for the Company's fixed assets revealed a capital surplus of £97,047 6s. 3d. The Directors were uncertain as to how to present this in the balance sheet, and it was consequently understated by charging much expenditure incidental to town development against the revenue account. This enforced greater financial caution than was strictly necessary. It was not until 1911 that the revenue account showed a profit, a mere £171, which grew to £3,034 by 1914. In 1913 a 1 per cent dividend was paid, but the outbreak of war prevented further payments. Purdom's analysis revealed an operating profit of £401 in 1904, £4,545 in 1911 and £6,017 in 1914. He privately circulated proposals for a revised accounting procedure: the unintended consequence of his tactless action was the resignation of Aneurin Williams, the F.G.C. Chairman, who had accepted personal responsibility for the slow growth of the town. Purdom also, more successfully, negotiated with the Inland Revenue over income tax on the Company's trading activities, reducing a claim from several hundred to a few pounds at a time when the tax was 1s. 0d. in the pound.

Broadway and The Town Square   In 1910 a delegation from the R.I.B.A. Town Planning Conference criticised Letchworth for lack of civic design.[8] The following year, influenced by a visit to the United States, Unwin announced 'Letchworth 1914', a project to commemorate the 10th Anniversary of the First Garden City with public buildings including a cottage hospital, public hall, boys club and institute. He also redoubled his efforts to urge completion of Town Square. At the 1912 A.G.M., Aneurin Williams declared that 'considerable attention has been given during the year to the laying out of town square'.[9] Unwin had by then prepared a definitive layout, and had convinced Gaunt that the time was ripe for positive action. In a 1913 article in *Garden Cities and Town Planning*, nominally by Gaunt, but almost certainly ghosted by Unwin, the new plan was unveiled.[10] The three-acre square was compared to Grosvenor and Belgrave Squares in London and had room for gatherings of 6,000 to 8,000 citizens. Formal planting was put in hand and the outline of the central civic and religious buildings was picked out in Lombardy poplars. Alas the buildings never progressed beyond a perspective showing their designs 'freely adapted from the works of Wren and other masters', a Baroque composition capped by cupolas and a

77. Central Square (Town Square). A 1912 design with buildings based on 'the works of Wren and other masters'. The concept shows the influence of formal classical design, notably the work of Lutyens at the Central Square in Hampstead Garden Suburb.

soaring spire dominating the Broadway axis. Colonnades linked the central buildings to the simpler facades surrounding the square. A *caveat* lay in Gaunt's statement that the Company should not give the impression of wastefulness, to businessman and labourer alike. Letchworth was placed at a disadvantage by Bournville and Port Sunlight, where their creators had provided ample formal buildings of a civic character.

A design policy was introduced for Broadway between Town Square and Station Place. The preference for the Georgian style to attain visual unity was undoubtedly influenced by Lutyens's central buildings at Hampstead Garden Suburb. Purdom, not himself an architect, felt that the Georgian style was the most out of keeping with the character of the town.[11] It appears that Parker and his staff prepared a less grandiose layout for the Town Square. The First World War postponed building on even the peripheral sites, and the Square was fitfully developed by the Museum (Parker and Unwin, 1914, first phase completed 1920), the Grammar School (Parker, 1931), and the Council Offices (Bennett and Bidwell, 1935), all conforming to the Georgian style. The Library (Crickmer, 1938) represented an uneasy interpolation of a mild 'moderne' style alongside the Museum, whilst later buildings on gap sites were related only by their inappropriate character for their context. Likewise along Broadway, the Estate Offices (Parker and Unwin, 1914), together with Barclays Bank (Hugh

Seebohm, 1908), set the Georgian tone, matched by the Boys Club (Parker and Unwin, 1914), and the Methodist Church and Police Station. Post-1945 buildings in Town Square and Broadway were largely an aesthetic jumble of the kind which the original policy was designed to avoid.

Letchworth Urban District Council   As early as 1912, Sir John Gorst advocated Urban District status.[12] In April 1913 a group of Parish Council candidates, the 'Letchworth XI' demurred, arguing that Letchworth would only gain higher rates — 7s. 6d. in the pound as against 5s. 0d. (37p against 25p) — in the process. The group included Charles F. Ball, J. Van Hooydonk, Howard Hurst and Norman MacFadyen. It became increasingly evident that the economies of the Parish Council were shortsighted. Roads were neglected, street lighting was 50 per cent below the expected standard, and construction of a cemetery required under the Burial Acts was delayed. Storm water drains were urgently required, and extra housing was needed, due to the influx of munition workers and Belgian refugees. In 1917, George Brown was authorised to apply to the County Council[13] for the conversion of the parish into an Urban District Council independent of Hitchin R.D.C., comprising 'the freehold of the Letchworth Parish known as the Garden City Estate, owned by First Garden City Limited', 3,652 acres, 1 rood, 25 poles (1478 ha.). The population in 1917 stood at 10,212 (5,324 in 1911); with 2,242 houses (1,315); rateable value £60,336 (£30,406).

Letchworth U.D.C. was created in 1919, with elections for 15 Councillors on 9 April.[14] The town was not divided into wards for many years, and electors could vote for up to five candidates. There were 15 Labour, an 'All Party' 15, and several Independents to choose from. 9 'All Party', 4 Labour and 2 Independents were elected, five of whom would retire

78. Letchworth Urban District Council, 1919. Charles Ball, the first Chairman of the U.D.C., had opposed the original move towards the new status of Letchworth.

annually. Charles F. Ball became the first Chairman and served until 1924 to be succeeded by Norman MacFadyen until 1927: both had originally strongly opposed the creation of the U.D.C. Mrs. W. H. Gaunt topped the poll with 1,014 votes. Remaining members were Miss Bartholomew, Messrs. C. F. Ball, J. van Hooydonk, H. D. Clapham, H. Bond Holding, E. H. Whiteman, W. G. 'Bill' Furmston , The Rev. H. Cubbon, C. E. Foster, Mrs. Margaret Steen, Messrs J. T. Openshaw, P. W. Bichener, J. J. Kidd and C. J. Hill. George Brown was appointed Clerk. In the early 1920s elections were hotly contested, but the new Council settled down by 1925 when *The Citizen* reported the now customary apathy with less than 50 per cent turnout.

Housing for Heroes During the War the Howard Cottage Society had made valiant efforts to continue with 'Little Belgium' and the R.D.C. had also completed 110 houses, but shortage of working class housing was acute, both locally and nationally.[15] Unwin's key role in advocating the construction of state subsidised, local authority owned working-class housing, based on Garden City standards, has already been noted, as has the formation of the Ministry of Health under Christopher Addison, and the open-ended financial arrangements under the 1919 Housing Act. The Letchworth U.D.C. enthusiastically pressed ahead with its housing schemes notwithstanding rapidly escalating costs and scarcity of materials.[16] There was urgent need for 600 houses; the programme under the 1919 Housing Act involved 707 houses built 1919-22. Despite high costs, the subsidies enabled the rents to be fixed at 7s. 3d.-8s. 6d. (38-42½p) per week for a non-parlour three-bedroom house, rising to 11s. 9d.-13s. 6d. (58-67½p) per week for a parlour four-bedroom house. The schemes were designed by architects with Garden City experience — Jackmans Place by Bennett and Bidwell, Pixmore by Crickmer and Foxley; and Westbury by A. O. Cave and R. S. Bowers. In design terms the estates were models of their kind. In particular, Jackmans Place, north of and partly fronting the Baldock Road, enabled Bennett and Bidwell to demonstrate their skills in natural progression from Rushby Mead. The articulation of the housing and the use of gables and dormers was masterly in producing a varied yet aesthetically coordinated townscape, set off by the colour washed roughcast walls and rich red clay tiled roofs. The layout involved a loop road with spur culs-de-sac, and road junctions and greens were effectively handled following the layout diagrams from Unwin's *Town Planning in Practice*. A quarter mile further west, Crickmer's site occupied the triangular area between Rushby Mead, Pixmore Way and Baldock Road. Pixmore Way was an important arterial route into the town centre, and Crickmer was content to use simple hipped roof groups similar to those at Gretna, stepped slightly back and forward, accented by 'M' gables. The Westbury scheme was on a neighbourhood scale, and pushed residential development westwards from Campers Road. The street layout approximated more to a regular grid which Cave and Bowers relieved by small setback tapering greens.

After termination of the 1919 Act subsidies in 1922 and Addison's resignation, new terms were offered in the Housing Acts of 1923 and 1924, promoted by Neville Chamberlain and John Wheatley, the first Labour Minister of Health, respectively. Housing designs were simplified to stereotypes from the Ministry *Housing Manuals*. Letchworth U.D.C. built 48 houses under the 1923 Act and 476 under the 1924 Act. Costs fell from an average of £900 for the 'Addison' Act schemes to £400 in 1924. Construction then ceased until the 1930s when additional Council housing was built between Bedford Road and Icknield Way. Limited use was also made of subsidies to private builders under a supplementary 1919 Housing Act. Housing society construction virtually ceased, but under the 1923 Act the Howard Cottage Society completed Meadow Way Green and built 20 flats between Broadwater Avenue and Spring Road. By the end of 1924, 755 local authority houses had been constructed which, added to the R.D.C. housing stock of 110, gave a total of 865 or

79. Jackmans Place housing, 1919-21. Bennett and Bidwell updated their excellent housing designs from Rushby Mead for this pioneer Letchworth U.D.C. Council Estate.

28 per cent of the 3,064 Letchworth total. Cottage society housing accounted for 1,086 houses, or 35 per cent of the stock. It is not known what proportion of the 1,113 privately built homes were owner-occupied.

Highways, Open space and Public Health   The U.D.C. began to take over the Company's highways. F.G.C. Ltd. had allowed space for widening, and the increase in traffic made this necessary in Station Road, Works Road, Gernon Road, Commerce Avenue and Eastcheap. Only 1¼ miles of road had been constructed during the First World War, but almost five were completed between 1919-24,[17] bringing the total to 18, rising to 26 in 1940. It was agreed that the Company would build to the Council's specification, following which the roads would be adopted and maintained at public expense. The variety of highway treatment and planting was continued, which matured into the verdure of the Garden City. Perhaps the most symbolic act was the making up of Broadway between Sollershott Circus and Town Square in 1924. The central section had remained a cinder path for bicycles and pedestrians through the war. The 100ft. reservation allowed a 24ft. carriageway, with 21ft. greenswards, 6ft. footways, and 9ft. 6in. margins. A double line of lime trees provided a tangible indication that Letchworth was at last acquiring a centre, after years of peripheral and lopsided development.

Open spaces passed from Company to Council. F.G.C. Ltd. had acquired the manorial rights of the 70-acre (28.3 ha.) Norton Common, and created a furore in 1909 by posting notices 'Temporary footpaths: Sufferance only'.[18] Howard was amongst the protestors and suggested that the land be formally declared public open space. In January 1922, the

IX.   'The Hitchin Bus, Station Place, 1946 — souvenir of the war years': a cartoon by Francis King evoking the transport difficulties of the austerity period, when a trip to 'Sleepy Hollow' was a great adventure.

X. 'High Tech' Letchworth. The Wynd Arcade, 1986, designed by Baldwin Brattle Connelly Partnership. Initially controversial, but tucked unobtrusively behind Station Road, this new development represents the latest variation on Howard's 'Crystal Palace' theme.

XI. The Letchworth Business Centre, Phase II (1989), Avenue One, the Business Park. The architects were Eric Askew and Partners. The sleek buildings of the Business Park symbolise the regeneration of the economic base of Letchworth after the recession of the early 1980s.

VIEW FROM SOUTH

SITE PLAN

PARKING

GARDEN

DOCTORS SURGERY
WITH FLATS OVER

NEVELLS ROAD

NORTON WAY NORTH

VIEW FROM SOUTH-WEST

PROPOSED DEVELOPMENT AT NORTON WAY NORTH, LETCHWORTH

FOR HIGHACRE CONSTRUCTION COMPANY LTD

ARCHITECTS – PENTANGLE DESIGN GROUP

XII. The Garden City revival. Surgery and flats in Nevells Road and Norton Way North by the Pentangle Design Group, completed in 1989.

80. Broadway, the cinder path, c.1923. The double lime avenue has already been planted and the road was made up shortly after this evocative photograph was taken.

81. Howard Park Gardens, the paddling pool, c.1933. Always a popular spot for young children, photographs of the paddling pool were widely used for Garden City publicity.

Company reiterated that the Common was private property, but allowed residents to enjoy the amenities provided no damage occurred. They reserved the right to withdraw the concession at any time, however. The Council was perturbed and in June 1923 acquired a long lease for 60 acres, but the Company retained the margins for potential building sites. At this time Barry Parker prepared a plan which included boating lakes. The axial avenue was planted in accord with the original layout plan, and tennis courts, bowling greens and, in 1935, a new open air swimming pool were provided. The U.D.C. had acquired Howard Park in 1934, and had taken over the area south of Hillshott, including the old swimming pool — now the Ball Memorial Gardens — in 1919. A bowling green and an ex-servicemen's club were established.

The 'official' definition of a Garden City included a claim that it was 'a town designed for healthy living'.[19] Infant mortality and death rates had long been accepted as a measure of the health of the population as a whole. At the time of purchase of the Letchworth Estate, the Hertfordshire County Medical Officer of Health, Mr. F. E. Fremantle, had advised the Company of the healthiness of the surrounding area. In 1912 the infant mortality rate was claimed as half that of the large industrial towns.[20] In 1912 there was an overall death rate of 95 for every 1,000 births of children dying in their first year, the lowest on record, but the Letchworth rate was 50.6. Fremantle also claimed that the health of children had greatly improved after their arrival in Letchworth, borne out to some extent in a survey undertaken in 1919 comparing the health of groups of children in Hitchin and Letchworth. The death rate per 1,000 population also showed a significant improvement over that for England and Wales, 8.0 as compared to 13.0, with a figure of 14.1 for 95 large industrial towns including London. The death rate was declining due to improvements in public health, and the situation in Letchworth may not have been as favourable as was claimed. In 1925, Purdom, who had enthusiastically quoted the 1912 figures in *The Garden City*, conceded that the earlier data were not sufficiently reliable. Later figures indicated a fluctuation of death rates of 5.5 per 1,000 population in 1919, rising to 8.4 in 1922 then falling to 7.4 two years later, and infant mortality rates per 1,000 births of 90 in 1919, reducing to 34.93 in 1922 and rising to 47.8 in 1924. The small population and post-war influenza epidemic accounted for the fluctuations. Purdom claimed that on the whole the high reputation for public health in Letchworth was justified. The water supply and sewage disposal facilities were comparatively new and, together with the open layout of the housing which encouraged circulation of air, assisted public health and the promotion of the benefits of 'the health of the country with the comforts of the town'.

Letchworth and Statutory Planning   Letchworth was the creation of a private landlord laying out his land as he wished. The Parker and Unwin plan was no more than a statement of intent and its land-use allocations had no statutory backing. The fundamental principle of a limited 'Town Area' within a larger agricultural belt preserved against building was entirely voluntary, and depended upon the good faith of the Company. An indication that commercialism sometimes attained primacy was given by their attitude to Norton Common. Statutory town planning made a modest beginning in 1909 when urban and borough councils were empowered to prepare schemes for land where development appeared imminent.[21] The 1919 Housing Act introduced the additional provision that any urban district or borough with a population greater than 20,000 after 1 January 1923 would be required to prepare a scheme within three years. With its 1921 population of 10,000, Letchworth U.D.C. fell outside the scope of compulsion, although co-operation with the Company over an agreed scheme based upon its master plan would have been possible, particularly given Parker's consultancy role. However, the Council did not address itself to town planning resolutions or acquire 'interim development control' powers under the 1925 and 1932 Planning Acts.

The Company made significant adjustments to the master plan, particularly in the Bedford Road area, and south of Baldock Road during the 1920s, and added almost 200 acres to the original 'town area', without any expression of concern by the Council. Statements by Sir Edgar Bonham Carter, F.G.C. Chairman, emphasised the junior position of the Council:

> The planning of the town has been carried out by F.G.C. Ltd. by means of its powers as sole owner of the estate and not by the local authority under the powers of the town planning Acts. The U.D.C. has, however, a voice in the town plan. To ensure this, the Company has deposited with the Council a 'layout' plan of the town, together with an explanatory memorandum defining user, character of building and density etc. and has agreed not to depart from the provisions of the plan without first consulting the Council.[22]

W. R. Davidge (d.1961), an eminent planning consultant who had prepared the first advisory Hertfordshire County Plan in 1927, was retained by Letchworth U.D.C. in 1938. He recommended that the Council now consider its own scheme. Building control was largely in the hands of the Company. Unwin's bye-laws had been progressive for their date, but the 1936 Public Health Act had introduced the compulsion for every district authority to adopt model bye-laws for streets and buildings. The deposit of building plans with the Hitchin R.D.C. and Letchworth U.D.C. had been little more than a formality. It was not until after the Second World War, however, that Letchworth U.D.C. took a more positive role in town planning and building control.

Chapter Ten

A Living From the Land

Co-operative Cultivation   One of Howard's principal objectives was to stem the tide of rural depopulation by building up a strong rural economy. The 1890s witnessed rural stagnation and an increasing flow of labour to the Colonies, particularly Canada, Australia and New Zealand. This stimulated trade in food, which further depressed British agriculture. The wide choice of estates available to the Garden City Pioneer Company reflected this. Following his own inauspicious experience of farming in Nebraska, Howard saw the opportunity for a wide range of agricultural activities in the Garden City, 'in large farms, smallholdings, allotments, cow pastures etc; the natural competition of these various methods of agriculture tested by the willingness of occupiers to offer the highest rent to the municipality, tending to bring about the best system of husbandry'.[1] Furthermore, the existence of the developing town area would bring a ready market of 30,000 residents into being, without the disadvantage of high transportation costs. Howard's theory of substitution of higher value cash crops including fruit and vegetables for basic staples such as wheat matched the work of the economic geographer, von Thünen, who envisaged intersection of varied angled concentric demand cones indicating a tendency to grow more lucrative crops on the fringes of a settlement. Howard calculated that a community of 30,000, consuming only one third of a pint of milk a day, would account for 1,250 gallons each day, which would save the farmers £1,900 each year on railway charges. This would encourage higher rental, without increasing the price to the consumer.[2]

The Garden City Pioneer Company announced the intention of 'the provision of a broad belt of agricultural land round the town under such restrictive covenants as may secure to the inhabitants the enjoyment for all time of the combined advantages of town and country life, while the agricultural tenants may have a market for their produce brought to their doors'. How did it all work out in practice?

The Letchworth Estate and its Farms   In contrast to the detailed investigation of the suitability of the Letchworth site for industry, comparatively little seems to have been done to assess its potential for agricultural diversity.[3] Almost all of the 3,820 acres (1546 ha.) purchased in 1903 was in agricultural use — 9 farms of between 252 (102 ha.) and 842 acres (340 ha.), four smallholdings from two (0.809 ha.) to 79 acres (32 ha.), and 15 allotments on five acres. Rents were low, ranging from 8s. 6d. to £1 10s. 0d. per acre for the farms, and 16s. 0d. to £2 3s. 0d. for the smallholdings. The modest rent roll of £3,172 19s. 0d. for the whole estate averaged 16s. 8d. (83p) per acre per annum. Given this 1.6 per cent return, it is scarcely surprising that the £40 15s. 0d. average per acre purchase price had been criticised as being unduly high. The farms were neglected and poorly cultivated, with buildings in disrepair. The average weekly wage for a farm labourer was 15s. 0d. (75p), and many of the 400 inhabitants were employed elsewhere. The situation represented a classic case of rural deprivation which the Garden City movement aimed to alleviate.

The under capitalisation of First Garden City Ltd. affected the agricultural strategy as profoundly as the development of the 'town area'. However, there was no overall master plan as in the case of the latter. Even Howard had referred to his 'absence of plan' for agriculture almost as an advantage, and at Letchworth matters proceeded on an *ad hoc* basis. On completion of purchase all existing tenants were given notice to quit, and new tenancies were negotiated under which they agreed to give up possession of one tenth of their holdings in any one year, subject to compensation. The two tenants of the major part of the town area were co-operative, although the area did not come fully under company control until 1910, when it was laid to grass or farmed directly. The tenancies were re-arranged, larger farms divided into holdings related to the existing homesteads, the buildings

82. Garden City Agricultural Conference, 1905. H. Rider Haggard sits in the centre, with Howard and Thomas Adams immediately to his left. Near the back, on the left of the picture, are Barry Parker and Raymond Unwin.

were repaired and an attempt was made to obtain more economic rents. Thomas Adams attempted to formulate a coherent farm strategy. His upbringing on a lowland Scottish farm, and his experience on a 48-acre smallholding stimulated his political interest in the 'Land question'. He arranged a conference on 'Garden City in relation to agriculture' on 10 September 1904,[4] hosted by the Company which, however, took little direct interest in it. The attraction of H. Rider Haggard, novelist and leader of the 'back to the land' campaign, reflected Adams's flair for publicity. Other leaders of the rural lobby attended — Constance Cochrane of the Rural Housing and Sanitation Association, J. Nugent Harris, Secretary of the Agricultural Organisation Society, and Alderman Richard Winfrey, Chairman of the South Lincolnshire Smallholdings Association. The conference presented a coherent argument for 'back to the land', based on the promotion of smallholdings.

'Back to the Land'   At the conference Adams outlined his ideas for the agricultural belt. He visualised 'a just and equitable system of tenure . . . giving the labourer a potential interest in the land'.[5] He urged the Company to create 200 smallholdings of five acres (2 ha.) each and ample allotments for factory workers, in addition to the generous garden spaces enjoyed by each house. Local farm credit banks and co-operatives would provide capital and develop marketing skills. Cottage industries allied to agriculture would employ wives. The example of Belgium, where this system had successfully combined agricultural and industrial labour, was no doubt familiar to him. There were also to be 10 large farms of 150 acres each, with the Company providing a lead by establishing a demonstration farm, technical institute, tree nursery and research centre. The total outlay of about £10,000 was double what the Company had initially invested in maintaining the existing farming pattern.

The Company did little to put these new ideas into practice. Purdom squarely blamed the lack of capital.[6] Publicity about smallholdings had brought hundreds of applicants for land, but most lacked the capital to build their own homes. Those who could build were offered 99-year leases on $\frac{1}{4}$ acre cottage plots, with a contiguous area of agricultural land on a 21-year tenancy. In 1905 a 152-acre (61.5 ha.) smallholdings centre was established at Norton Hall Farm under the direction of E. O. Fordham, Lord Lucas, Alderman Richard Winfrey and C. R. Buxton. The Norton Cooperative Smallholdings Society paid the Company 25s. 0d. an acre and sub-let parcels up to 20 acres (8 ha.) at 35s. 0d. Twelve cottages were built in Norton village, pig sties were constructed and 10 acres planted with fruit. The experiment was not successful, neither was a bank and a smallholdings and allotments society. After Adams's replacement by Walter Gaunt, agriculture was accorded very low priority. Even Howard became irritable over Adams's continued championing of the cause in *The Garden City*. Nevertheless, in 1907, an attempt was made to include model smallholdings in the 1907 Cottage Exhibition, mostly located south of the Baldock Road. None were successful in the long term, and in the 1930s the land was infilled with ribbon development. Adams's vision of 'a new race of sturdy English Yeomen . . . to form the bulwarks of our Empire'[7] faded, to be replaced by Howard's resignation to expediency — 'The right development of the rural area may be far more safely left with a little timely help here and there to adjust itself to new demands as they rise'. Any remaining enthusiasm for smallholdings was dampened by soil conditions. Contrary to expectation, raised by successful market gardening a few miles north in Bedfordshire, the Letchworth estate consisted largely of clay or chalk, and crops were both late and sparse.

A Small Country Living   A few hardy pioneers did overcome the difficulties. W. G. 'Bill' Furmston has already been mentioned as the genial 'Mine Host' of *The Skittles*.[8] In the early 1900s, he was a skilled craftsman and pattern maker at Doultons, the London based-sanitary engineers. Married, living in rooms with a growing family, ultimately 11 children, Furmston considered emigration to New Zealand. He learned of the Garden City project through the editor of *The Clarion*. At Whit weekend 1904 he joined a party of 200 from Ruskin College on a special excursion. Raymond Unwin met the party on the wooden plank platform and explained the scheme. He introduced Purdom, F. J. Cole, the estate forester, and the Rev. J. Bruce Wallace. They toured the estate from Willbury Camp to Norton, to Willian and Letchworth Corner, returning to the station along Spring Road. The Furmstons leased 6, 'Alpha Cottages', and convinced two of their fellow lodgers at St Pancras, Miss Revell and Miss Priestley, to follow suit — Miss Revill was in fact the first official resident of the Garden City.

The Furmstons leased a plot on Baldock Road, to build 'Pine Cottage' for £300, on a loan raised from the Co-operative Building Society. They rented $2\frac{1}{4}$ acres (0.91 ha.) on a

21-year lease, originally on behalf of a friend who failed to take it on. Bill initially commuted to London, often lodging with his mother during the week. He hired an agricultural labourer for 7d. an hour, more than double the going rate, who dug the plot and planted 400 apple trees, 400 nut trees, plums and pears. The local farmers were sceptical, chaffing at the fancy prices of Furmston's rent and his expensive hired help. His London colleagues called him 'barmy leaving a place where you have been 20 years and going down to a God-forsaken place like that'. He worked the holding less than one day a week, and sub-contracted his labourer, and estimated that he grew enough food for 40 people. Over a 25-year period he calculated that £3,000 had been spent in wages, £1,000 on seeds, plants and bushes; manure and fertilizer; greenhouse, bees, ducks and fowl; and ground rent. His family of eight lived off the produce and 'even in years when the accounts showed a money loss there was a net gain in terms of life'. There was never any large profit, merely an attempt to balance the outgoings. In 1941, the wages bill was £156, other outgoings £34, receipts £178, a loss of £12. Nevertheless he had been able to show to his own satisfaction 'How to bring up a family of eight children, and keep a bit of Old England cultivated as it should be'.

The Furmstons were not wholly an isolated case. Amongst Benoit-Lévy's neighbours on Wilbury Road, a Mr. Jones rented a five-acre (2 ha.) plot, at £30 per annum for his cottage plot, and £5 per annum for the remainder in the rural zone.[9] A saddler by trade, Jones had lived near Epping, had read Howard's book, and had brought his family, with five children ranging from 2-16 years, to Letchworth. He had built his home at a cost of £370. The produce supported his family, and provided a margin for sale. He was considering dairy farming, but did not have sufficient capital to purchase four cows. Jones had been a founder of Garden City Smallholdings. He employed two men at £1 each per week, higher than the prevailing average. His crops were primarily fruit — he had found the land too exposed for early vegetables and fruit. Early strawberries sold at 7½d. per pound, but those from Letchworth came later when the price had dropped to 2d. Potatoes were, however, an excellent money spinner, particularly if they could be saved until Christmas. He considered it would be preferable to divide the estate partly into 20-hectare farms for cereals and dairy produce, and the remainder into smallholdings for orchards, a division which suggested familiarity with Adams's plans.

A Horticultural Cornucopia   The provision of generous gardens enabled the produce to make a worthwhile contribution to the family budget.[10] Garden sizes for small cottages, and later for Council houses, varied from two to 10 poles (61 sq. yards/$1/80$ acre to 302.5 sq. yards $\frac{1}{16}$ acre). Many tenants allocated a third to grass, a third to flowers, and the remainder to vegetables. Almost all had fruit — there were about 3,500 apple, pear and plum trees. Above this, there was a demand for allotments — in 1925 there were 38 acres, giving 230 plots and, after 1945, 606 plots, by which time the Allotment Cottage Garden Association had a membership of 500.

The amount and variety of crops was remarkable. A ten-pole garden or allotment produced two dozen spring cabbages, 10 lb. broad beans, 8 lb. French beans, 20 lb. runner beans, 8 lb. carrots, 10 lb. peas, two dozen lettuces, 10 lb. Brussels sprouts, 10 lb. cauliflowers, 10 lb. parsnips, 10 lb. beetroot, and 20 lb. onions, total 156 lb. By concentrating on a more limited range it produced three cwt. (336 lb.) potatoes, 28 lb. tomatoes, 14 lb. carrots, 14 lb. parsnips, 10 lb. turnips, 20 lb. beetroot, and 56 lb. onions, total 478 lb. Wartime restrictions, particularly the 1939-45 'Dig for Victory' Campaign, stimulated production. In 1953, an attempt was made to estimate the total volume and value of garden produce. Writing in the Jubilee Issue of *Town and Country Planning*, H. Brewer stated that there were 6,000 gardens in Letchworth. Basing his estimate on a ¼-acre ($1/10$ ha.) garden, the following produce had been grown:

40 lb. rhubarb 13s. 4d, eight dozen lettuces £1 12s. 0d., 16 lb. gooseberries 10s. 8d., 15 lb. redcurrants 15s. 0d., 16 lb. raspberries £1 0s. 0d., 24 lb. peas 12s. 0d., two cwt. [224 lb.] onions £3 14s. 8d. 14 lb. parsnips 4s. 8d., 7 lb. turnips 2s. 8d., two cwt. [224 lb.] apples £5 12s. 0d., 8 lb. blackcurrants 10s. 0d., 5 lb. golden plums 2s. 6d., 20 lb. Victoria plums 10s.0d. Total 623 lb.; £15 19s. 6d.

A ten-pole (0.025 ha.) garden had produced 397 lb., worth £6 12s.8d. Estimating an average of one third of that figure for each of the 6,000 gardens, Brewer speculated that these could produce 794,000 lb. of food with a value of £13,200. Nobody queried this, and however wide of the mark his figures may have been, there was no doubt that, particularly during and after the Second World War, many families were self sufficient for fruit and vegetables. In addition to this he recorded 32 bee keepers owning 117 hives, each contributing 30 lb. to the food pool, and more than 1,000 poultry keepers, with an average stock of six birds, each yielding 160 eggs per bird per year, in addition to a good supply of meat. Added to this 160 greenhouses might produce 120 cucumbers and 160 lb. of tomatoes each season. A veritable horticultural cornucopia!

Mixed Farming   In contrast to the increasing productivity of domestic gardens, farming remained relatively static, reflecting national conditions, rather than, as had been hoped, a response to the stimulus of a ready market. The depressed condition of the farms has already been noted and although there was some stimulus to production during the First World War, when undeveloped fields either side of Broadway were turned over to wheat, the post-war depression reached its nadir during the early 1930s. Purdom quoted rentals of 25s. 0d. to 60s. 0d. per acre in 1925, high figures which were not borne out by a report commissioned by the Company in April 1928, when they had become seriously concerned about the return from the agricultural belt.[11] Conversion to dairy farming was seen as the salvation of agricultural enterprise, through which one farmer would be able to handle more extensive holdings, enabling rationalisation into fewer, larger units. On the north, Norton Grange, Wilbury and possibly Standalone Farms would be dispensed with; on the south, Lower Farm, New Farm Baldock, Letchworth Hall and Lordship Farm, particularly if the town area was extended southwards, which eventually came to pass in the 1960s and 1970s.

Rental levels in the late 1920s were low, but it was suggested by the land agents, Hardings of St Albans, that 16s.0d. per acre north of the railway and 21s. 0d. per acre to the south was all that was justified by conditions, a substantial reduction and more than contemplated. The Company proposed new agreements on the basis of 22s. 6d. and 25s. 0d. respectively, which the farmers queried. The rental levels had, at best, remained relatively static since 1903, when the overall average had been 16s. 8d. per acre. It was to take a more extensive changeover to dairy farming, which entailed substantial expenditure of £52,614 on cow sheds and milking parlours, and another World War, before farming became more than barely viable.

Agricultural Industries   A variety of industries related to agriculture on the estate sprang up over the years. The Company did not establish its own research centre as recommended by Adams, but, in 1910, the Country Gentlemen's Association moved to Letchworth. This was an organisation which advised landowners, and issued a monthly magazine and annual handbook. The concern leased two sites, one on Birds Hill, just west of the main industrial area, and the other on Icknield Way, to the west of Spring Road, which included extensive seed testing grounds. The propagation of cuttings was also carried out. The handsome Tudor-style offices, reminiscent of a country house, were designed by R. J. Johnston.

Dairies flourished early on due to the proximity of the market, even before the widespread changeover to dairy farming was stimulated by the Company. Cole's Garden City Central

Dairy was established in Station Road by 1907, and others operated from the farms themselves — Wilbury Farm, Letchworth Farm, Norton Grange Farm and Pixmore Farm. Between the Wars, the Bancroft Dairies of Hitchin established a branch in Station Road, whilst T. Squire was well-known locally. In the mid-1930s the Cooperative Wholesale Society built their own dairy on the newly opened Letchworth Gate. A distinctive building, rather reminiscent of a progressive pithead bath, resulted, designed by a Barnsley architect. Its tower formed a focal feature on the approach to Letchworth from the Great North Road. Operations ceased in the early 1980s, and the building was demolished in 1988.

The local production of livestock brought about the need for an abattoir. The Company resisted local butchers slaughtering on their premises, and in 1925 a model abattoir was built on Works Road, capable of handling 300 head of cattle, 400 sheep and 250 calves, and more than 3,000 pigs per week. Associated with the abattoir, a processing works produced fats, fertilizers, and dried blood. The Letchworth Bacon Company diversified from sausages and pies into food and scientific, and even medical, research, and in addition opened a bakery. Amongst local bakers, Notts, Leys Avenue and subsequently Eastcheap soon became dominant, to be joined by the Co-operative Society in the inter-war period.

Chapter Eleven

Garden City Comes of Age

Howard's Final Years   Within a decade of the foundation of Letchworth, Howard began to press for a second Garden City.[1] In 1910 he had the idea of developing a Garden City in memory of King Edward VII. Influenced by the success of Hampstead Garden Suburb and the attendant legislation, the Garden City Association was renamed the Garden Cities and Town Planning Association, and re-wrote its objectives to include garden suburbs and garden villages. In March 1912, G.C.T.P.A. honoured Howard with a public dinner attended by the leading figures in the emergent town planning and housing movements, whilst, in 1914, he became an Honorary Member of the newly formed Town Planning Institute, whose first President was Thomas Adams. Although wartime plans for reconstruction were based on low density suburban housing, rather than self-contained Garden Cities, the 'young lions' of the G.C.T.P.A., 'New Townsmen', Purdom, Osborn, and W. G. Taylor wrote a pamphlet on *New Towns After The War*, advocating 100 new settlements, a milestone in progress towards state developed new towns, finally implemented after 1945.

In October 1918, Howard confided to Purdom and Osborn that he had identified the site for his second Garden City:[2] a gently rolling tract of countryside immediately south of the Digswell Viaduct on the Great Northern Railway, running through Hertfordshire from Kings Cross to the North. Fourteen miles nearer to London than Letchworth, it seemed an ideal location. The Desborough Estate put a large part of the site up for auction in May 1919. Howard successfully bid for 1,500 acres (607 ha.), and even convinced the estate agent, Norman Savill, to advance him the £250 balance of the deposit. Howard, Purdom and Osborn threw in their lot with the new project — named Welwyn Garden City to distinguish it from 'Old' Welwyn, the small coaching town on the Great North Road a mile or two to the west. The settlement in 'the heights of Hertfordshire' was designated 'the First Satellite Town', both to distinguish it from Letchworth, and also in recognition of its closer proximity to London. History repeated itself with the flotation of Second Garden City Ltd. to develop the town, and the preparation of a master plan, initially by Crickmer, but later in 'definitive' form by Louis de Soissons (1891-1962). A further parallel was a housing exhibition, the Daily Mail Ideal Home Model Village, held 1921-2. Friendly rivalry characterised relations between the two Garden Cities, but many influential pioneers moved to the new settlement, to a degree sapping the vitality of Letchworth.

Howard received international honours. In 1913 he was elected President of the newly formed International Garden Cities and Town Planning Federation, an internationalist body which in the 1920s held an influential sequence of conferences in Europe and the U.S.A., beginning in 1919 in war-torn Belgium. In 1925, in New York, Howard suddenly announced his intention to persuade Henry Ford to build a Garden City. 'I'll take a taxi to Grand Central Station: there is bound to be a train to Detroit in an hour or two', was his parting comment.[3] He succeeded in meeting Ford, though with no very positive outcome. *Garden Cities of Tomorrow* was published in all major European languages.[4] The Russian translation by Aleksandr Block, published in 1911, was widely used after the 1917 Revolution, whilst Block, ironically, spent his exile in Welwyn Garden City.

In 1926 H.R.H. Duke of York (later George VI) was noticeably impressed by the Letchworth achievement during his Civic Week visit. In the New Year Honours for 1927,

Howard received a Knighthood. Not before time; according to Shaw, he had merited a Barony for the book, an Earldom for Letchworth and a Dukedom for Welwyn! The Minister of Health, Neville Chamberlain, visited Letchworth with Howard, and toasted his achievement in non-alcoholic wine. Time was running out, however. Howard worked on producing his shorthand typewriter, and wrote cryptic notes for '3rd GC', which would be funded by the success of his invention. In March 1928 a chest infection and stomach cancer were diagnosed. He died on 1 May. Four days later his funeral service was held at the Free Church Letchworth, and he was laid to rest in the town cemetery. The procession was filmed, and edited into views of Garden City life. Shaw cautioned the family about expecting a fortune from the typewriter, adding that Howard was 'one of those heroic simpletons who do big things whilst our prominent worldlings are explaining why they are Utopian and impossible.[5] And of course it is they who will make money out his work'. In May 1930 a Memorial Stone was unveiled in Howard Park Letchworth, and a plain brick wall in Howardsgate, Welwyn Garden City, represented his Memorial there until replaced with a handsome bronze relief plaque many years later. The G.C.T.P.A. introduced an Ebenezer Howard Memorial Medal in his memory, to be awarded for outstanding planning achievements. Appropriately both Unwin and Parker were amongst early recipients.

83. The Ebenezer Howard Memorial Medal, awarded to Barry Parker at Oxford in March 1941 for services rendered to the Garden City movement.

Moving into profitability   The First World War disrupted dividend payments by F.G.C. Ltd.[6] In order to meet essential development costs, the Company had, in 1915, created £50,000 second debentures, with $4\frac{1}{2}$ per cent interest, as a second floating charge on the assets. In 1916 they issued 10,000 of the £5 unissued Ordinary shares as Preference shares bearing a fixed cumulative dividend of 5 per cent. In May 1920 an issue of 50,000 7 per cent gas works mortgage debenture stock was created, to be repaid in 1925. Mortgages on the original 1903 land purchase totalled £83,934 at 4 per cent, repayable with other loans from the late 1920s. The availability of loans influenced the pace of development, whilst the complexity of voting powers attached to the restructured shares was to become crucial during the 1950s takeover struggles. Dividend payments were resumed: 2 per cent in 1918-21, 4 per cent in 1922, and the maximum 5 per cent in 1923, maintained thereafter. In 1923 the total capital stood at £549,141: £194,649 in Ordinary Shares, £25,160 in Preference Shares, and £329,332 from mortgages and loans. It was not until 1937, however, that clearance of dividend arrears began, and was not completed until 1946.

The financial situation of the Company drew conflicting conclusions. In 1922, Purdom again argued that development expenditure brought a greater return than reflected immediately by revenue, and its allocation to the revenue account depressed real profitability. The public utility subsidiaries had assisted overall viability, notwithstanding a miners' strike and post-war depression. Purdom disagreed with the Board's view that their disposal would enable them to concentrate upon development of the town. He laid great stress on the creation of subsidiaries at Welwyn until he was ousted in an acrimonious power struggle in 1928. The U.D.C. also pondered over the apparently poor performance of F.G.C. Ltd., which contrasted with the continued growth of the town, and their own investment in housing construction. The Council felt that the town should be transferred to them, as corporate representative of residents' interests. A Committee examined the matter, but could find no financial basis for the transfer and the matter was shelved.[7]

Industrial diversity   There was an immediate post-war depression whilst the economy adjusted to peacetime conditions. The ambitious Council housing schemes and the reconstruction of the sewage works helped to relieve local unemployment, but economic vitality was dependent upon regeneration of the industrial base. By 1926 this had largely been accomplished: there were 52 factories, compared to 26 in 1913. Spirella, Phoenix Motors, Heatly-Gresham and Ewarts had all extended their works post-1919, and new firms commenced operation, including several which were to remain key employers over the next half century. The severe economic depression of the late 1920s and early 1930s affected Letchworth comparatively little, and the pattern of its industrial estate was examined by government committees — the Greater London Regional Planning Committee visited the industrial area in 1928, and the Marley Committee on Garden Cities and Satellite towns followed in 1932.

Inter-war industries continued the trend towards products with a high value to weight ratio, and a significant input of skill. The British Tabulating Machine Co. Ltd. had begun operations in Lambeth, south London in 1907. They acquired a large plot on Icknield Way in 1920, and Cecil Hignett designed their factory, partly completed the following year. The 'Tab' were leaders in the office revolution.[8] Their Hollerith machines used punched cards to record information on transactions, or census data statistics, which could be electrically sorted and classified. Employment peaked at almost 4,000. The Lacre Motor Company had gone into voluntary liquidation in 1913, following its notorious industrial dispute, but kept operational through war work. In 1919 they pioneered a mechanical road sweeper, a fearsome contraption with revolving brush beneath the driver's cab. It vanquished 'Sir Gadabout' in the cartoon-saga of 1923, but the firm left Letchworth in 1926. Two of their key staff had defected in 1922 to found Shelvoke and Drewry, a firm whose product was also related to public cleansing. Their transverse engined, tiller steered 'freighter' had semi-automatic transmission, and could carry two tons of refuse. By 1930 they had been supplied to 350 Councils and exported throughout Europe and the British Empire.

Phoenix Motors had undertaken government work during the war. In 1921, Joseph van Hooydonk introduced a three-litre car, retailing at over £500, followed by a 12-25 model in 1925. He confidently asserted that his only problem was to obtain land for expansion of his Pixmore Avenue factory.[10] However, the cars neither challenged quality marques such as Daimler or Rolls Royce, nor were they competitive in the emergent mass market with Austin, Ford, Morris or Standard. Production ceased in 1928, and the factory was taken over by the Ascot Motor Company, manufacturers of motorcycles and small cars. They, too, failed and a creditors' meeting was called at the factory on 10 December 1929, whilst the employees milled about outside. The premises reopened as

84. 'Sir Gadabout and the Lacre Monster', cartoon by Fitzwater-Wray, c.1923. Shortly after the cartoon was drawn two key staff left Lacre to found the rival street cleansing firm, Shelvoke and Drewry.

one of the first government training centres the following year. Chater-Lea was founded in London in 1890. In 1928 they moved to Icknield Way, and concentrated upon motorcycle manufacture. They supplied Automobile Association 'Scouts' until 1935, when manufacture of motorcycles ceased, although the firm continued to produce components. The Westinghouse Morse Chain Company located in Works Road in 1920, and expanded into Pixmore Avenue three years later. Their rocker joint chain drive was widely used in electric and internal combustion engines, steam and water turbines or manufacturing machinery. Allied to gear changing, the chain drive formed the basis of automatic transmission, and the firm was absorbed by Borg Warner after the Second World War.

The post-war slump of 1921 sapped the viability of the K. & L. Foundry, and the 1926 General Strike caused cancellation of many of its contracts. Following voluntary liquidation, K. & L. Steel Founders and Engineers Ltd was reconstituted in 1928 as part of the Cohen 600 Group. By 1930, it was claimed as the best equipped steel foundry in Britain, making carbon steel castings up to eight tons for hydraulic cylinders, valves, turbine casings, cars locomotives and wagons, bridges and cranes.[11] In 1938, its associates Jones Cranes pioneered the manufacture of a diesel driven mechanical mobile crane.

In 1930 the employment profile of the town was as follows:[12]

Engineering	1,300
Construction of vehicles	700
Body Building: Prams	280
Furniture	170
Metal Trades	400
Instrument manufacture	120
Printing and Bookbinding	550

Silk and Embroidery	120
Figure Training and other Garments	1,050
Building	600
Constructional work, Contractors etc.	140
Transport	50
Gas, Water and Electricity	140
Local Government	80
Distributive Trades, Shops, etc.	700
Other Industries, including Restaurants, Laundries, Box-making, Parachutes, etc.	500
TOTAL	6,900

Improved Communications   In the inter-war period Letchworth emerged as part of a sub-regional grouping in North Hertfordshire, with Hitchin and Baldock. Improved road and rail transport also developed connections with Luton, Bedford, Royston and the villages in between. In 1920 Road Motors Limited introduced six daily buses to Luton, and the National Bus Company improved internal routes. London Country Green Line buses established long-distance links with London. Faced with competition, the railway, from 1923 the London and North Eastern Railway (L.N.E.R.) smartened itself up. In the 1930s, new 'buffet trains' were introduced, calling at Letchworth en route to and from King's Cross to Cambridge. The fastest completed the 34-mile journey from Letchworth to Kings Cross in 43 minutes, and there were 60 'up' and 'down' trains every weekday. The new rolling stock included a cocktail bar with Bauhaus-influenced tubular chrome and black leather seating.

To improve internal communication across the railway a permanent bridge was constructed to link Spirella with Station Place. Regrettably it was not the fanciful fortified bridge shown in Unwin's *Town Planning In Practice*, but a more functional triple-arched structure, designed by Barry Parker. Named in memory of Sir Ralph Neville, the bridge was opened in May 1930

85. The L.N.E.R. buffet trains, *c*.1935. The modernity of the interior of the buffet car, with its smart cocktail bar, was offset by the welcome reassurance of the old fashioned L.N.E.R. engines.

by Herbert Morrison, returning to Letchworth as Minister of Transport in Ramsay MacDonald's Labour Government. In 1927, the north-western sector of the town was replanned by Barry Parker, with Bedford Road thrust purposefully towards the junction of Wilbury Road and Stotfold Road, providing a convenient link with Bedfordshire via the Arlesey New Road. Parker had become interested in highway design both from a functional and amenity viewpoint, during his 1925 visit to the U.S.A. In 1929, his inaugural address as T.P.I. President, given in Letchworth, included slides of the landscaped parkways of Westchester County, New York.[13] He had included parkways in his master plan for Wythenshawe, the Manchester satellite. At Letchworth, links with the Great North Road, newly designated as the A1 trunk road, were poor. The 1927 *Hertfordshire Regional Planning Report* prepared by W. R. Davidge continued to recommend the diversionary route from Graveley to Willian, along Willian Way and Norton Way, rejoining the historic Great North Road at Radwell. Whilst this by-passed Baldock, the Letchworth residential roads were hardly suitable for

86. The freedom of the road: Letchworth Gate, newly opened, *c*.1933. A lone limousine poses alongside Letchworth Gate with no other vehicle in sight.

heavy long distance traffic. In 1931 a different solution emerged, with the construction of a gently-curving landscaped road from north of Jacks Hill on the Great North Road to the Baldock Road/Pixmore Way junction, on the fringe of Letchworth. Constructed by the County Council, with a Government grant and a contribution from the Company, and opened in 1933, Letchworth Gate was designed by Barry Parker with landscaped reservations either side of the 30-foot, three-lane carriageway. Allied to extensive improvement further south, including the Welwyn and Barnet by-passes, this gave a fast connection to the West End. Keen motorists, such as Parker's daughter-in-law Barbara, were able to rival the best train times!

87. 'Advertising is the Magnet': consumer products of the 1920s.

XIII. The Letchworth Shop, 1986. The architects were Pentangle Design Group. The Garden City Corporation Information Centre has represented a design prototype for the refurbishment of early shops in the town centre.

XIV. a) The Estate Office — now Garden City Corporation offices — designed by Parker and Unwin 1913-14, and mixed town centre development in Station Place. b) The Council Offices. Built by Letchworth U.D.C. in 1935 and designed by Bennett and Bidwell, the building now houses the North Herts D.C. Housing Department.

XV. The 'greening' of the Garden City. The 'Broad Walk' Broadway. The central path, originally intended as a tramway reservation, is flanked by mature trees which screen the buildings.

XVI. An aerial view of Town Square — now John F. Kennedy Gardens. The Lombardy poplars define the intended site for the central group of civic buildings. The unsympathetic character of 1960s buildings is highlighted by the I.C.L. offices on the right.

The Dawn of Consumerism The 1920s witnessed a rise in disposable incomes in the South-East, and a demand for consumer goods and services maintained even through the 1929-31 depression. There were 162 commercial concerns in 1925, reflecting Letchworth's expanding role as a regional shopping centre. Fifty new shops were opened between 1924-6 alone.[14] The most comprehensive development filled in the area between Station Road and Leys Avenue. Bennett and Bidwell designed the Georgian-style buildings. With the London Joint City and Midland, at the apex, the parades of shops stretched away either side, terminating in the entrances to an arcade framed by giant triumphal arches. Visually, the arcade was disappointing, although the octagonal centrepiece and roof light were effective. Eastcheap emerged as a major commercial street in the 1920s, when the *Icknield Halls* were built, designed by Bennett and Bidwell in a free Queen Anne style. On the opposite side, the Co-operative Society extended in a Tudor style, designed by L. G. Ekins in 1921.

The local press broadcast availability of goods and services:[15] 'Advertising is the magnet' proclaimed *The Citizen* in June 1930, lending distinctly commercial overtones to Howard's concept of the irresistible force. In 1929 a free paper, *The Garden City Advertiser*, was delivered regularly to 3,600 households. It lasted ten years but was about half a century too early!

Garden Citizens became increasingly fashion conscious in the '20s and '30s. In 1926 'Civic Week millinery' could be purchased from Ida in the Arcade. Parker Perry, Colonnade Buildings, had dresses for day, dinner and evening wear from 29s. 6d. (£1.49), but ladies had to journey to Hitchin for the latest lace-trimmed celanese cami-knickers, at 8s. 11d. (44p). In 1930 Lillian Reed, in the Arcade, boasted of 'Useful frocks for sports, business, home or outdoor wear. Delightful lingerie which will appeal to the woman of taste'. Spirella were omnipresent, and a 1935 advertisement commended the corsetière as 'the only intermediary between designer and client'. Permanent waves were available at the Metro Salon, Station Road, to complete a well groomed appearance. Menswear advertising was lower in key. Peters Menswear in Eastcheap had boys' and mens' flannel trousers from 8s. 11d.-21s. 0d. (44p-

88. 'Fashions of 1935' — Spirella.

£1.05); and tennis flannels from 2s. 11d. (14½p). Tweed suits were available ready made at 39s. 11d. (£1.99½) from the Co-op, or made to measure from 50s. 0d. (£2.50) from Rawlinson's in Leys Avenue. Foster and Scott, in the Arcade, stocked the new 'Aquatite Raincoat'. Smokers' requisites were widely available from Fenner and Fenner or Sidney Thacker, both in Leys Avenue.

In 1935 the Co-op claimed patronage by two-fifths of Letchworth families for food and clothing. For the former there was severe competition from Moss's, and the International

89. Everything for your convenience. Interior of the Co-op, *c.*1925.

stores. Price cutting of leading lines was already well established by 1930 when International offered canned peaches or apricots for 9½d. and 10½d., jellies at 3d., and blancmange powders at 1½d. and 4½d. — no doubt snapped up for Sunday tea. Fancy cakes and pastries were available at Nott's, who also offered ice cream sodas and sundaes at 6d.(2½p), and their home-made chocolates at 3s. 6d. (17½p) per pound. To cope with the effects of over eating, patent medicines were available from Russells' in Station Road or Boot's in Leys Avenue. Deliveries of the 'demon drink' were widespread; in 1935, G. B. Christie of Hitchin boasted of their supplies to Letchworth 'day in and day out' over many years. With a *frisson* of guilt, comparable to Americans visiting a 'speakeasy', Garden Citizens discreetly rang Hitchin 122 to place their orders, their hidden vices known to the telephone operator in those pre-dialling days.

Home ownership was widely canvassed. J. L. A. White developed Bedford Road in the early '30s and he offered a house for £50 deposit, legal costs of £25, and a £1 1s. 0d. (£1.05) weekly payment. Brookers fitted out the 'all electric' 'Civic House' in South View in 1926. A Revo electric cooker, daily running cost 4d. per day to cook for a family of four, was available for £15 15s. 5d. (£15.77) or a quarterly hire charge of 7s. 6d. (37½p) from the F.G.C. Electricity Showrooms. For lounging about in the garden, deckchairs cost 2s. 11d. (15p) from Underwoods in Leys Avenue. For home entertainment, the 'Phonos' portable gramophone, at five guineas (£5.25), was 'perfect for Summer outings, holidays, river trips and dancing'. Doubtless Charlestoning flappers annoyed their elders just as much as their

90. Advertisements from the 1930s.

91. 'The Effect of Matter on Mind': cartoon portrait of Barry Parker by Charles Crombie.

1980s counterparts with ghetto-blasters. Hodgsons of Commerce Avenue offered Brown's wireless receivers, and by 1935 H.M.V. radiograms, available from D. R. Stevens in Leys Avenue, were the ultimate domestic status symbol. Pianos were still popular, and relatively cheap with the elegant Gors and Kallmann overstrung baby grand at 42 guineas (£44.10). Operatic, ballet, tap, limbering and ballroom dancing lessons were available from Diana Robinson in Nevells Road — she was no mean artist, either!

Motor cars were already being heavily promoted. In 1926, the best deal was the £165 four-seater Peugeot ('pronounce it pur-jo'), 50 m.p.h. and 60 m.p.g., and available from Exell Service Garage, Pixmore Avenue. 'Buy British and be proud of it!' proclaimed Mason's Garage, Eastcheap, established 1920. An 11.9hp Morris 'Bullnose' Cowley cost £190 and was perfect for 'carefree holidays'. Mason's also sold Humber cars and B.S.A., Rudge, Sunbeam and Raleigh motorcycles. Their great rival, Bennett's Motor Works, opened in Station Road in 1919. Leslie Woodbridge Bennett (1894-1972) became a civic and business leader. He was a Ford main dealer and imported V8's from the USA in addition to selling the home-built Dagenham product. Car ownership grew rapidly in Hertfordshire, faster than the national ratio. In 1925 there were 14,417 motor vehicle licences issued in the County,[16] one motor vehicle for every 245 residents, which gave 562 for Letchworth. This figure rose sharply and in 1935 the U.D.C. provided the first off-street car park behind their new offices. Bicycles were popular, sold by Munt's, Eastcheap, where the Raleigh all-steel bicycle was available for £1 down, and easy payments or £6 7s. 6d. cash (£6.37½).

Marmet prams sold widely in the 1920s, manufactured locally since 1913, with the prestige of supplying a scale miniature for Queen Mary's Dolls House in 1924. Photography had always been popular, and local pharmacists pressed the merits of the latest folding Kodaks to record Civic Week events. Locally-produced Kosmos paper was advised for high quality prints. Amongst professional photographers, the Clutterbucks, with their home and studio facing the Common on Icknield Way, Brunts in Leys Avenue and Julian and Violet Tayler at Howard Park Corner were chief rivals. Cartoon portraits by Charles Crombie of Baldock Road were also popular, and published in the press and Civic Week Programmes.

Mass entertainment was dominated by the cinema.[17] The Picture Palace was updated in 1924 when a new front was added, with a balcony to the auditorium. Seats cost 4d. (2p), 8d. (4p), 1s. 2d. (6p), and 1s. 9d. (9p) for the best seats and private boxes. Chaplin's comedies were universally popular and *The Gold Rush* played to packed houses in June 1926, a welcome relaxation from Civic Week. The 'Palace Gem Orchestra' provided accompaniment. Somewhat delayed, the 'talkies' arrived on 31 March 1930, with the stentorian tones of Victor McLaglen in *King of the Khyber Rifles* booming out over the British Thomson-Houston reproducer. *Fox Movietone Follies*, *Applause*, *Mammy* with Al Jolson, and *Innocents of Paris* — the debut of the elegant Maurice Chevalier — brought the delights of '100% — all talking — all singing — all dancing' entertainment. A barrage of American accents counterbalanced the BBC's received pronunciation and clipped vowels. By 1935 a second cinema was needed, and Howard Hurst built the Broadway — despite its name located at the junction of Gernon Road and Eastcheap. Wilson Bidwell designed a mild Art Deco building, structurally adventurous, exploiting its builder's enthusiasm for reinforced concrete. The Broadway was opened on Wednesday 26 August 1936 by Sir Arnold Wilson

92. The Broadway Cinema, bathed in neon-light, *c.*1937.

M.P., with a black tie gala screening of *Follow the Fleet* starring Fred Astaire and Ginger Rogers.

The theatre was sporadically successful, but after the opening of the theatre at the St Christopher School (St Francis), in Broadway, there was in the late 1920s an attempt to establish a Letchworth Repertory theatre on a semi-professional basis. This was short-lived and folded in 1932. Amateur theatre flourished, however. The Letchworth Operatic Society was founded in 1921, and its first president was Barry Parker who was a skilled amateur singer. The Society was active until 1940, and concentrated on light operetta — their first production in 1923 was, appropriately, *The Arcadians*, and they also presented Gilbert and Sullivan. The Settlement Players were formed as a play-reading group in 1923 by Miss Pym, and concentrated upon Shaw, pre-1939 giving *Pygmalion*, *Major Barbara*, *Caesar and Cleopatra*, *St Joan* and *Arms and the Man*. A Drama Festival was held in 1937 with participation by the Operatic Society, Settlement Players and The Spirella Players. The following year the Y.P.F. Players were formed, out of which grew the successful St Paul's Amateur Dramatic Society (S.P.A.D.S.).

'Whit Week is Civic Week'   The official 'Coming of Age' of Letchworth was set for 17- 22 May 1926, rather belated for the estate had been opened in October 1903. An ambitious week-long programme focussed on key aspects of civic and community life.[18] The main attraction was the first official Royal visit to Letchworth, by H.R.H. Duke of York. The

93. Special stickers for local post.

General Strike in May put back the event until June. The fostering of civic consciousness and community service had been a priority with many of the pioneers. The Letchworth Rotary Club, formed in March 1924, also stressed that Letchworth demonstrated 'How a better England can be built up'. Introducing Civic Week in *The Citizen*, Ralph Pearsall emphasised the responsibility to proclaim Howard's message widely. The principal objective of Civic Week was the foundation of a Civic College as a permanent tribute to Howard and his co-pioneers. The college would evolve a co-ordinated system of education from primary school to university, including adult education. Grants and endowments would overcome financial impediments. There were only four Council primary schools, and a secondary school, to be funded by the County Council, was integral with the college project. £40,000 from public donations was required above the cost of the secondary school. A site had been selected on the vacant western frontage of Town Square. Barry Parker prepared a formal classical design, with a long central block linked by colonnades to wings, one of which incorporated a theatre. In the centre a domed Hall of Memory perpetuated the names of all who had 'deserved well of their town'.

Civic Week included lectures by eminent speakers, formal luncheons and dances, and culminated in the Civic Ball, held at the Spirella Assembly Hall, under the patronage of the Marchioness of Salisbury. The roof terrace was laid out as an Italian garden, and guests

94a. & b. Eminent guests at Civic Week, 1926 and 1935. *Above*, H.R.H. The Duke of York in Eastcheap, 1926. *Below*, 'Miss Letchworth' (Betty Hills) presents Herbert Morrison with a green belt, 1935. As L.C.C. Chairman, Herbert Morrison had recently obtained a resolution for a Greater London Green Belt.

danced to Howard Aynstey's No. 1 Band until 1.30 a.m. Lesser mortals attended a 'popular dance' at the K. & L. Canteen for 1s.6d. The town centre was decorated, under the supervision of Barry Parker, and the traders participated in a window dressing competition.

The week's highlight was the Duke of York's visit on Wednesday 8 June.[19] He arrived punctually at 12.45 p.m., and, after reviewing a British Legion Guard of Honour, he entered the Icknield Halls for the Civic Luncheon. After the Loyal toast, the Duke rose to speak. He commended Letchworth for 'a splendid contribution . . . to human progress by the Garden City pioneers'. Howard had not only 'been granted the vision of this promised land; but he has also been allowed to witness its realisation'. He continued, 'the wealth of the town is in her people. Therefore I am glad to know that the conditions here, under which men and women live are so good . . . in conclusion I congratulate you upon the choice of a civic college as a memorial of your 21st anniversary'.

The Duke toured the town centre, Pixmore Hospital, Jackmans Place, Works Road, Green Lane, Common View and Icknield Way. He toured the Spirella factory where he was presented with a Morocco-bound album of photographs of the works. Councillor Charles F. Ball, Chairman of the U.D.C. Housing Committee, received him at the Hillbrow Estate. The Duke returned to the town centre and left Letchworth at 4.15 p.m. H.R.H. Duchess of York (Queen Elizabeth the Queen Mother) had not resumed engagements following the birth of Princess Elizabeth (H.M. Queen Elizabeth II) on 21 April 1926. At least one enthusiastic Garden Citizen called out to the Duke, 'Why haven't you brought the baby?!'

Regrettably the Civic College did not materialise. In October 1927, Councillor J. Wick raised money for planting the Town Square Gardens (renamed John F. Kennedy Gardens in 1964) and F.G.C. Ltd. promised no building in the centre for a further 25 years. Barry Parker was chosen as the architect for the Secondary School, a more utilitarian building than the elegantly proportioned classical college. The Letchworth Grammar School was opened on 7 October 1931 by the Right Hon. J. H. Whiteley, Chairman of the B.B.C.

Another Civic Week was held in 1935, the Silver Jubilee year of George V. This time funds were raised to assist the hospital.[20] The week began with a united town service in Town Square addressed by the Dean of St Albans. On Monday 10 June the keynote theme was 'The relationship of Letchworth to the Town Planning Movement'. Herbert Morrison, leader of the L.C.C., returned to Letchworth to be presented with a ceremonial 'green belt' by Betty Hills, Miss Letchworth, to commemorate the recent resolution of the L.C.C. to acquire land for a Green Belt. Tuesday was 'Industry Day', opened by Harold Macmillan M.P., a future Conservative Prime Minister. The afternoon was enlivened by the Girls Club Junior Gymnastic Display in Town Square and a folk dance festival in the evening. Unwin returned to declare 'Letchworth Points the Way' on Thursday. On Friday, 'Health Day', the new Council Offices, designed by Bennett and Bidwell, were open for inspection, and George Pepler from the Ministry of Health addressed the Sanitary Inspectors Conference at Howard Hall. *Merrie England* was staged at St Francis' Theatre that evening. 'Children's Day' brought the festivities to a close on Saturday, with a final carnival that evening. There were no more Civic Weeks, but the Coronation of George VI was made an event for an elaborate historical pageant.

Chapter Twelve

Post-war Expansion

Wartime Prelude In September 1939 life in Letchworth was again disrupted by international conflict.[1] 4,000 evacuees arrived from Islington, Stoke Newington, Tottenham and Hackney, the crowded urban districts of north and east London, whence Howard had hoped to attract Garden City residents. The newcomers were often less than enthusiastic about the tree-lined streets and open spaces. 'The Gracie Fields Home and Orphanage' took over 'Wilbury Turrets', having considered Peacehaven, Sussex, vulnerable to attack. Schools from Bexhill, Sussex shared Pixmore and St Francis' premises. Eighty-six bombed-out Londoners dossed down in the Commerce Avenue Church Rooms. Life in Letchworth regained something of the pre-1914 community spirit. Food rationing, blackout and the embargo on private motoring were endured with grumbling. The 'dig for Victory' campaign, amateur poultry and even pig keeping supplemented the depressingly monotonous food of factory canteens and the British Restaurant on Icknield Way. Clothing coupons brought a drab uniformity to civilian clothing, sweets were 'on points', and daily conversation was inhibited by the warning 'careless talk costs lives'. On the wireless, *I.T.M.A.*, the comedy programme starring Tommy Handley, offered relief from depressing, censored war news, interspersed with stirring speeches from the Prime Minister, Winston Churchill. At least the cinemas dispensed escapism, and were packed out twice nightly. The 'phoney' war gave way to the air battles of 1940, the conflicts in the Far East, Mediterranean and eventually the liberation of Europe. Letchworth was remote from conflict, with few enemy aircraft sighted, and in October 1940 a German bomb killed one rabbit, one bird, and damaged a minor road and hedge.

The factories increased shifts to ensure maximum output. K. & L. Foundry and Engineering produced armaments, the Morse Chain Company made Churchill tanks, Shelvoke and Drewry built miniature submarines, and Irvin's parachutes were at peak demand. Leslie Irvin had demonstrated his parachute to the U.S. Air Force in 1919, and founded his British subsidiary in 1926. It was calculated that his products saved 45,000 lives in the Allied forces during the Second World War. The town's Spitfire Fund presented one of these legendary fighters, proudly named *Letchworth*, to the R.A.F. On 25 September 1941, King George VI and Queen Elizabeth visited the Government Training Centre in Pixmore Avenue. Eventually it was all over. Flags fluttered over Letchworth on V.E. Day, 8 May 1945. The transition to peacetime continued for several years. Fundamental changes were brought about by the Labour Government, under Clement Attlee, elected with a majority of 146 on 26 July 1945. The Hitchin Division had a Labour M.P. for the first time, Philip Asterley Jones. Letchworth U.D.C. also had a Labour majority, and its first female Chairman, Mrs Margaret Harvey. Individual idealism and voluntary co-operation were eclipsed by public initiative as the foundations for the welfare state were laid.

The Council Throughout the war Leslie Bennett had been U.D.C. Chairman. In 1944 he paid for a Coat of Arms from the College of Arms, which conferred civic dignity of Letchworth, and reflected links between the Garden City and the ancient manorial families. The Letters Patent described the Arms thus:

95. 'Bombs a Daisy' from K. and L.   A 4,000lb bomb made in 1942.

96. Miniature submarines from Shelvoke and Drewry. These top secret craft carried four crew members and were used for naval espionage.

The Arms following, that is to say, Argent three chevronels gules over all on a Chief embattled azure two roses of the first barbed and seeded proper. And for the Crest on a Wreath of the colours an owl affronty argent between two sprigs of oak vert fructed or.

The Shield is a combination of the Arms of Barrington and Montfichet Lords of the Manor of Letchworth in the 15th and 16th centuries, represented by the red chevronels on the silver ground. The Chief (the band in blue) typifies blue sky and sun which, with the roses, represent the Garden City. The Helmet and the Wreath are heraldic emblems. The Crest exemplifies the firm foundations upon which the Garden City is planned, and this is represented by the oak sprigs in the supporters of the Crest. The Owl, the bird of wisdom, emphasises the Motto *Prudens Futuri* ('Thoughtful for the Future').[2] In 1950, the Town Clerk, Horace Plinston persuaded F.G.C. Ltd. to present Badges of Office to the town, formally handed over on 16 July 1951 by Sir Eric MacFadyen, F.G.C. Chairman, to Ernest Gardiner, U.D.C. Chairman.[3]

If the Arms and Regalia symbolised the past, the Council concentrated upon planning for the future. There was a concerted attempt to accelerate growth to achieve Howard's 32,000 population target, and to provide housing for Greater London overspill. Local politics became more fully aligned with national parties, particularly after the division of Letchworth into five wards in 1946. Mrs Harvey held sway until 1949, when she was succeeded by George Woodbridge. Ernest Gardiner, a Conservative, became Chairman in 1949-50, and

97. Letchworth Urban District Council coat of arms.

alternated with Woodbridge over the next few years. The role of Town Clerk and Solicitor became crucial. Horace Plinston had been appointed in 1948 and readily adapted to the 'cabinet' style of administration, gaining the confidence of both parties, which was to stand the Council in good stead during the Company takeover battle.[4] The Council's housebuilding priority created arduous tasks for professional officers, notably the Surveyor, E. L. Johnson, and Housing Manager, G. W. Mulvenna.

The Company's post-war vicissitudes In the political context of 1945, the continued existence of F.G.C. Ltd. seemed anachronistic to many. Company and Council had enjoyed a cosy working relationship pre-war, but this could no longer continue. Initially, however, Company affairs resumed normality.[5] At the 1946 A.G.M. it was announced that the dividend arrears of £113,224 18s.11d. would be paid off. In anticipation of post-war growth the issue of a further £200,000 share capital was authorised, to bring the total to £600,000, but was never implemented, possibly due to the consequences of the 1947 Town and Country Planning Act for development land. The Company's utility subsidiaries were nationalised.[6] By 1945 the power station served Biggleswade and Baldock and the surrounding Bedfordshire villages, but had not been taken into the National Grid. In 1947, its capacity was 7,500kv and in 1945 it sold 40,726,844 BTh. Units. The gasworks had supplied 200,000,000 cu. ft. in 1945, with a peak weekly demand of 5,000,000 cu. ft. — the total 1906 output! In 1947 the power station made £45,662 profit, and the gasworks £14,176, a sizeable proportion of the pre-interest revenue balance of £68,160. Compensation of £1,129,858 was agreed for the power station, £268,814 over book value. Although this enabled repayment of a bank overdraft and mortgages, a lucrative asset had been lost, and this was repeated when the gasworks was requisitioned. A degree of local loyalty disappeared. In February 1947, during a harsh winter, with fuel shortages and extensive power cuts throughout the country, the Ministry of Fuel and Power initially allowed the Letchworth Power Station to use its coal stocks, but compelled it to switch off three days later.

Letchworth Development Corporation? The Labour Government implemented the recommendations of Patrick Abercrombie's 1944 'Greater London Plan' for a ring of 'New Towns' around Greater London.[7] This strategy developed the concepts of Purdom and Osborn, Unwin's pioneering work on the Greater London Region, and the recommendations of the 1940 Barlow Commission Report. Abercrombie proposed 10 new towns, each of 60,000 population, to enable the rebuilding of war-damaged central London and slum clearance. The outward spread of the conurbation would be halted by a strict Green Belt policy. A government Planning Authority had been created during the War, and in 1946 the New Towns Act was passed to enable their designation. This would be pursued 'wherever the Minister is satisfied that it is expedient in the national interest to do so'. Following this there was consultation with local Authorities and landowners. The first, Stevenage New Town, strategically located between Letchworth and Welwyn, was fraught with confrontation between local and national government.[8] Lewis Silkin, Minister for Town and Country Planning, fought the matter to the House of Lords against Stevenage U.D.C. In August 1946 Silkin prevailed — Stevenage New Town was long referred to as 'Silkingrad'! Following designation, a development corporation was appointed 'to acquire, hold, manage and dispose of land ... to carry out building and other operations, to provide water, electricity, gas, sewerage ... and generally to do anything necessary or expedient for the purposes of the New Town ...';[9] in fact, the complex roles of the private companies which had created both Letchworth and Welwyn Garden City. The corporations were not local authorities, and were accountable to the Minister. They gained a reputation for remoteness. Silkin emphasised that they protected the public interest, and pressed ahead to take control of Welwyn Garden City, despite assurances that the development company would harmonise its operations with those of the public corporations.[10] Silkin demurred, and publicly declared that despite his 'greatest admiration for the pioneering work of the Welwyn Garden City Company ... [it] would not be the right instrument for continuing the task ... the Company is answerable only to its shareholders and to no one else ... only to people with financial interests ... The character of the town ... would be just what the Company would like and not what the people would like. This is opposed to any sense of democracy'. He pressed ahead with the draft designation order in January 1948.

That month, Letchworth U.D.C. passed a resolution requesting the Minister to create a Letchworth Development Corporation.[11] As 'the first New Town ... it would be appropriate that it should be completed before other New Towns proposed; and ... land was available for 'overspill' from the London area, ... the New Towns Policy was the *raison d'etre* of Letchworth's existence'. Silkin promised careful and sympathetic consideration of the matter. F.G.C. Ltd. had not been consulted and expressed their grave doubts whether such a step would be in the best interests of the town. Silkin and his Permanent Secretary, Miss Evelyn Sharp, met Company representatives on 9 June 1948. On 29 July he recalled the

Council and stated that 'the Company's Board had assured him that they were anxious to play their part in completing the development of Letchworth', having undertaken to receive industry and population from London. On completion Letchworth would be conveyed to the Council, as was then envisaged with development corporations The Company had offered two seats on the Board for Ministerial nominees. Silkin accepted these assurances and informed the Council that he did not intend to appoint a development corporation, the antithesis of his action at Welwyn. He hoped that Council and Company would in future co-ordinate their activities to the mutual benefit of the town.

The U.D.C. invited F.G.C. Ltd. to nominate representatives for a Joint Consultative Committee, to discuss future development, and resolve differences amicably. The compulsory purchase of the Grange estate land had soured relations and, in December 1948, the Company offered to the Council, subject only to their paying legal charges, the freehold interest of Norton Common, the Ball Memorial Gardens, Town Square, Howard Park and other open spaces. This was accepted as an article of good faith of the ultimate intention to assign the whole estate. An Extraordinary General Meeting was held on 15 September 1949 to approve the resolution:[12]

> That the stockholders approve in principle the ultimate transfer, when the development of Letchworth is substantially completed, of the Company's undertaking to the Local Authority, or other suitable public body, subject to satisfactory terms being agreed.

At the same meeting there were danger signals in resolutions to alter the Memorandum of Articles of Association to restrict the surplus to be paid to the town, after winding up the Company, to 10 per cent, on contention that development value of the estate had been nationalised through the 1947 Town and Country Planning Act. This proposition was accepted, virtually *fait accompli*, although the Chairman, Sir Eric MacFadyen, later told Plinston that, had he known the Council's feelings before the meeting, he would not have put the amendments to the vote. Plinston took Counsel's opinion but was informed that the U.D.C. had no standing to raise the matter. The ultimate community benefit was now restricted to 10 per cent. For the present, MacFadyen initiated a joint Trust, the 'Common Good Fund', into which F.G.C. Ltd. paid £14,000, and subsequent voluntary contributions, to assist the Town's voluntary organisations. It was a case of 'crumbs today' with a declining hope of 'jam tomorrow'.

Planning and Land Values   The issue as to whether land values created by planning should be retained by the owner or taken by the community in whose name the planning decision had been taken, has long remained a political shibboleth.[13] Community benefit from enhanced land values created by development was the foundation of Howard's concept. Unwin wrote extensively on the necessity to recoup a portion of the enhanced values to enable designation or purchase of amenity land and provide compensation for removal of development potential. During the Second World War the Uthwatt Committee examined the question afresh. Under the 1947 Town and Country Planning Act, land remained in private ownership, but development rights in undeveloped land were nationalised. Development now required planning permission. If refused, no compensation was payable. Any permission granted which brought an increase in land value, or 'betterment', would be subject to a development charge. A £300,000,000 fund was created to compensate owners who could demonstrate to a Central Land Board that their land had some development value on the appointed day for the Act. The development charge was a 100 per cent levy. Locally, this halted land transactions except for public development. Resale prices were at existing use value, and the purchaser who carried out the development with planning permission had to pay the difference between purchase price and development value through the development charge.

Under the 1947 Act, the County Council, as planning authority, prepared a town map showing approved primary land use zoning for Letchworth. The draft statement was issued in 1951, and fundamental differences between the Company and Council emerged.[14] F.G.C. Ltd. claimed the right to develop the Norton Common road frontages and received compensation for loss of development value when the area was zoned for open space. The cricket ground had received residential zoning and, following refusal of planning permission, the Company successfully claimed compensation for loss of development value. The same occurred over the cycle park at the corner of Commerce Avenue, where refusal of planning permission to build shops brought £6,000 compensation for loss of development rights. By the mid 1950s, the Company had become more concerned by commercial gain than the longer term community benefit.

Letchworth and Statutory Planning   The post-war era of statutory planning overlaid the landlord powers exercised by F.G.C. Ltd. Abercrombie had referred to the development potential of Letchworth in his *Greater London Plan*, and envisaged rapid population and industrial growth. He felt that the 1938 estimated population of 15,000 could be increased by 19,000. But he considered the Company's proposed 100 per cent increase of industrial land excessive, bringing the danger of the coalescence of Letchworth with Baldock along the A505. He recommended a town boundary along a line drawn northwards from the Baldock Road pumping station to the railway.[15] The Company's post-war plan was shown in Osborn's newly edited re-issue of *Garden Cities of Tomorrow* published in 1946. It defined a 'town area — (ultimate)', with 'green Belt' beyond, neither of which was of statutory significance. Residential land included the Grange and Standalone estates on the north and Lordship/Manor Farm and Jackmans estates on the south, and additional areas which did not appear in the County Development Plan or any subsequent plan, including a 50-acre tract south of the Baldock Road, eventually partly developed by the North Herts Leisure Centre.

Under the 1947 Act, 145 local planning authorities were defined, with the Shire counties and County Borough Councils empowered to prepare plans, compared to a potential 1,441 under the pre-war system. The responsibility for forward planning for Letchworth passed to the Hertfordshire County Council, who were required to consult the districts, and could delegate development control. The County Development Plan naturally followed national policies on decentralisation and new towns,[18] and incorporated Hemel Hempstead in addition to Stevenage and Welwyn/Hatfield. The plan covered the years 1951 to 1973. In 1951 Letchworth U.D.C. covered 4,697 acres (1,900 ha.) had a population of 20,321, and £167,589 rateable value. A natural increase of population of 1,420 by 1971 was forecast, with provision for inmigration of 10,259 to achieve Howard's projected 32,000 population. To provide employment maximum industrial zoning was included, ignoring Abercrombie's cautionary remarks. Public sector housing would take priority, and the Grange estate, already commenced, was to be completed by 1958-62, together with the newly zoned Jackmans estate. The Manor and Lordship Farm estates would follow in 1963-73. A total of 3,964 houses on new residential sites was envisaged, with a further 230 on infill sites. The overall population density was 13 persons per acre (5.26 per ha.) within the 2,483 acre (1,004 ha.) town area, within which were 1,698 acres (687 ha.) residential land including local shops and schools, and access roads, 273 acres (110 ha.) industrial land, 52 acres (21 ha.) shopping and town centre buildings, 34 acres (13.75 ha.) major educational facilities and 348 acres (140 ha.) major public and private open spaces. An extension of the main shopping area, a central hotel and a sports stadium were proposed. An A1 Baldock By Pass was proposed with an interchange on the Baldock to Letchworth Road.

Church End

Newnham

Stotfold

Arlesey

Roman Way

R. Ivel

GREEN BELT

Letchworth
Garden City

Norton

Baldock

BELT

L.M.S.R.

L.N.E.R.

To Cambridge

Town Area ~
(ultimate)

Willian

GREEN

Great North Road

Hitchin

To London

Scale of feet

0   1000 2000 3000 4000   5000   6000   7000

0   ¼   ½   ¾   1 mile

Residential   Industrial   Shopping
                             Centres   Towns and
                                        Villages

98. The Company Plan, 1946. A further expansion of the urban area, together with an
industrial belt linking Letchworth almost to Baldock, was envisaged.

99. The County Development Plan, 1951. The plan made provision for the construction of The Grange and Jackmans Estates and showed the Baldock by-pass with a surface-level interchange for Letchworth on the A505.

Grange and Jackmans Estates Letchworth U.D.C. faced a substantial demand for housing in 1945. By 1950, 669 Council houses, 47 private houses, and 16 elderly persons bungalows by the Howard Cottage Society, had been completed. Post-war construction had begun in 1945 with the Warren Estate off Wilbury Road. There were 1,570 on the housing waiting list in 1950. 'Pre-fabs' were built off Icknield Way and lasted for 30 years. The Grange Estate north of Wilbury Road had been begun pre-war when the Howard Cottage Society had built semi-detached houses along Grange Road. In 1945, Geoffrey Jellicoe, the eminent landscape architect, prepared a new layout for the 237-acre (96 ha.) site, which included areas for housing association and private development as well as local authority housing. The Company declined to sell the freehold and the Council made a compulsory purchase order.[19] County Council school sites had always been freehold, and were held as a precedent. Moreover, in seeking the freehold, the Council claimed it was anticipating the ultimate transfer of the whole estate. F.G.C. Ltd. maintained that this would break the integrity of the estate and opposed the order, supported by the Letchworth Manufacturers' Association, who feared a burden on the rates. A compromise was accepted under which the Company surrendered the freehold of land required for Council housing but retained

100. The Jackmans Estate. The pedestrian footpath network was the most notable feature of this post-war layout.

the remainder. Development proceeded following Jellicoe's plan, a modified grid layout providing the customary 12 houses to the acre, giving continuity with established standards, and including generous greens and verges. The Letchworth U.D.C. panel of architects included Crickmer, who updated traditional designs, using prominent gables on some housing groups. The extremity of the estate lay two miles north of the town centre, and a selfcontained neighbourhood, with schools, shopping centre and playing fields, resulted. In March 1948, U.D.C. Chairman George Woodbridge inaugurated construction by John Mowlem and Co. Eastern Way was cut through Eastholm Green to serve the estate, leading into Gaunts Way, named after W. H. Gaunt the Estate Manager, and Western Way. 1,431 new houses were completed by the early 1960s.

Accommodation for London overspill awaited solution of the local housing shortage. The Town Development Act of 1952 was passed by a Conservative Government, and promoted by Harold Macmillan as Minister for Housing and Local Government.[20] It encouraged 'Town development in County districts for the relief of congestion of over-population elsewhere', through local authority agreements 'by friendly negotiation and not imposed by arbitrary power'. The 'exporting' authority could contribute towards infrastructure and public service costs. Schemes in conjunction with the London County Council, which had 246,000 families prepared to move home provided a job were available, benefited from financial and technical assistance. The farmland around the Jackmans plantation, stretching south-east along Letchworth Gate to Baldock Lane had been added to the 'town area' and appeared in the County Development Plan. Initially set at 944 houses, an estate of 1,500 was agreed, with development to be phased over 1958-63.[21] In July 1955, agreement in principle with the L.C.C. was announced, to house a population of 5,000 with the estate conveyed to Letchworth U.D.C. after 10 years. Infrastructure grants rose from £60,000 to £105,000. The following year it was revealed that the L.C.C. would finance the £3,000,000 initial expenditure, and would be reimbursed as properties were handed over. Tenant selection would be geared to employment, with the L.C.C. endeavouring to promote industrial mobility. An Exchequer subsidy of £24 per dwelling for 60 years was available, with an additional London grant of £8 per dwelling for 10 years. Land acquisition again created friction. An extension of the industrial area, Blackhorse Road, was to be developed in conjunction with the estate. Whilst F.G.C. Ltd. was prepared to sell residential land, it refused to part with the industrial land. The Ministry and the County Council insisted that the U.D.C. must control the land. Although comparatively remote from Jackmans, a Compulsory Purchase Order for the land was confirmed following agreement that 20 acres of K. & L. land, already zoned for industry and almost bordering the estate, would not be used for 20 years. The District Valuer's report of 7 September 1959 required the Council to pay £62,960 plus fees and legal expenses for the freehold of 212.38 acres (86 ha.), with the Jackmans land priced at £347 per acre, and the Blackhorse Road land at £465. Purchase was completed shortly before the 1959 Town and Country Planning Act restored full market value for development land transactions. The Council had benefited from the dual system whereby, under the 1954 T. & C.P. Act, land was acquired for private development at market value, but for public purposes at existing use value. A few months later the market value of Jackmans was £5,000 per acre.

Planning and design of the Jackmans Estate was undertaken by a local consortium — The Associated Architects — William Barnes, Martin Priestman and Leonard Brown. The layout introduced the principle of pedestrian and vehicular separation, based on the plan for Radburn, New Jersey, U.S.A., the 'New town for the motor age' designed by Henry Wright and Clarence Stein in 1928-9.[22] The adoption of the principles at Letchworth was reflected in the main distributor road being named Radburn Way. Subsidiary culs-de-sac were named in alphabetical sequence — Allison, Bayworth, Chatterton, Denby, Ellice . . .

101. The Grange Estate. This post-war housing design and layout represented continuity with pre-war estates.

through to Vincent and Yardley. The estate had its own schools, and a shopping and community centre, with five storeys of flats above, and a circular pub — originally named *The Carousel*. The introduction of modern residential architecture to Letchworth was not an unmixed blessing and the individuality of earlier housing was replaced by a bland reflection of the Parker Morris housing standards. The most successful part of the estate was around Chatterton, Denby, Ellice and Fleetwood, with paths leading upwards from Radburn Way, where existing trees and hedges were retained. The least successful housing was a prefabricated system built by Hawthorn Leslie, the Sunderland shipbuilders. Construction began in 1959, and the estate was half completed by 1965, when the Greater London Council was created, and completed in 1973.

Private development resumed in the mid 1950s after the repeal of building licences and the restoration of market value for private development. Pleasant, if bland, semi-detached and detached houses of Longmead and Hawthorn Hill off Wilbury Road, Cloisters Road, Lawrence Avenue, Bowershott, Lordship Lane and Howard Drive, between Baldock Road and Letchworth Gate, were typical of the period.

Golden Jubilee On 1 September 1953 First Garden City Limited celebrated its Golden Jubilee. The Town and Country Planning Association brought out a special edition of *Town and Country Planning* edited by F. J. Osborn, who drew attention to the uncertainty and excitement of early development financed by 'industrialists and professional men who combined idealism with daring practicality, supported by investors willing to risk their money in an imaginative project'.[23] The ultimate vindication of Letchworth lay, he believed, in the 1946 New Towns Act, a theme brought out by others, so well entrenched was the principle of state initiative. Osborn had assembled a choice collection of articles on virtually every aspect of Letchworth life, with emphasis on pioneer memories. Reminiscence also featured in a Jubilee edition of *The Citizen*.[24]

Celebrations emphasised commerce and industry. Virtually all wartime restriction had disappeared and shopping was in full swing, with a three-guinea prize for identification of mystery articles in 63 shop-windows. The new Ford Zephyr Six was available from Bennetts, the Austin Hereford A70 from Whiteheads in Commerce Avenue, whilst a Daimler Conquest could be ordered from Dickinson and Adams in Eastcheap for £1,066 plus Purchase Tax. Television sets sold briskly from 40 guineas (£42) upwards, for this was Coronation Year. Yet cinemas were still popular, and in 1955 the Broadway was converted for the new wide screen CinemaScope films. A Jubilee Fair of Industry and Trade was held on the Arena, the muddy patch between the Co-op and the Town Hall Car Park, from 1-3 September, opened by U.D.C. Chairman George Woodbridge. Additional attractions included 'Jubilarity' a revue by the S.P.A.D.S. (St Paul's Amateur Dramatic Society), a service in Howard Park, a fashion parade by Spirella, and a Letchworth display at the Museum. The opening of the first workshop block of the new North Herts Technical College must have recalled the unfulfilled Civic College project.

That's Entertainment   Amateur theatre continued to flourish in the 1950s. The Letchworth Arcadians were formed in 1952, and, not surprisingly, their annual programmes began with Lionel Monckton's evergreen light operetta from which they took their name. Over the years they performed many of the most popular musical shows of the century, ranging from *Chu Chin Chow* to *Hello Dolly* via *Showboat* and *Oklahoma!* The first President, R.S. Kellaway, was succeeded by Horace Plinston who found the company an admirable relaxation away from the vigours of the take-over battle. The Drama Festival was revived in 1946 after the War, and made its home in the Kincaid Hall, constructed from the legacy of the founder of Spirella. Kenneth Spinks and Florence Thompson were leading lights, and Hugh Bidwell, architect son of Wilson Bidwell, became President as the Little Theatre Drama Festival evolved. The Settlement Players also broadened their repertoire, giving *Ebenezer's magnetic dream town* in 1983 to celebrate the 80th Anniversary of the Garden City, *The Killing of Sister George* in 1987, and *Stevie* in 1988.

The 1950s also witnessed the capitulation of the Garden City to the liquor trade. On 17 May 1957 there was a vote in favour of a licensed hotel with residential accommodation, public lounge, restaurant, ballroom, bars etc! This materialised a few years later as *The Broadway Hotel*, a neat if somewhat pedantic Georgian-style building designed by Sidney Clark. Construction began in 1961, and the hotel was opened on 17 October 1962, hosting a Civic Dinner to celebrate the passing of the Letchworth Garden City Corporation Act a few weeks later.

Full Employment   The industrial theme heralded the complete post-war industrial recovery.[25] Between 1945 and 1953, 12 new factories ranging from 3,000 to 30,000 sq. ft. were built, giving a total of $2\frac{1}{4}$ million sq. ft. industrial floorspace, with over 10,000 employees. In the 1950s many firms consolidated their operations, amongst them Shelvoke and Drewry and K. & L., whilst Spirella still retained its pre-eminence for female employment. Expansion of the industrial estate eastward brought a new length of Works Road and of Jubilee Road which led to Baldock Road. In 1955, Borg Warner, a Division of the American company manufacturing automatic transmissions and linked with Morse Chain, built a £4,000,000 factory along the entire eastern side of Jubilee Road, backing onto the reservation for the future Baldock By-Pass. They obtained contracts from many of the leading motor manufacturers and became one of the leading employers in the town. Opposite them, Armco, the English Division of a Company from Ohio, U.S.A., built a major new plant which

102. I.C.T. Type 1202 computer. Early computers were extremely bulky and demanded the energy resources of a miniature power station.

manufactured small diameter double walled steel tubing for automotive and engineering industries. In 1958 'British Tab' was reconstituted as International Computers and Tabulators Limited, evidence of the growing importance of computers for financial and administrative purposes. Early electronic computers were unwieldy, with information stored on punched cards similar to the earlier tabulators, and a control console the size of a large office desk. The firm outgrew its Icknield Way premises, and in 1964 completed a visually insensitive office block in Town Square.

Modern Architecture in Letchworth   Post-war architecture incorporated concrete and steel framed structures, large glazed areas, with multi-storey forms and flat roofs increasingly predominant. Housing designs were simplified by the elimination of chimneys, bay windows and non-functional ornament, with roof pitches brought down to 30 degrees or less. Traditional materials were often reduced to a veneer. Substitutes such as concrete panels or concrete tiles were widely used. Architecture lost its strong local affinity for a bland 'anywhere' character or a deliberately assertive iconoclasticism. Many new Letchworth buildings lacked a regard for their context.[26]

Educational buildings showed a remarkable visual and functional transformation.[27] In the 1940s traditional materials were scarce, and the County Architect, C. H. Aslin, was faced with an unprecedented demand for new schools in the new towns and rapidly expanding residential estates. The outcome was a lightweight system of pre-fabricated construction, with an 8ft. 3in. modular steel framework (later 3ft. 4in.; 1.0 m.), clad with precast concrete panels, extensive glazing and flat roofs. Used for primary schools, the system allowed considerable freedom of planning to form classroom groups with associated cloakroom spaces, adaptable assembly halls with generous lighting, and courtyards for outdoor teaching. At their best, the county schools were outstandingly elegant, and created an informal and high quality environment for innovative teaching. The Wilbury School off Bedford Road (1949) and the Northfields Infants School on the Grange Estate (1951) are fine examples of the system at its best. The results were not so happy in larger buildings. The Willian School on the Jackmans Estate (1963) was more impersonal, whilst the additions to Norton School clashed with the innovative design of the first purpose-built Garden City school. Most unfortunate of all was the North Herts College campus, with an outlook to the Town Square and a Broadway frontage following demolition of the old Methodist Church. The design was no doubt functionally based, with its combination of low rooflit workshop blocks, and two-storey and four-storey teaching blocks. The college opened in 1958 and provided long needed higher education facilities for day, evening and industrial day release courses for 5,000 students. The cost to the character of the town centre was considerable. A grouping to achieve visual enclosure for the town square frontage, or to balance the Town Hall, was studiously avoided, and the two-storey block set back from Broadway was an apologetic recognition of the street frontage. Significantly, nothing was done to link up to the well proportioned Georgian-style Boys Club, where the blank fletton brickwork side elevation is a reminder of an opportunity missed. The siting of the college also removed the possibility of developing Westcheap.

The town's first post-war commercial development showed a similar disregard for its context. Arena Parade, on the vacant site twixt Co-op and car park, designed in 1958 by Eric H. Davie, represented an updating of the pre-war shopping parades, sensibly planned with rear servicing to enable the pedestrianisation of Eastcheap. Visually it claimed modernity with a flat roof and brick and artificial stone cladding, and window treatment suggesting the fashionable curtain walling. It would have fitted without comment into Stevenage town centre only six miles away, but it had no affinity with Letchworth. The same was true of office blocks. The I.C.L. Offices in Town Square were designed by Trehearne Norman, Preston and Partners. Completed in 1964, the plans had been approved by the U.D.C. after rumours of pressure from the Company. The monotonous grid of windows and blank purple brick ends above a slightly recessed ground floor represented another building almost perversely determined to reject its context. A wedge-shaped office block in Station Place was equally uninspiring, whilst the offices in Norton Way South, on the site of the old St Michael's Church, compounded a depressing saga.

Churches were happily more individual. St Michael's developed their permanent site on Town Square between 1966-68, with a neat polygonal brick church, with windows ingeniously provided in the angles, and a roofline enlivened by a cupola and spirelet. The architect was Laurance King. Internally the church was undemonstrative, with a central altar below the cupola and a suspended crucifix, and stained glass by John Hayward. The Roman Catholics also built their permanent church, St Hugh of Lincoln, facing Town Square, a pre-war design by Nicholas and Dixon Spain, but not built until the early 1960s, and consecrated in 1964. The setback from the frontage was a serious visual flaw, exposing the 'temporary' end as likely to remain permanent. Barry Parker had wrestled with the problem in 1938, but to no avail. Once built, the new church was a handsome traditional structure, with its walls treated as a serious of receding planes, but the pale brickwork was

103. St George's church, Norton Way North, 1963. This church with its soaring concrete spire remains one of the most notable modern buildings in Letchworth.

distinctly out of harmony with the predominant red of the majority of buildings in Town Square. Nor was the design improved by the addition, in 1985, of dark grey concrete tiled pitched roofs.

A third new church was perhaps the most uncompromising in design and ultimately the most successful. A small church hall had been built at the corner of Norton Way North and Common View. In the early 1960s, St George's church was designed by Peter Bosanquet of Brett, Boyd and Bosanquet. It ingeniously exploited the acute angle of the corner site and its change in level, with the church situated above ancillary accommodation. Externally, the building had bold geometrical form, with a low sweeping roof, complementing the vernacular forms of nearby housing. The walls were rather blandly treated and might have justified a bolder, more sculptural approach. The handling of the concrete spire was very successful, formed of two angles of a triangle, which sheltered a rooflight between, and penetrated the structure to form the backdrop to the altar, with an impressive crucifix above. At the west end, a tapered concrete pier supported the circular ring of the font and the roof. A fine organ gallery concealed the main entrance a level below. The church was consecrated on 27 July 1964. It proved that 1960s architecture could carry conviction and yet be responsive to its surroundings. Regrettably it was an exceptional achievement in Letchworth.

North Hertfordshire Technical College, officially opened on 15 June 1958.

Chapter Thirteen

Save Letchworth Garden City

Danger Signals Post-war growth, particularly after the dismantling of the development charge, raised the overall value of the estate, and made it an attractive target for speculators.[1] In 1955, the net profit reached £24,702, modest enough, but which brought a substantial increase in the price of Ordinary Shares; the £1 stock jumped to 26s. 0d. (£1.30). Suspecting the possibility of a take-over, the Council requested a meeting with the Board but this was refused. A group of shareholders, fearing possible nationalisation of the estate, suggested disposal of assets, which in turn alarmed the Company, whose Board feared intense speculation to obtain the remaining developable land. The Board determined to hold firm and bring the project to completion for the benefit of shareholders as 'a substantial reward for their faith and patience during the years of growth'. The social purpose of the original development was progressively dismissed. At an Extraordinary General Meeting on 6 April 1956 Sir Eric MacFadyen pronounced that a joint stock company was 'a very inappropriate method of carrying out a social experiment'. It was also proposed to remove dividend limits, strongly opposed by the Council and the Town and Country Planning Association. Sir Eric reiterated that the assets were the property of the shareholders and that 'we have learned on good advice . . . that there is no binding obligation to carry out the original policy'. The Board's proxies enabled the resolutions to be passed overwhelmingly.

A Public Meeting held the following July, addressed by Lord Silkin, urged the Company to recognise their moral obligations. Horace Plinston was asked to find a way to protect and restore the community's interests. Although the Council were assured that the estate would ultimately pass to them, relations with F.G.C. Ltd. continued to be uneasy. The 10 per cent surplus for charitable purposes, following the winding up of the Company, added to the articles in 1957 was viewed by Purdom as 'knocking nails into the coffin of the Garden City, supposing it to be dead!' Dividends rose steadily, $4\frac{1}{2}$ per cent, 5 per cent, $7\frac{1}{2}$ per cent — equivalent to 9 per cent, 10 per cent and 15 per cent on the original capital. In 1959, $8\frac{1}{2}$ per cent was declared with a 'special dividend' of 3 per cent, a total of $11\frac{1}{2}$ per cent representing 23 per cent on the original capital.

In January 1960, the £2 shares were divided into four 10s. 0d. (50p) shares, but voting rights remained unaltered; 20 of the new Ordinary Shares were required for one vote. The new shares immediately rose in value — 37s. $7\frac{1}{2}$d. (£1.88) in May, 50s. 0d. (£2.50) in August. The following month a take-over struggle was in progress.

The Take-over On 2 September 1960, the Raglan Property Trust made a requisition for an Extraordinary General Meeting to restructure the Company, removing the Ministerial nominations of two Board places, and urging the approval of a more swift development of the remainder of the estate, and winding up of the Company. This was a direct consequence of the final restoration of market value in land transactions. Drivers Jonas had valued the Company's assets at £1,635,000 in 1958, and the recent rise in share prices indicated a total of at least £2,000,000, compared to nominal share capital of £650,000. Raglan's Chairman, and Vice Chairman, Group Captain Maurice Newnham and Brigadier Eric Flavell, stood for election to F.G.C. Ltd. Board.

This appeared to represent an attack on the town's inheritance. The Council alerted the Divisional M.P., Martin Maddan, and on 4 October 1960 met Dame Evelyn Sharp at the

Ministry of Housing and Local Government. She again discounted the possibility of forming a development corporation, but suggested that the promotion of a private bill to create a non-political trustee body, in whom the estate might be vested, might be sympathetically considered. Three days later at the A.G.M., the F.G.C. Chairman emphasised that the Company wished to continue the development of the estate with regard to the green belt and other constraints, but contracts for large commercial and industrial premises, both within and beyond, would bring higher dividends. The Garden City supporters were between Scylla and Charybdis — they were fundamentally opposed to the Raglan overtures, yet F.G.C. Ltd. was also treading the entrepreneurial path. Ernest Gardiner of the Letchworth Civic Trust felt that the 'break up boys' were about to move in. Horace Plinston pointed out that the £2,250,000 Company investment should be set against the £6,500,000 spent by the Council on provision of services and property development: to a large degree the enhanced value of the estate was a reflection of the Council's investment in town development. The resolutions were defeated, and Newnham and Flavell were spurned.

However, the result was a reverse rather than a defeat. The Company remained vulnerable. Plinston assessed the acquisition costs at £2,000,000, raised at $6\frac{1}{4}$ per cent, which would represent an annual charge of £128,000, and a deficit of £48,000, which with a penny rate product of £2,200 would require a 2s.0d. (10p) rate. Even if a Parliamentary Bill were successful, would ratepayers accept this? In the midst of uncertainty there was renewed attack on 4 November 1960. Forty Lane Securities, a Raglan subsidiary controlled by Newnham, offered £1 5s. 0d. (£1.25) for each £1 of Preference Stock, which with its superior voting rights represented the cheapest way of obtaining control. Ernest Gardiner appealed to shareholders to pass their stock to the Civic Trust. A new contender entered the lists, Mrs. Amy Rose of Hotel York Ltd. Few suspected that this concern would shortly acquire the assets of the Company.

104. Mrs. Amy Rose outside the Estate Office.
Sold, one Garden City, to the lady in the fur coat!

Hotel York was a London-based property holding company, entirely owned or controlled by the Rose family, who had become directors in December 1958. Two London hotels, the *Welbeck Palace* and the *Berners*, had been sold and Mrs Rose, a shrewd business operator, sought further investments to enhance the assets of her 'Family Trust'. On 19 November 1960, Hotel York indicated to shareholders its willingness to purchase the entire £150,000 6 per cent cumulative Preference Stock for 32s. 0d. (£1.60) for each unit, and 260,100 Ordinary Shares for 50s. 0d. (£2.50) each. Mrs. Rose undertook to ensure the integrity of the Letchworth estate although many including Plinston and Purdom doubted the veracity of this, given her propensity for lucrative asset stripping. The Board warned against acceptance of the offers, although the Company Secretary, J. D. Ritchie, was thought to be more receptive to Mrs. Rose's proposition. F.G.C. Ltd. was doubtful whether the proposed Letchworth Bill would succeed and Mrs. Rose became aware of this. She told Plinston that she could not understand opposition to her take-over bid; Plinston informed her that, whatever happened, the Council would press ahead with the Bill. His parting shot was, 'the Bill will be accepted and I do not think your Company will lose money. If I were a betting man, I'd have my usual golfing stake of 2s. 6d. (12½p) on each'. Three days later Raglan sold out to Hotel York. On 16 December, Mrs. Rose was invited to take a seat on the Board. The lady, whose abiding image is of an imposing fur-swathed presence transported to the offices in a glossy limousine, had won. She became Managing Director on 5 January 1961, with her son, Michael Balfour Rose, alongside her on the Board. At the Company A.G.M., a few weeks later, Mrs. Rose and her son were re-elected over the Civic Trust candidates, Edwin Nott and Florence Thompson.

Save Letchworth Garden City!   The Council had already been alerted to the dangers. On 22 November 1960, a letter was published in *The Times* and locally, signed by party leaders on the Council, which indicated unanimity in defending the ideals of Letchworth against the speculators, irrespective of political belief, through the formation of a non-political trustee body to hold and manage the assets of F.G.C. Ltd., for the benefit of the community.

Whilst the cost of acquisition by a trustee body would be considerable and would result in deficits in early years, the venture would ultimately prove profitable and the 'rich harvest' would be garnered. Ernest Gardiner called a 'Save Letchworth Garden City' Public Meeting for 1 December 1960 at the newly completed Grammar School Hall, attended by over five hundred. The Divisional M.P., Martin Maddan, authorised the release of a Press Statement indicating his support for the proposed Parliamentary Bill, which he believed would gain Commons approval. Lord Pethick-Lawrence and Purdom addressed the meeting. Ernest Gardiner emphasised the urgency of the situation, picturing speculators walking away 'with a profit of £1,000,000 leaving Letchworth with nothing but its name'. It was evident to Cllr. Charles Sax, leader of the Labour majority, that residents were strongly behind moves to promote a Private Bill. He was concerned about the pressure on Plinston and his department, and hoped that the matter would proceed to a successful conclusion. The meeting approved a formal petition to the Minister of Housing and Local Government.

> Letchworth was the first 'New Town' and the vesting of the entirety of the land assets of a New Town in a body which is removed from the sphere of commercial gain is a principle recognised by the Government. We therefore petition the Minister . . . to take statutory action to secure that the Company and its lessees are protected from the activities of property speculators so that the intention of vesting the undertaking in a public body for the benefit of the community can be implemented.

The petition attracted 8,319 signatures. U.D.C. Chairman, Colin Bywaters called 20 'formal signatories' and the petition was despatched and presented to the House of Commons by Martin Maddan on 24 January 1961. A political truce was declared locally, pending resolution of the fundamental question of the future ownership of the Letchworth Estate.

The Parliamentary timetable did not permit hearings until after November 1961. Meanwhile, following the A.G.M., Mrs. Rose had *carte blanche* for action. The Board decided to obtain a new valuation, and also offered freeholds for auction. Hitherto only Church, amenity, County Council and, latterly, U.D.C. housing land had been disposed of in this manner. A Company prospectus offered a 10-acre (4 ha.) parcel of Howard Drive, and 2-acre (0.80 ha.) plots in Cloisters Lawns and Howardswood, all with outline permission for residential development. £50,000 was obtained for the Howard Drive site, notwithstanding the Council warning that it would re-possess the land if the Bill were successful. F.G.C. Ltd. threatened a libel action against Horace Plinston. They had also discussed a population target of 60,000 with Ernest Doubleday, the County Planning Officer, suggesting that lucrative development of additional Green Belt land was envisaged. Freehold reversions were offered, and Howard's objectives appeared under attack on all fronts.

Protracted Preparation   Howard had been sceptical of Government as a vehicle for social reform. It was perhaps ironic that 'this cumbrous complex piece of machinery' should ultimately have proved the saviour of Letchworth Garden City. It was doubly ironic that the measure should have been presented to, and enacted by a Conservative Government. Preparatory work and propaganda were considerable. For once, the devil did not always have the best tunes. The acrimonious A.G.M. of 16 February 1961 was linked to a leader in *The Times* which drew attention to 'A town based on principles', and concluded that 'it would indeed be a matter for dismay if purely commercial considerations were to prevail'. The Company tactics were directed towards maximum expansion, and raising the value of the estate in an effort to deter the Council. Plinston requested the Hertfordshire County Council to consider a penny rate contribution as a loan to be paid back with interest once profits materialised, on the basis that Letchworth had contributed greatly to the County's overall prosperity and rateable value. Although the County Council were sympathetic, they were wary over the principle involved, and declined support. Through the tactful fence-mending by Claude Barker, the recorded decision expressed sympathy with the endeavours of the U.D.C. to secure the passage of the Bill.

In January 1961, the U.D.C. retained Sharpe Pritchard and Company as their Parliamentary Agents. Wentworth Pritchard took personal responsibility for the Bill. Private Bill procedure had been followed by many local authorities since the 18th century. It was initiated by deposit of the Bill on petition at the Private Bill Office for scrutiny by the Examiners. It then required a promoter to introduce it in Parliament. Geoffrey Lawrence, Q.C. was engaged as Leading Counsel, with Eric Blair as his junior. Stanley Hill was appointed as the Council's Finance Adviser. Plinston approached G. M. P. Williams, the St Albans District Valuer, to prepare a valuation of the estate. Williams had been responsible for the valuation of Welwyn Garden City when taken over by the Development Corporation, and had also valued the U.D.C. compulsory purchase of the Grange and Jackmans land.

The Council continued regular contact with Evelyn Sharp. In July 1961 she emphasised that acquisition terms and valuation methods constituted crucial points. Stanley Hill explained the distinction between a 'break up' and a 'going concern' valuation, at which the Council wished to acquire the assets. Martin Maddan suggested use of Stock Exchange value, but Dame Evelyn disagreed, and suggested that current value be used. The valuation by the District Valuer represented this basis and was also close to share price valuation. Dame Evelyn was unable to offer assistance through the Ministry, nor provide a reference to the Public Works Loan Board. On the constitutional question, Martin Maddan emphasised the proposed independence of the body from the local authority and party politics, and stated that the Minister should appoint a majority on the Board. Dame Evelyn felt that the Minister would not accept responsibility for a corporation which was not a

Government creation. In conclusion she rated the chances of success at slightly below fifty-fifty.

The U.D.C. appointed a Sub-Committee — Councillors Sax, Askew and Talbot, to take day-to-day decisions relating to the Bill, and Plinston was appointed as policy witness for the Parliamentary hearings. Maddan met his Conservative colleagues, allaying fears that the Bill might establish an undesirable precedent and represent municipalisation of a registered public company. Omens were not favourable at this stage for, unless the Bill had the co-operation of the Minister, it was regarded as a non-starter. Yet it could be pointed out that the Bill sought to protect the interests of residents and householders; if the Government were to preside over its defeat, the example would not be lost on the opposition, not least for its propaganda value. Maddan briefed Henry Brooke, Minister of Housing and Local Government, on the Bill, who indicated that he would not object in principle, but wished to be satisfied that the measure was both fair to shareholders and a viable proposition for ratepayers.

Locally, the question of additional rates loomed large. Sidney Stapleton, an 'Independent Ratepayer' candidate in the May 1961 elections, estimated a 10s. 0d. rate. Although this was wildly exaggerated, nobody knew for certain what the figure would be. The unwillingness of the County Council to assist was serious, as their penny rate was equivalent to a local rate of 2s. 3d.

On 10 October 1961 the Council met the Company, Councillors Gay, Askew, Saxon, and Talbot with Mrs. Rose and Messrs. Rosevear and Smedley. Presentation of the Bill was expected after the Parliamentary recess. The U.D.C. was prepared to discuss a price if the Company was prepared to implement the 1949 promise to transfer the undertaking to a local authority or public body. Smedley replied that the Board was interested in the benefit of the community only insofar as it benefited shareholders. 'I do not believe that in the changed circumstances one can expect implementation of the Ebenezer Howard ideals . . . There is no sentimental Ebenezer miasma — we are a commercial company'.

Valuations were far apart — the *Evening Standard* had disclosed a U.D.C. figure of £2,000,000 whilst Smedley hinted that Cluttons' valuation for F.G.C. Ltd. would be above £3,500,000. There was no basis for a negotiated agreement. In reporting to the Council in November, Plinston had to tackle the thorny question of valuation. It was essential to avoid extravagant compensation claims, and all methods posed problems, with share valuation fluctuating in response to the Stock Market. The draft Bill had incorporated values based on 50s. 0d. (£2.50) for Ordinary Shares and 20s. 0d. (£1.00) for Preference Shares (the book value), giving a total of £2,650,000. The Council substituted 'market value as a going concern' on 16 November, and Stanley Hill calculated that a purchase price of £2.3m would, at the prevailing interest rate of $6\frac{3}{4}$ per cent, give a 1s. 3d. (7p) rate surcharge. F.G.C. Ltd. countered with Cluttons valuation of £3,712,582. The U.D.C. considered the possibility of acquiring only the town area, excluding the 2,000-acre (809 ha.) green belt, which had acquired statutory protection through the County Development Plan. However, this would infringe the unity of the Letchworth estate which was one of the key points in the argument. Plinston's calm grasp of detail at this stage was remarkable. In the midst of fears of escalating valuations, he inserted a clause exempting the ultimate transaction from Stamp Duty, and saved the Corporation almost £60,000 in the process.

The Views of the House   Parliamentary Standing Orders required notice of the Bill to be served on 4,000 separate interested parties, whilst a Book of Reference and a large scale Plan identifying every separate interest had to be deposited before Parliament. The latter was compiled under the leadership of Plinston's Deputy, Michael Kelly, using rating records as a base. The Book was deposited on 20 November 1961, the Council formally resolved to promote the Bill on 22 November, and the Bill petition was deposited a week later. Notices were published locally and in the *London Gazette*, served on all owners, lessees and occupiers, and on 4 December the Bill was deposited in the Commons Private Bill Office, with a statement confirming compliance with Standing Orders. On 17 December there was a town meeting of electors at the Grammar School Hall. The Company forecast a 5s. 0d. (25p) rate increase and urged residents to 'Ban the Bill'. The meeting was addressed by the U.D.C. Chairman. Stanley Hill explained its financial provisions, and was inevitably challenged by Sidney Stapleton. Whilst risks were recognised, the overwhelming tenor of the meeting was positive and the resolution was carried: 442 for, 24 against. However, F.G.C. Ltd. obtained 100 signatures, and requisitioned a poll, held 6 January 1962, at which 3,183 were in favour and 903 against, on a low 25 per cent turnout. However, this cleared the last hurdle before presentation to Parliament. On 24 January 1962, it was deemed to have received its First Reading, through being placed on the Speaker's table.

The Bill provided for the creation of a Letchworth Garden City Corporation as a public authority, with members appointed by the Minister, by the County Council, and by the U.D.C. The estate would be managed as an entity in accordance with the principles in operation until 1960. The estate would be conveyed as a whole to the new body, following which any adverse balance in revenue would be made good by the Council. After meeting all claims, any balance would be spent in favour of the community. The Company counter-petitioned, claiming a lack of justification for confiscation of private property, in the interest, not of the community, but merely that of the Council. A meeting of the Back Benchers Committee decided not to oppose the Bill. Charles Sax and Plinston met Labour M.P.s who, not surprisingly, indicated their sympathy. Plinston ensured that all parties received briefing notes on the significance of the Bill and of Letchworth itself.

The Second Reading was deferred several times, and an attempt was made by Ray Mawby, M.P. for Totnes, to defer the Second Reading by six months. However the debate took place on 20 March. At 7.04 p.m., Lord Balniel introduced the Bill and moved the Second Reading. Dr. Barnett Stross (Labour, Stoke-on-Trent) reiterated that unified ownership of Letchworth should be preserved. Ray Mawby saw the Bill as an effort to nationalise an ordinary property company. Speeches from all sides often mingled personal memories of Letchworth life with the necessity to perpetuate its founder's ideals. The Minister, Dr. Charles Hill, recommended that the Bill be examined in Select Committee. Before the Division, Martin Maddan paid tribute to Howard's ideals which had been translated into three-dimensional reality at Letchworth. He quoted Osborn, a Socialist, on the benefits of planning and unified site ownership, coupled with leaseholds, reconciling public interests with freedom of choice and enterprise. He noted that the F.G.C. Ltd. Annual Report dated 13 March 1962 stated that 'the vast majority of the present shareholders have invested in this Company to obtain maximum increase on their investment and it is the Board's policy to act in the interest of these shareholders', urging passage of the Bill to remove the town from the mercy of speculators and to benefit from strong management divorced from political interference. The House divided at 9.59 p.m. The Reading was carried: ayes 246, noes 13. Plinston felt he was dreaming when he named the tellers' announcement. Conservatives such as John Biffen, John Biggs Davidson, W. F. Deedes, Charles Hill, Iain Macleod, Gerald Nabarro, Francis Pym and Geoffrey Rippon rubbed shoulders in the division lobbies with Labour stalwarts including Bessie Braddock, Fenner Brockway, James Callaghan, Barbara Castle, Judith Hart, Jennie Lee, Philip Noel-Baker and George Thomas. It was a remarkable night both for Parliament and for Letchworth.

The A.G.M. of F.G.C. Ltd. was held on 6 April 1962. Osborn and other prominent shareholders had drawn attention to inaccuracies in Mrs Rose's statements. At the meeting, Christopher Cadbury moved the rejection of the Report and Accounts, but although passed by a show of hands it was lost on a poll. Osborn moved a resolution asking the Directors to withdraw opposition to the Bill, which was carried 40 to 27 on a show of hands, but defeated 45,853 to 2,119 on a poll. Osborn's proxies from 248 shareholders, with 246,864 Ordinary and 16,312 Preference Shares, represented 20 per cent of the voting strength, but were declared invalid on a technicality.

Timing of the A.G.M. ensured further ammunition for the Examination in Select Committee. The Parties were represented by Counsel, with expert witnesses cross-examined. The Committee sat on Tuesdays, Wednesdays, Thursdays, from 11-1 and 2-4.30, commencing 2 May 1962. It comprised five Conservative and four Labour members, under the Chairmanship of Sir Samuel Storey on behalf of the U.D.C. Geoffrey Lawrence, Q.C. presented an opening statement giving the history of the Company and its recent actions, summarising the provisions of the Bill, particularly the compensation arrangements, and claiming the overall fairness of measure. The Minister had reported favourably and, whilst ordinarily he was critical of compulsory purchase of private estates, there was much to be said for the ownership being a trustee for the citizens. The management arrangements appeared likely to prove satisfactory, the Minister was prepared to accept his responsibilities if the Bill were passed. This positive start was compounded by Plinston's expert testimony and astute response to cross-examination. Stanley Hill brought out the relevant financial details and revealed that investors had had ample warning of the possibility of public ownership from such an impeccable source as the *Stock Exchange Yearbook*, which noted that in September 1949 the shareholders had 'approved in principle the ultimate transfer, when development is completed, of the undertaking to public ownership subject to satisfactory terms being agreed', information provided by First Garden City Ltd! Under cross-examination he maintained that Cluttons' valuation represented asset stripping. Sir Frederic Osborn appeared and stated that Letchworth had pioneered the official British policy on decentralisation and that the protection of its integrity was of world-wide significance. For the Company, C. P. Harvey, Q.C. challenged the claim that the Corporation brought any lasting public benefit. The U.D.C. case was pure hypocrisy for they had forced the F.G.C. Ltd. to sell the freehold of the Grange Estate. The Bill challenged the right of a company to manage its affairs in the best interests of its shareholders, and the provisions for compensation were not in accord with the Land Compensation Act 1961. Few modifications were made in Committee. On 21 May it was stated that the Bill would be addressed to the house. It received its Third Reading and passed to the Lords.

F.G.C. Ltd. launched a propaganda war — a four-column tirade in the *City Press* circulating in London, headed 'Prejudice or Justice — Facts for the House of Lords in the Letchworth Dispute', and petitioned the Lords against the Bill. Again the Council prepared its case thoroughly. Business followed the pattern of the Lower House and the Second Reading commenced at 6.30 p.m. on 28 June 1962. Lord Molson moved the Reading, supported by Lord Silkin, now reconciling his 1948 opinion that a public corporation was not appropriate in the present circumstances, stating that Sir Eric MacFadyen's undertaking that Letchworth would be run in accordance with Howard's principles had now vanished. Earl Jellicoe, on behalf of the Government, recommended the formal Reading which was unopposed. The Lords Select Committee under Lord Strang commenced on 3 July 1962. Speaking for F.G.C. Ltd., Michael Wheeler, Q.C. withdrew opposition on principle, but remained opposed to the compensation arrangements, and examination of detail continued. Clause 15 of the Bill envisaged a transaction between a willing seller and a willing buyer and was subject to close scrutiny. Much time was spent on the divergence between the U.D.C. and F.G.C. Ltd. valuations. At a late stage Wheeler attacked the 'Letchworth principles' referred to in the Bill as being vague and uncertain. Although recounted by Plinston under cross-examination they were not to be found in the Company's Memorandum of Articles of Association which referred to Howard's book in the vaguest terms. F.G.C. Ltd. were also concerned about the definition of 'going concern'. After the Third Day, the Chairman concluded that the preamble was proved without amendment and the Bill returned to the House.

The Report Stage and Third Reading on 18 July 1962 were formalities, and on 1 August 1962 the Royal Assent was given.[2] The struggle was over for the present. The Council held

105. Horace Plinston (right) presented with a copy of the Letchworth Garden City Corporation Act, by Cllr. William Askew. Plinston's deputy, Michael Kelly, arranged for the second presentation copy of the Act to be made in secret for a surprise event at the civic dinner held on 8 December 1982.

a special meeting on 3 August 1962 to celebrate a unique historic event, recording thanks to Martin Maddan and all concerned. A Civic Dinner was held at the *Broadway Hotel* on 8 December 1962. Bound copies of the Act were presented to Martin Maddan and Horace Plinston. Donald Howard, Mabel Barry Parker and many pioneers were present to toast the new Corporation.

Notwithstanding the passing of the Act, First Garden City Ltd. showed a perverse determination to be awkward and the last few months passed in open warfare. In July 1962, when it was evident that the Bill would succeed, an E.G.M. was called to amend the

Articles to remove the 10 per cent surplus payable to a charitable concern after winding up, which had been agreed in 1957, and a poll carried the matter with a large majority. Plinston had to obtain an injunction to restrain the Company from selling or granting new leases on several sites. On 1 January 1963 snow covered the Broadway pavements as Horace Plinston, accompanied by Laurie Freeman, entered the Estate Offices. Amy Rose had stripped out office furniture and stationery. 'What a dump' was Humbert's reaction as he arrived to find Plinston working at a borrowed desk and chair. Four weeks later the Corporation sent a lorry to collect the furniture from one of Mrs Rose's London hotels. Post, on her insistence, was delivered to London, which meant that she saw many letters requiring the Corporation's attention.

Appointees to the Corporation were discussed with Evelyn Sharp. Colonel R. A. Humbert, a member of Welwyn Development Corporation and a St Albans-based surveyor, was appointed Chairman. The remaining members were Sir Harold Fieldhouse, Leslie Bennett, D. G. Haddow, Claude Barker and Alderman County Councillor Charles Sax. Board meetings were initially held at Welwyn Corporation offices to preserve confidentiality. Plinston's secondment as Solicitor and Legal Adviser to the Corporation, initially for a six-month period, was agreed. Shortly after its formal take-over of the Estate Offices, he requested Plinston to remain their Chief Officer. His deputy, Michael Kelly, was appointed Town Clerk to the U.D.C. Laurie Freeman was appointed Corporation Estate Officer.

The Letchworth Garden City Corporation Act 1962   The Act constituted the Letchworth Garden City Corporation to acquire the undertaking of First Garden City Limited, as of 1 January 1963. The Preamble referred to the incorporation of the original company and its objectives 'to promote and further the distribution of the industrial population upon the land according to the lines suggested by Mr. Ebenezer Howard's book entitled *Garden Cities of Tomorrow*'.

The Act was divided into five parts. Part I dealt with interpretation and definition; Part II described the establishment and constitution of the Corporation. It comprised a Chairman and five members; the Chairman and three other members being Ministerial appointments, one County Council, and one District Council, member. The Corporation was 'to manage, to turn to account, to carry on, develop and extend the undertaking . . . as a public service', with powers 'to acquire, hold, manage and dispose of land . . . to carry out building and other operations' but was required to 'have regard to the maintenance of the undertaking . . . as an entity in accordance with the principles upon which Letchworth Garden City was founded' (Section 11). Part III dealt with the transfer of the undertaking, with S. 15 containing the much debated but unamended provision for a 'going concern' approach. Failing agreement, the matter would be referred to the Lands Tribunal. Part IV dealt with finance. The Corporation was empowered to borrow and to spread repayment over 60 years. S. 27 harmonised the Corporation with local authority finance. The District Council was empowered to lend to the Corporation (S. 29). Section 32 dealt with revenue disposal. After meeting all establishment charges, interest payments, repayments of borrowing, providing working capital and a reserve fund, the Corporation might apply 'any balance . . . to the provision of traffic facilities, lighting, drainage, markets, libraries, baths or otherwise for the embellishment of the Corporation, the provision of means of education, recreation or amusement for the people or for any other purpose which the Corporation may deem to be a requisite public service'. This provided the framework for the disbursement of Howard's legacy.

The Lands Tribunal   The difference between the Company and Corporation valuations was fundamental. In 1964 payment on account of £1,000,000 was made. The money was raised from the Shell Investment Department. This made it possible to raise 25 per cent of the figure, £250,000 from the Public Works Loan Board, which was used for development. On 2 June 1964 the Corporation applied for the compensation question to be referred to the Lands Tribunal, with hearings fixed to commence on 5 October 1965. Detailed evidence was again prepared, but the Corporation case was affected by the appointment of its leading Counsel as a High Court Judge in August 1965. By contrast, the Company's team remained intact. Shortly before the hearing commenced valuations were exchanged. Cluttons' valuation of the Company ran into 462 pages, and a second by Gerald Eve and Son grouped the assets into categories. A final figure of £3,620,951 was tabled. The Corporation's valuation showed deductions for management costs, and a profits tax was also deducted. Their offer had adjusted Williams' valuation to £2,510,000, plus professional charges and legal costs. There was thus a gap of more than £1.1m between the two parties.

The hearing lasted 77 days over a six-month period, forcing Plinston to stay in London from Mondays to Fridays, studying the daily transcripts supplied to him at 9 p.m. The Tribunal, Erskine Simes, Q.C. and John Watson, considered over 1,000,000 words of testimony. The Company's leading evidence alone took five days to present, and seven days in cross-examination. Much hinged on the fact that 'going concern' was not defined, nor were limitations placed on the term in the Act. By 10 November, after 26 days, the Corporation's Counsel, Reginald Goff, believed that it would be impossible to envisage an award lower than £2,900,000, and quite likely for it to be above £3,000,000. Counsel advised the Corporation to authorise an offer of £2,950,000 plus costs, with an absolute maximum of £3,050,000. If this were accepted, the Corporation would save substantially on legal costs. The Corporation believed that their valuation would stand up to extended cross-examination, and decided to press onwards. The case lasted a further 51 days. Stanley Hill was in the witness box for 10 days, followed by G. M. V. Williams. Under cross-examination the latter almost agreed that the Letchworth rents were those of a 'benevolent' landlord; just in time he reiterated that he had used open market values prevailing throughout North Hertfordshire. He was then taken through a gruelling 12-day examination of detail.

In December 1965, leading Counsel R. W. Goff was appointed a High Court Judge. The replacement Counsel worked over the Christmas recess, only to fall ill, then a member of the tribunal succumbed to mumps. Submissions were not completed until 5 April 1966. At the final session on 27 July 1966, the Lands Tribunal made an award of £3,060,000, midpoint between the divergent figures, and close to the amount recommended the previous November. The Corporation accepted that their 'going concern' basis had been rejected, but appealed over the 'bricks and mortar' aspects, particularly the valuation placed on the Letchworth Cottages and Buildings property. Mrs. Rose had liquidated the Company on 17 March 1966, and shareholders were pressing for payment. The Liquidator accepted a figure of £3,115,000 in full settlement and, as the Corporation was liable for the Company's costs which untaxed stood at £160,000, the result was favourable, leaving £2,995,000 as the residual value. Although disappointed, Plinston must have reflected that the County Treasurer, John Alexander, had told him 'if you can get the undertaking for £3,000,000 you will be buying a gold mine'. Mrs. Rose also expressed this opinion in a press interview.

It was ironic that the integrity of the estate should have been threatened in 1967 by the Leasehold Reform Bill, which enabled long leaseholders to acquire their freeholds. Despite lobbying, Letchworth was not excluded from the operation of the Act. The Corporation appealed to the High Court for an introduction of a Scheme of Management, which was granted.[3] The scheme applied to all enfranchised property, with the objective of preserving the standards of amenity of the estate. It imposed covenants which required the maintenance of the exterior of buildings and their boundary fences and hedges in good condition. Owners could not alter, extend or rebuild without written Corporation consent. This enabled continuity with the previous leasehold covenants. Many of the early Letchworth leases for residential property were of only 99-years length. As the unexpired period shortened, and land values rose, the cost of obtaining freeholds under the legislation rose steeply. The introduction of a scheme for deferred payment provoked arguments with a Leaseholders and Freeholders Association in 1989, and this will be discussed further in the next chapter.

A final consequence concerned liability of the Garden City Corporation for Corporation Tax and Capital Gains Tax. It had been defined as a body within the Local Loans Act 1875, analagous to a local authority for the purposes of raising loans and making precepts. Under S. 66 of the Finance Act 1965, local authorities were to be exempt from Income Tax, Corporation Tax and Capital Gains Tax. The Inland Revenue did not accept this in the case of Letchworth. The matter was followed through the assessment and appeal procedure, involving a lengthy discussion of the definition of the 1875 Act and subsequent legislation. The Commissioners found in favour of the Corporation. From 1973, the Corporation was not to be liable to taxation upon revenue or capital surpluses, and later obtained exemption from Development Land Tax, and partially from the 1975 Community Land Act. The forecast of a 'gold-mine' moved nearer to fulfilment.

SAVE
Letchworth
Garden City
PUBLIC MEETING
called by **ERNEST G. GARDINER**
THURSDAY DECEMBER 1 at 7.30 p.m.
GRAMMAR SCHOOL
Assembly Hall

The Old Order Changeth

Environmental Appraisal During the 1960s and early 1970s the planning framework of Letchworth was re-appraised.[1] In December 1965, the County Planning Officer, Ernest Doubleday, published a *Letchworth Central Area Appraisal Plan*, the first to be undertaken in a 'New Town'. Town centre planning in the early 1960s was influenced by *Traffic in Towns* by Sir Colin Buchanan, which emphasised definition of a principal road network, within which were traffic-free zones and pedestrianisation. These principles were advocated in Letchworth which had accommodated a tenfold increase in motor traffic between 1935-65. The generous highway reservations, and absence of principal routes through the town centre, had helped to absorb the traffic without the serious pedestrian/vehicular conflicts found in Hitchin and Baldock. The gross shopping floorspace of 330,400 sq.ft. indicated an efficient use of the existing premises. Emphasis was placed on improving servicing, parking and introducing pedestrianisation. Five possible redevelopment areas were proposed, including the congested areas east and west of Commerce Avenue, and The Wynd. 'Silver Birch Cottages' in Station Road were considered to provide a poor residential environment. Development of rear servicing areas would enable pedestrianisation of Eastcheap and Leys Avenuue where traffic levels were excessive. To keep pace with population growth, provision of an additional 100,000 sq.ft. gross shopping floorspace was suggested by 1973. Townscape improvements were based on a choice between 'trees or traffic'. It was suggested that the gaunt flank of the Broadway Cinema to Eastcheap should be screened, the Arena car park built over, and comprehensive shopping be developed between Eastcheap and Commerce Avenue. The *Appraisal* was adopted in 1967 as the basis for town centre development control.

In the late 1960s, the County Council undertook a land use/transportation study of Hitchin, Letchworth and Baldock, following American techniques which predicted vehicular movement generated by land use zones and assigned it to a highway network. *Letchworth — People and Traffic* was published in 1970. The A1 (M) Baldock By-Pass, running from Corey's Mill, Stevenage to rejoin the A1 Great North Road at Radwell, had been opened in August 1967, and included an interchange with Letchworth Gate. Connections with the industrial area remained poor, with an elevated section of the by-pass running over the A505 Letchworth-Baldock Road, without connecting ramps. *People and Traffic* included a 'Willian Route' diverging from Rosehill, Hitchin, swinging round south-east of Willian, across Letchworth Gate and running north to a junction with the Baldock Road opposite Jubilee Road. Although approved in principle, it would have brought severe environmental conflicts at Willian, and was eventually dropped, in favour of a diversion from the A505 to Corey's Mill and thence via the A1(M) to Letchworth Gate, but with no new connection to the industrial area. The history of this route indicates the regional significance of traffic problems in Letchworth. The remainder of the principal network defined in the report used existing roads to sub-divide eight environmental districts from within which through traffic would be removed. Some radical improvements were proposed and implemented, the most significant being the 'longabout' on A6141 Letchworth Gate, built 1972, in effect a short length of dual carriageway, with a pedestrian underpass, picking up access to the Lordship and Jackmans estates. Most controversial was a proposed gyratory around the Free Church at the foot of

Gernon Road and Leys Avenue, partly implemented to give access to the multi-storey car park, in 1973. The report also recommended the closure of many subsidiary junctions. Convenience appeared to be sacrificed to theory, and few closures were implemented.

The County Development Plan was approved in 1958, and underwent a First Review in December 1963, which worked its way through a six-month public inquiry in 1965, ministerial modifications in 1968, a second inquiry in 1969, attaining final approval in May 1971. The 1968 Town and Country Planning Act had introduced a broader brush 'structure plan' as the vehicle for strategic policies concerned with population prediction and balancing housing with employment.[2] More detailed matters were the subject of local plans. In Hertfordshire, the 1973 terminal date of the County Development Plan was extended by eight years through an informal policy statement, *Hertfordshire 1981*, to span the period until the County Structure Plan became operable. Letchworth was predicted to grow from its 30,945 population in 1971 to 36,121 by 1981, with completion of the Jackmans, Lordship and Manor Farm and Standalone Farm Estates.

Enter North Hertfordshire District Council   By the 1960s local government in England represented a patchwork of authorities, with widely differing resources and responsibilities, ranging from the rural district councils, with their constituent civil parishes, urban districts, municipal and county boroughs, to shire county councils and the London County Council, all created by 19th-century legislation. The Greater London Council was created in 1965, with a second tier of Borough Councils. The 1969 Redcliffe-Maud Royal Commission recommended 58 'unitary' authorities, and three further Metropolitan areas.[3] The 1972 Local Government Act, passed by a Conservative government, adopted a different system which retained shire counties, albeit with some boundary changes, within which district councils were created by amalgamation of the old urban and rural councils. The Hertfordshire boundary had already been adjusted with the creation of the G.L.C., and ten new District Councils were created, with effect from 1 April 1974.

In 1930, the Boundary Commission had proposed to amalgamate Letchworth with Baldock, which was huffily rejected. Now it was to be grouped not only with Baldock, but also with Hitchin, Royston, and the 33 Hitchin R.D.C. parishes, to form the new North Hertfordshire District Council, covering a broad 155 sq. mile swathe wrapped northwards around Stevenage New Town. This ended the geographic conjunction between U.D.C. and Corporation. The 31,000 Letchworth residents were absorbed into a district total of 99,500. In June 1973, 48 Councillors were elected to represent 19 wards for an initial three-year period. The first meeting of the new Council was convened on 21 June 1973. In May 1979, 25 new wards were created, represented by 50 Councillors, the number in each reflecting its population. Letchworth's five wards each had three members, giving one more overall than the 14 representing Hitchin. The old rival had been absorbed and with Letchworth made up almost two thirds of the Council. There was ample scope for both geographical as well as political loyalties to be reflected in Council decisions. The first N.H.D.C. Chairman, Bill Miller, was a Letchworth councillor, and the new authority was Labour-controlled until 1976. Letchworth was chosen as the administrative centre due to the availability of a six-storey office block in Gernon Road. Modified to include a Council Chamber, and with the air conditioning omitted as an economy measure, the extensive glazing gave a dramatic demonstration of 'passive solar gain' in the sweltering summer of 1975, with internal temperatures of 120°F recorded.

Michael Kelly, U.D.C. Clerk wondered 'Who will mourn the passing of this U.D.C.? A few of us perhaps, particularly the survivors of the 181 Councillors ... since 1919 ... the hope is that in the brave new world of Local Government we shall get more of everything'.[4] In 55 years, the U.D.C. had built nearly 5,000 dwellings, 3,700 since 1945, and extensive

106. Presenting Arms, March 1974. U.D.C. Chairman Charles Sax and Corporation Chairman Robert Humbert. Michael Kelly, U.D.C. Clerk (left), was to become the first Chief Executive of North Hertfordshire District Council.

civic facilities and public utilities. Some assets were dispersed — the Anglian Water Authority took over sewage disposal, whilst the County Council absorbed the library. As its farewell gesture in March 1974, the U.D.C. passed its Coat of Arms into the safe keeping of the Garden City Corporation. Many N.H.D.C. Chief Oficers were drawn from the old constituent authorities. Michael Kelly, as Chief Executive, headed the corporate management team, with Don Woolston from Hitchin U.D.C. as Solicitor, Wilfred Hammond from Hitchin R.D.C. as Secretary, Keith Sutton from Royston as Treasurer, Fred Such, the Letchworth U.D.C. Engineer and Surveyor as Technical Officer, Trevor Thompson from Hitchin as Housing Officer, and Derek Coyne from Cheshunt U.D.C. as Environmental Health Officer. N.H.D.C. became a planning authority in its own right, and Brian Hull, from the County's East Divisional Planning Office, was appointed Planning Officer.

The honeymoon period was short. Residents outside Letchworth, particularly from Royston, found the new authority remote. On the first birthday of N.H.D.C, the *Letchworth Comet* declared 'Local Authority spending has never been higher, the image never lower. Of almost equal importance is the total loss of faith by individual townships in an authority which no longer represents their particular problems . . .'. A harsh judgement and somewhat premature. Local Government has suffered from a poor image since reorganisation, exacerbated by the attitude of national government in the 1980s. There were gains, not least in a timely emphasis on conservation, which included the early Garden City achievements.

An Area of Special Architectural or Historic Interest   Widespread dissatisfaction with comprehensive town centre redevelopment brought pressure for improved legislation to protect historic buildings and areas. The 1968 Town and Country Planning Act introduced the obigation to obtain prior consent to demolish, alter or extend buildings listed by the Minister as of special architectural or historic interest. The previous year, Duncan Sandys, a Conservative M.P., promoted the Civic Amenities Act through a Labour Government. This introduced 'Conservation Areas', which the local authority had a duty to identify, designate, and to administer policies for their preservation and enhancement.[5] Although the County Council had designated Conservation Areas in Norton and Willian, no action had been taken to protect Letchworth itself, possibly due to the U.D.C.'s role in the redevelopment of Commerce Avenue. Whilst most early Conservation Areas were largely concerned with historic towns and villages, both Hampstead Garden Suburb and Welwyn Garden City preceded the designation of Letchworth.

In 1966, publication of *The Search for Environment* by the American scholar Walter Creese focussed attention on the international significance of the Garden City movement.[6] Mabel Barry Parker lived at 296 Norton Way South, the old Parker and Unwin offices, and carefully catalogued her husband's papers and drawings.[7] Active in Letchworth life into her 90s, Mrs. Parker moved to St Catherine's Nursing Home in 1973, following which the Corporation purchased the Norton Way building for extension and reopening as the First Garden City (Heritage) Museum in 1977. The Garden City lifestyle had been kept alive by the, now elderly, band of pioneers and their first generation offspring. Kenneth Johnson, an assistant librarian, chronicled the events and personalities of Letchworth history, and for over 25 years wrote a lively column in *The Citizen*. In 1976 his *Book of Letchworth*[8] presented a kaleidoscopic view, compiled by serendipity, juxtaposing the significant with the memorably trivial.

N.H.D.C. inherited 31 Conservation Areas including Baldock, Hitchin and Royston, and most of the historic villages in the district. It seemed anomalous that the First Garden City was not recognised as historic. Consequently, in 1974, an extensive Conservation Area was defined, including the town centre, pioneer residential areas, and Old Letchworth, and was linked in designation to the Diamond Jubilee of the Royal Town Planning Institute, the formation of which the development of Letchworth had done much to foster.[9] This was followed by detailed research on the buildings, using early bye-law records, for reference to the Department of the Environment for listing.[10] Over 300 separate properties were included in the published list of September 1979.[11] Examples included the Spirella building, the Parker and Unwin Studio (First Garden City Heritage Museum), Baillie Scott's 'Tanglewood', 'The Cloisters', the concrete cottage at No. 158 Wilbury Road, and the Stanley Parker house, Wilbury Road, all as Grade II* items, whilst groups such as Westholm, or the fine 'L' blocks in Sollershott East framing Field Lane were Grade II. In 1977, N.H.D.C. published an illustrated Broadsheet history of Letchworth.[12] Visits proliferated. In 1976 the Town and Country Planning Association brought a major group, including Sir Frederic Osborn; in 1977 the international meeting of the Urban History Group followed. Japanese parties had an insatiable appetite for Garden City history, translated by their inscrutable and tireless interpreters. After such a visit in Autumn 1987, N.H.D.C. Chairman Anthony Burrows, and a Corporation Board member, John Stoddard, were invited to attend a Japanese conference on Garden Cities for the 21st century.

For the 75th Anniversary of Letchworth in 1978 a major commemorative exhibition was

107. Letchworth Garden City, 1903-1978. Walter Crane's evocative drawing, originally produced for the cover of *Garden Cities of Tomorrow* in 1902, was used to commemorate the 75th anniversary of Letchworth.

108. Sir Frederic Osborn and Robert Humbert at the 75th Anniversary Exhibition. On one of his last public appearances, Sir Frederic made an impassioned speech about the significance of Letchworth.

mounted at the First Garden City (Heritage) Museum. This included Howard's desk and one of his typewriters, with his original diagrams, and Hunter's fabrics and Cockerell's bookbinding to represent early craft industries.[13] The exhibition was opened by Corporation Chairman Robert Humbert. Sir Frederic Osborn, aged 93, was present. Despite his frailty, he made an impromptu speech, fired by memories of the Howard Cottage Society and Letchworth life. He stressed Letchworth's continued significance for civilised living, but emphasised that its message had been least understood in the town itself. It was his last public appearance. He died in Welwyn Garden City on 1 November 1978. Sir Frederic had earlier agreed to become President of the Letchworth Garden City Society, founded on 3 May 1978, by participants in a series of lectures on Garden City history, given by the author at North Herts College. Hugh Bidwell, son of the architect Wilson Bidwell, was elected Chairman, and founder members included Horace Plinston. The Society aimed at fostering the ideals of the founders of Letchworth, encouraging civic pride and the protection of the Garden City environment.

This latter objective was easier to achieve in theory than in practice. Although controls over property alteration were drawn both from the planning legislation and the Corporation's scheme of management, alterations continued to proliferate, particularly on smaller properties, often abetted by aggressive home improvement advertising. The sale of council houses without covenants over subsequent alterations, and N.H.D.C.'s own housing improvement policies, which were not always sensitive to Conservation Area locations, exacerbated matters. Visually unsympathetic alterations included concrete interlocking tiled roofs, metal and plastic windows. Where residential properties were unlisted, designation of a Conservation Area did not remove the householder's rights to undertake minor alterations, unless an 'Article 4 Direction' had been approved by the Secretary of State. In 1988 N.H.D.C. resolved to seek these powers. These 'minor' alterations were also seemingly beyond the scheme of management, too. Modest grants help to bridge the cost between modern substitutes and the more expensive handmade tiles and timber windows, but a significant problem remains.

Moving into surplus — the Howard Legacy Section 32 of the Letchworth Garden City Corporation Act required that any balance after payment of operating expenses should be used for community benefit. In 1968 F.G.C. Ltd. had been paid off, and the Corporation's operations were moving into surplus. Although a large debt to the U.D.C. remained, a modest £1,000 was distributed as the first instalment of Howard's bequest on 11 September 1968. The Wilbury Wanderers Football Club, the Youth Club, the Guides Building Fund, the Settlement, and the Old People's Welfare Committee were beneficiaries.[14] In 1973 sale of the Standalone farmland more than wiped out the remaining debts of £3,000,000. In 1974 and 1975 balances available for distribution were £359,546 and £384,805 respectively. The time had come to look forward to spending major surpluses.[15] A town meeting held in December 1974 produced priorities for a leisure centre/swimming pool, a community hall and a day hospital. Provision was postponed due to economic uncertainty which began with a freeze on rent reviews and mounting inflation. Matters revived in 1979 when the surplus reached £2,598,000. £502,000 had been distributed since 1974. The reconstruction of the town's industrial base again depressed the surplus, and it was also depleted by withdrawal of large tranches for the major projects. By 1988 Section 32 disbursements of £732,000 were made including £370,000 enterprise subsidies, and £140,000 grants.

The major capital expenditure was absorbed by five major projects — the First Garden City Heritage Museum, the Ernest Gardiner Day Hospital, North Hertfordshire Sports and Leisure Centre, Plinston Hall, and Standalone Farm Centre. The day hospital involved lengthy discussions with the Area Health Authority. By 1982 costs had increased to a point

109. Ernest Gardiner Day Hospital. The first matron, Mrs. Jean Hyde, poses with one of her green-fingered day patients.

110. Britannia Rules the Waves! North Herts. Leisure Centre — the official opening by H.M. The Queen, July 1982.

where the Corporation withdrew its offer both to build and equip the hospital. Agreement was reached to pay for its construction, with £60,000 to be raised for essential equipment — in the event £75,000 was donated. The hospital opened in October 1984. Although privately built, equipped, and staffed, it catered exclusively for National Health Service patients. Twenty places were provided in a domestic scale, single-storey building off Pixmore Avenue, with a welcoming non-institutional atmosphere developed by the first Matron, Mrs. Jean Hyde. The emphasis was on rehabilitation of the elderly, sick and disabled, for the most part over a six-week period. Physical and occupational therapy sessions formed an important part of activities at the Hospital. The building was named after the former U.D.C. Chairman, who called the 'Save Letchworth' meeting in December 1960. The nearby Cottage Hospital closed in August 1988, and in Spring 1989 it was announced that it would be refurbished as a hospice at a cost of £750,000, to provide 15 residential places, a day care centre and a base for two home care nurses. Public donations quickly raised over £400,000, including a donation of £100,000 by Letchworth Garden City Corporation, handed over at a reception in Plinston Hall.

The Leisure Centre was the most ambitious Section 32 project, and was the subject of lengthy discussions with N.H.D.C. who were to be responsible for its running and maintenance, with the Corporation initially undertaking to meet up to 25 per cent of any annual deficit on running costs, up to £35,000, over the first five years. The £3.5m Leisure Centre was designed and built by package contractor, Module 2, and provided a wide range of facilities within its impersonal red brick exterior. The major attraction was the 'T'-shaped combination pool, with wave-making machine and a 25m. central section for serious swimming. In addition, a large multi-sports hall, squash courts, weighttraining fitness room and sauna were provided. The complex was officially opened by H.M. Queen Elizabeth II in July 1982. Plinston Hall was named in memory of Horace Plinston who died in 1980. It was perhaps a surprising choice as Letchworth has never lacked such buildings, and provision of a new facility could only relegate the Howard Hall still further. The Plinston Hall in Town Square took the shell of the 1960s Grammar School Assembly Hall, with a new frontage block, and ancillary accommodation at the side and rear. Retractable seating was installed, and the stage improved to allow concerts and theatrical events. Opened in June 1982, the Hall quickly proved very popular with an estimated usage of 250,000 people in 1985.

The Best Laid Plans ...   The 1970s witnessed preparation, submission and approval of the Hertfordshire County Structure Plan, and preparatory work on the North Hertfordshire District Plan.[16] Strategic planning at best involves aiming at a moving target: prediction of human activities remains notoriously inexact, however sophisticated the hardware and information technology applied. By the time of approval of the N.H.D.C. District Plan in March 1984,[17] certified, as required, as in accord with the Structure Plan, the County Planner, Geoffrey Steeley, freely admitted that few of the policies of the Structure Plan remained valid. The original planning context was the high growth rate enjoyed since 1945. The Plan aimed at securing a better balance between employment and housing, controlling the growth spiral through limiting job increases, and encouraging industrial relocation to development areas. Only Hertfordshire firms whose location met a national interest would be allowed to expand. Similar restrictions affected office development. Housing would be constructed only to match the projected natural population increase, with the hope of discouraging immigration. The Metropolitan Green Belt was extended along the A1(M) corridor northwards from Hatfield to envelop Welwyn Garden City, Stevenage, Hitchin, Letchworth and Baldock.

Preparation of the N.H.D.C. District Plan began against this background, using the 1981-91 period operable for the County Structure Plan. By the time the Draft District Plan was published for public comment in January 1981, it was evident that the Letchworth economy was undergoing a profound structural change, with widespread redundancies and closures. The detailed implications of this will be discussed in a later section, but the immediate effect on the plan preparation was a difference between the Council and Corporation as to whether the industrially zoned land north of Baldock Road should be re-allocated for housing, thus easing provision for the initial part of the plan period and meeting the obligation to identify a five-year land supply. This point was raised at the District Plan Inquiry during October-December 1982, but the point over the Baldock Road land was conceded. This increased the difficulty in meeting the requirement for housing land. Demographic analysis indicated an increasing demand for smaller dwellings in line with national trends. Letchworth was grouped in a plan policy area with Hitchin and Baldock, and although a substantial part of the requirement could be met on a large site east of Baldock, allocated in the County Development Plan, but not used, there was still a need for sites which added to the edge of Letchworth, where the District was also defining the extended Metropolitan Green Belt in detail. The additional allocations, particularly east of Green Lane, and near Letchworth Gate on proposed school playing fields, brought protests from the Letchworth Garden City Society.[18] The Council pointed out that Howard's original land allocation had been based on the large Victorian family, and that it had subsequently been necessary to increase the town area for the Grange, Standalone, Jackmans and Lordship estates to house the anticipated 32,000 population. The modest increase in housing land was necessary to enable fulfilment of obigations. Major pressure on the perimeter of Letchworth would probably arise in the 1990s, beyond the first period of the Plan. This point was taken and the allocations were confirmed.

Recession and Recovery   As already noted, Letchworth prospered through mixed manufacturing and engineering with a high value-added content. A few key firms became dominant — Spirella, Dent's, British Tab (I.C.L.), K. & L., Shelvoke and Drewry, and Borg-Warner. In the mid 1970s high inflation followed by economic recession, coinciding with declining demand for several Letchworth 'staples', brought widespread unemployment. Spirella production was confined shrinking enclaves in Castle Corset. I.C.L. went through painful reorganisations and shed a large number of employees, announcing its cessation of manufacture in Letchworth in Spring 1989. Borg-Warner, once a symbol of the vitality of the motor industry, suddenly closed, leaving an echoing mausoleum of 400,000 sq. ft. on a 14-acre (5.6 ha.) site. The 600 Group shut down the K. & L. Foundry, and Shelvoke and Drewry, hard hit by restrictions on local government expenditure, shed all but 10 per cent of their workforce, but later reorganised as Shelvoke Dempster, under the U.S.A. Krug International group. Unemployment had been virtually nil in the early 1970s but rose to an unprecedented 16 per cent in 1981-2.[19] Government-imposed regional controls were dismantled and local planning policies loosened. In the late 1970s a new industrial revolution, based on information technology and electronics, took place 25 miles away in the Cambridge science parks. The 'high-tech' industries blurred the distinction between office and manufacturing employment. A high quality, intensively serviced environment was required, and generated the opportunities for high skilled, high paid employment. Firms which survived the shakeout included Ogle Design who had become well known for innovative design work on cars and commercial vehicles, epitomising the importance of specialist skills, independent of the manufacturing process.

The Corporation perceived the outward ripples of the 'Cambridge effect', and sought to promote a Business Park on the 56 acres (22.6 ha.) of vacant industrial land north of

111. The Business Centre: Phase I (1985) from Phase II (1989). The 'high-tech' image and slick finishes contrast with the basic construction of the old K. and L. Foundry nearby.

Baldock Road. Andrew Egerton-Smith, appointed as Estates Manager during the 1970s, who became Chief Executive of the Corporation in 1986, led the initiative. Once the land allocation had been reaffirmed by the District Plan, the Corporation formed a development consortium with Bride Hall, and the Pos(t)-Tel(ecommunications) Pensions Fund, in 1984. A master plan prepared by D. Y. Davies Associates stressed the importance of a landscaped park to attract new industries without the financial incentives of enterprise zones such as Corby and Peterborough. Locationally Letchworth enjoyed excellent communications and

was situated midway between Milton Keynes and Cambridge. The objective was to provide
1½ million sq. ft. and create 2,000 new jobs — hence the original designation Enterprise
2000. Development began with the Business Centre, started earlier in a refurbished building
on Works Road.[20] The new headquarters was built by the Corporation, and included a
business consultancy service, central boardroom and conference facilities, computer and
word processing services, in a central block, with twin wings each housing 13 small
intensively serviced units, from 713 to 1,238 sq.ft., adaptable both as office or manufacturing
space. The centre was fully occupied by 1986. After a slow start, development of the
remainder of the park accelerated in 1987-8. A new 65,000 ft.headquarters for Sigma
Controls was opened in 1988, construction of new 18,000 sq. ft. headquarters for the Country
Gentlemen's Association, and for G.C.M. 600 (George Cohen Machinery Ltd.), and a back-
up national computer facility for Tesco began. A Phase 2 Business Centre with 40,000 sq.ft.
high tech space, with units between 2,300-5,000 sq.ft. was completed in June 1989, and an
'office village' on the edge of the park was proposed, whilst the possibility of an out-of-town
superstore was also mooted. A 7.5-acre development on 'Campus 5' of the Business Park
began in March 1989, to be completed in three phases and available from early 1990.
Nearby, off Dunhams Lane, Wheatley Developments began work on 'Letchworth Point',

112. The new industrial image: Letchworth Roofing Co. Ltd., Works Road (Architects: Pentangle
Design Group). High quality industrial buildings such as this brought a new image to the industrial
area.

with 17 varied units grouped around a courtyard with a central sculpture. The Business Park was also promoted through the County Council's 'A1 Corridor' programme as a counter magnet to the M4 corridor west of London.

Rebuilding of the older industrial area began in the 1970s, when the Letchworth power station was redeveloped with twin concrete chimney stacks which became a dominant landmark. Off Works Road, Such Close was the first small unit development promoted by the Corporation, followed by Saunders Close on the site of the old abattoir. Units became smaller — 5,000 sq.ft., to 2,500, and even 500 sq.ft. were viable. The Spirella factory was unofficially subdivided into over 100 separate occupancies. Efforts were made to refurbish existing factories. A good example of this was Ascot Close, south of Icknield Way, site of the old Camco factory. Its distinctively designed units in light grey brick, with bright red and blue metal cladding were popular, their marketing assisted by their rather gimmicky image. A major project involved the creation of the Jubilee Trading Estate from the 400,000 sq.ft. Borg-Warner complex. In contrast to the Business Centre, with its small but sophisticated and comparatively high rental units, the Jubilee Estate was adaptable for a range of unit sizes for sale — the slogan ran 'You don't rent your home — so why rent your factory?' One of the finest new industrial buildings was completed in 1986 on Works Road, the Letchworth Roofing Co. headquarters, designed by Pentangle Design, and which won a N.H.D.C. Civic Award in 1986. Its twin linked pitched roofed pavilions, with boldly overhanging roofs, gave ample scope for demonstration of craftsmanship by its owners, and its overall concept was less idiosyncratic than many of its contemporaries.

Employment training presented a challenge in the late 1970s. The Skills Training Centre was an important regional resource and the Skills Training Agency Group, of which it was a component, became the largest organisation of its type in Europe. In September 1988 the centre was expanded to include the Government's Employment Training initiative, successor to the Manpower Services Commission programmes. In the mid-1980s, the new business success rate in Letchworth was above 85 per cent, against a national average of 66 per cent. Between 1981-6, many firms had started, many had been rehoused, and the Business Park alone had brought more than 90 new units. The challenge of economic reconstruction appeared to have been met, but the sudden closure of I.C.L. in Spring 1989, with an anticipated loss of 660 jobs on two sites by September, brought a reminder of the difficulties earlier in the decade.

Home Base Housing passed through a volatile period in the 1980s. Already in the 1970s the first major price increase cycle had caused concern over availability of homes for first time buyers. The Council concentrated its efforts on sheltered accommodation for the elderly, but also built a few 'starter homes' for sale on the Jackmans Estate. The major private estates at Lordship Farm and Manor Park built by Wates Ltd.between 1973-9, to a layout by Shankland Cox, and developed by Wates Limited, concentrated on detached executive houses, but in 1974, 34 grouped houses priced at £10,750 were built, a minute proportion of the 700 total for the two estates. Availability of cheap housing was concentrated on run-down areas, notably the Pixmore Estate. No moves were made to use area improvement programmes and sporadic uptake of improvement grants exacerbated the overall appearance of the area.

The population of Letchworth grew more slowly than forecast -the 36,000 population projection for 1981 was matched by a census return of 31,848. Smaller households multiplied — single person households by 48 per cent, and two person households by 21 per cent.[21] There was a growing mismatch between the housing stock and demographic trends, but market response was not immediate. In the late 1970s the Fearnhill Park estate, on the

113a. & b. Housing refurbishment. *Above*, Norton Manor: barns reconstructed for sheltered housing, 1987-8. The grouping of the flats around a landscaped courtyard assists the development of a community feeling. *Below*, Birds Hill: 1905 housing refurbished in 1980. Sensitively landscaped, this housing remains in the rental section. Both projects were designed by Pentangle Design of Hitchin.

old school playing fields, north of Sollershott West, included luxury two-bedroom bungalows designed to attract the older residents, freeing larger houses for resale. The lack of large executive houses worried the Corporation for the perceived attractiveness of Letchworth housing was a vital element in their Business Park strategy. In partnership with the Nationwide Housing Trust, the Corporation developed Norton Hall Farm with 24 bungalows, 30 apartments and four houses, again designed to release larger homes for resale. The units were sold to the elderly, with a buy back provision of market value less 2 per cent. The bungalows were grouped in clusters of three units around entrance patios, whilst the apartments occupied the site of the farmyard and barns, regrettably destroyed by fire before the planned conversion could take place. The Corporation had also undertaken construction of conventional sheltered housing through its Letchworth Cottages and Buildings subsidiary, including 'MacFadyen-Webb House' on the fringes of Norton Common, and 'Robert Humbert House', named after the first Corporation Chairman. Other recent specialist housing schemes include a Methodist home for the elderly, and rental apartments for single people, under construction east of Green Lane in 1989.

The early 1980s saw several notable refurbishment projects. 'Silver Birch Cottages', Station Road had been considered a potential redevelopment site. The Corporation acquired them and promoted full restoration of these Parker and Unwin designed cottages. Roofs were stripped and retiled, chimneys rebuilt, and joinery replaced, revealing the visual delights of early Garden City housing. An attractive landscaped buffer area was planted along the street frontage. The refurbishment scheme, by Pentangle Design, received a N.H.D.C. Civic Commendation in 1981. The Corporation had acquired a substantial housing portfolio through Letchworth Cottages and Buildings Ltd. In 1981-2 they completely refurbished the Mansard roofed 'Noah's Ark' cottages on Birds Hill, built as 1905 Cheap Cottages exhibits. Unlike 'Silver Birch Cottages' they remained in the rental sector, and on completion in 1981 won a N.H.D.C. Civic Award. A notable feature was the landscaped parking area, provided in place of neglected allotments in front of the buildings. Comprehensive housing improvement was also undertaken in Common View.

The Council's dwelling stock was whittled down under the 'Right to Buy' of the 1980 Housing Act. The Letchworth local authority stock stood at 4,243 in March 1989, with 413 new Council dwellings built since 1974. Between 1974-89 they had sold 1,328 dwellings, 1,143 since 1980.[22] Massive increases in house prices occurred in the 1980s and by 1989 little was available under £80,000, £150-175,000 was common for semidetached properties, and £250,000 upwards for detached houses, depending on location. Broadway and Sollershott West with The Glade, and Pasture Road/Garth Road remained the most exclusive Letchworth addresses.

The Leasehold Reform Act of 1967 introduced the right of individuals to purchase the freehold of their properties. In the early years the leasing period was either 99 or 990 years. Modern estate leases as with 'Tabbs', Icknield Way are typically 125 years. With long leases, the purchase of the freehold represented a comparatively modest amount: however, enfranchisement becomes progressively more costly as the unexpired period shortens, and is related to the value of the land. Property values rose sharply after the mid-1970s and accelerated between 1985-8, but fell back with spiralling interest rates, and slackening demand, particularly for 'first time' properties. It was estimated that a house for sale at £28,000 in 1975 might cost £250,000 in 1988. However, there was evidence in Spring 1989 of reductions, sometimes of several thousand pounds in the advertised price of Letchworth houses, whilst building societies were becoming reluctant to advance loans on leasehold properties with less than 50 years to run.

It was against this volatile market that the Corporation introduced new schemes for deferred payment for freehold purchase. The first involved cases where the property owners were over 55, and had either lived in the house for 10 years, or in the town for ten. Payment for the freehold could be deferred until the property was sold, or the leaseholder or surviving spouse died. Annual interest would be levied at a ratio 4 per cent below the Midland Bank average base rate or a maximum of 8 per cent. A modified scheme for the under 55s required purchase by ten annual instalments. The schemes involved freehold purchases applied for between 1 December 1988 and 31 March 1989, subsequently extended through April. Valuations followed the procedure in the 1976 Act, based upon the land value at the date of claim, and the length of the unexpired lease, and using a 'residual standing house' approach, where the value of the bricks and mortar might represent 55 per cent of the total.

The levels of the valuations under the schemes provoked fierce controversy locally and were challenged by the Leaseholders and Freeholders Association, who held protest meetings and addressed the Corporation Board. Comparisons were instanced with Welwyn Garden City where freehold could be obtained for under £100. In those cases, however, 999-year leases were involved and no direct comparison was possible. With some properties having as little as 14 years left to run, the situation was seen as critical. It was claimed that valuations made in 1981 and 1985 of £3,160 and £3,613 had risen to £30,580 and £34,400 in 1989, and that the Corporation had changed its basis of valuation. This was refuted, but it was accepted that some high valuations had resulted from the correct application of the formulae — of 519 quotations made up to 2 March 1989, there were 51 between £10,000-£20,000, 12 between £20,000-£30,000 and one above £30,000, but the average figure of the batch was £4,193, with a considerable number below. By May 1989 a total of 2,860 properties were enfranchised. There were then 12,570 houses in Letchworth, of which 4,243 were Council-owned. Demands for freehold quotations remained brisk, notwithstanding the controversy.

Most post-war housing lacked Garden City architectural characteristics. In 1984 Barratt purchased the playing fields north of Letchworth Gate. The Corporation, N.H.D.C. and H.C.C. prepared a design brief which emphasised the importance of layout characteristics drawn from Rushby Mead and Unwin's *Town Planning in Practice*. The Letchworth Gate estate, developed by Barratt 1988-9, had a layout which produced well designed street pictures, whilst the houses used rendered walls, gables and dormers with accents of tile hanging and weatherboarding, representing a welcome revival of early Garden City designs. A comparable development by Wheatley Homes, Tabbs used the I.C.L. factory site on Icknield Way. Redevelopment of this and other surplus industrial sites represented a means of increasing the housing stock without infringing the Metropolitan Green Belt, but some infill proposals in established residential areas have provoked controversy.

The Green Setting   Farming has been radically reorganised over the past quarter century.[23] The Corporation inherited 2,200 acres (890 ha.) of farmland, with the 310-acre (125 ha.) Lordship farm with its dairy herd of 85 'in hand'. In September 1963 the Board decided to take on Manor Farm, Normans Farm and Letchworth Hall Farm as well, following notice of expiry, with the milking herd based on Lordship Farm, and cereal handling at Manor Farm. A farms manager, John Salwey, was appointed later to expand the farming enterprise, with the addition of Standalone Farm in 1973, Nortonbury and part of Paynes Farm in 1975. In 1976 purchase of the 230-acre (93 ha.) Grange Farm, north of the estate in Bedfordshire, was the first major increase in landholding since 1903. Additional agricultural land was later acquired at Wymondley, to the south of Letchworth. The Dairy used a 'cotel' cubicle milking parlour with 350 places, but its success was short-lived, closed down with an E.E.C. grant of £97,000, following the freezing of milk prices in 1979. Arable farming encountered similar problems of surpluses in the 1980s. Diversification, and the opening of a successful farm shop at Manor Farm, Willian, assisted a return to

114. Tree planting in the Business Park, March 1989: N.H.D.C. Chairman Alan Evens and Corporation Chairman Sidney Melman.

115. Standalone Farm Visitor Centre. David Marsh and his staff with new-born lambs and 'Warrant', the Shire horse, March 1987.

profitability. In 1987 a farming master plan designated Manor Farm, Willian, as the operations centre. Main crops included wheat, barley, oilseed rape, potatoes and soft fruit.

From 1979 the Corporation considered ways of enhancing the green setting and providing greater community access to the agricultural belt. A farm-landscape strategy aimed at softening the raw edge of the town, particularly northwards to the Bedfordshire plain. Wildlife conservation areas were identified, notably the meadows of the Ivel Valley, together with key views for enhancement and replanting after the Dutch Elm disease epidemic, which killed the majority of the 1,600 mature elms on the estate. Most of the Letchworth plantations were about 200 years old and followed the creation of fields under the Parliamentary Enclosures Act, and no new planting took place until the late 1970s. With the support of the Countryside Commission, 2,200 trees and 550 hedge plants were planted over three years, a prelude to a five-year programme using inaccessible field corners, filling gaps, and creating spinneys and windbreaks, involving 35,000 trees and seven miles of hedges. The Corporation and the Garden City Society collaborated on the identification of six countryside walks around the southern and eastern fringes of the estate, initiated on 3 June 1982. In the early 1970s Standalone Farm was reduced to 170 acres by the sale of land for housing development. In 1980 it was refurbished and opened as a Farm Visitor centre, intended both for school and family visits, with 2,000 visitors in its first six months, and 20,000 from April- November 1981. By 1987/8 this had risen to 80,500, including 13,500 school children. Facilities were originally centred on livestock, cows, sheep, pigs, poultry and working horses, but exhibitions of farm machinery were mounted in the farm buildings, a wildfowl area was added in 1982, followed by a forge, and other rural crafts. In terms of revenue Standalone approached a break-even point by 1988-9, with 5,000 visitors over the 1989 Easter weekend.

Education 2000   In the 1970s the County Council reorganised the ten junior and four secondary schools into a comprehensive system. The old Grammar School was closed and a large new comprehensive school, 'Fearnhill', was opened on the north-western fringes of the town. Two major private schools survived. The St Christopher School enlarged their campus south of Barrington Road to include a drama studio and its properties included 'Arunside' ('Laneside'/'Crabby Corner'), the 1904 Parker and Unwin houses, which were extended in 1985. In 1934, the St Francis School for Girls took over St Christopher's original premises and added a massive three-storey dormitory block facing Broadway. Originally

116. Education 2000 in action: the Japanese connection. This kind of computer link-up was the first of its kind.

run by an order of Nuns as a Roman Catholic Girls High School, its management was restructured as an Educational Trust in 1984. In that year there were 3,500 secondary pupils and 250 teachers in Letchworth.

Education 2000, a privately funded charitable trust, sought ways of promoting innovative education, and to provide school leavers with skills demanded by industry and commerce.[24] Developments in the U.S.A. had been studied, and the promotion of an experiment in Hertfordshire in 1987 stemmed from the innovative attitude of the education authority, with high achievement locally in both public and private schools, and the co-operation of the Corporation, who provided office accommodation for the Director of Education 2000, John Abbott, and his staff. The Corporation, through its education liaison consultant, Peter Macleod, had already assisted computer provision in junior schools and the development of a secondary school computer network. This linked with Education 2000's fourpoint objectives — community links; new technology; curriculum re-appraisal; and response to the needs of young people. Staff secondments to industry were assisted, computer provision increased to a ratio of one terminal to seven pupils, with word-processing encouraged. Curriculum development stressed interdependence in place of narrow subject barriers. Finally the decision-making and corporate ability of all pupils was to be fostered. £1.3m was raised from industry and commerce for teacher retraining and equipment. The Department of Education and Science observed the project, particularly its links with industry and its public/private sector co-operation, as they moved towards a national curriculum. In Spring 1989 one of the participants, The Highfield School, joined with the Shinmei School in Tokyo on a computer link-up, and live programme for Japanese television.

Letchworth Town Centre — The 1970s onwards   In the late 1960s, following many comparable towns, the U.D.C. and Corporation agreed on redevelopment of the area between Leys Avenue, Eastcheap and Gernon Road by the Laing Development Co. Ltd.[25] The existing jumble of shops and workshops was swept aside, but the line of Commerce Way was retained as the main north-south pedestrian route, with a connection to Eastcheap. The architecture, by Damond, Lock, Grabowski and Partners, reflected the current developer idioms in a mixture of low and medium rise blocks, and a six storey office block with red brick ends and dark bronze tinted glazing. In the centre was a utilitarian tiered 400-space multi-storey car park. In an attempt to relate the development to its context, tiled canopies and other cosmetic details, notably the 'lych gate' entrance from Leys Avenue were added. The scheme also included Letchworth's first purpose-built town centre public house, *The Black Squirrel*. It was possibly coincidental that this rodent had become as scarce as were licensed premises in the Garden City.

The precinct contained two major supermarkets, two further large units, a public hall used for little else but bingo, above a covered market, and 34 shops ranging from national multiples to the inevitable plethora of gift and card shops. The centre was opened by H.R.H. Duke of Gloucester, himself an architect, on 22 July 1975 in European Architectural Heritage Year. His Royal Highness made no design comments! Within 15 years the precinct suffered from over intense use. In 1987-8, the owners, Equitable Life Assurance, prepared a refurbishment scheme in conjunction with the Corporation and Council. The dull interlocking concrete block paving was replaced with more varied patterns. The tiled canopies were modified, and in the centre a tile-hung shelter was built, its form suggesting that the First Garden City was about to launch its first space probe. On the Eastcheap frontage, a glazed canopy was thrust outwards. To reduce vandalism the centre was closed at night, by ornamental gates, from Spring 1989, although not totally enclosed, and the multi-storey car was modified by large scale trelliswork to relieve its fortress-like appearance. No proposals were made to modify the office block occupied by the Council. Little

117. The Central Area Shopping Centre, Commerce Way Square, built 1973-5 and refurbished in 1989. The eye-catching folly appears to be an amalgam of traditional market cross and a space probe.

short of total redevelopment could mitigate its intrusion on nearby residential areas, perhaps second only to the I.C.L. building.

The Wynd was refurbished in the early 1980s. Traffic management produced one-way circulation along Openshaw Way, from Station Road to Norton Way South, with vehicle speed restricted by 'rumble strips', and The Wynd itself was pedestrianised, reinforcing its importance in linking Leys Avenue with Station Road. Surveys had indicated a preference for smaller shops and most of the existing buildings were retained, although several were updated in a jokey post-modern Garden City idiom. The *pièce de résistance* was undoubtedly the small 'high tech' arcade with its ingenious exposed tubular steel structure, and acid yellow and bottle green colour scheme, designed by Baldwin, Brattle and Conolly. Although it excited the wrath of the Victorian Society, its impact was muted. The forward thrusting canopy, breaking into the Station Road frontage, like the proboscis of a giant praying mantis introduced a foreign accent of limited extent, much less obtrusive than the large filling station canopy opposite. Howard would undoubtedly have been intrigued by the new arcade as a small-scale updating of his 'crystal palace'. During the refurbishment of the Arena Parade in the early 1980s, a red-painted projecting arcade was installed, running around from Broadway to Eastcheap, and linked to the Co-op with an arch motif and clock. Howard himself had envisaged glazed canopies like those at Victorian Southport or Harrogate.

The upgrading of individual shopfronts was a means of emphasising the quality of Letchworth shopping in the face of competition from nearby superstores. The Corporation's Information Centre in Leys Avenue, where a sensitively designed traditional shopfront replaced a poor 1950s example laid the foundations for a successful policy which sought to preserve the best examples from the past, and to introduce more sensitive new designs.[26] In 1988, a fine parade of shops in Leys Avenue, designed by Allen Foxley in 1909, was sensitively restored with a projecting canopy leading into a small internal precinct. In 1986 a large new retail unit in Eastcheap, on the site of the Palace Cinema, drew inspiration from the gables of pre-1914 shopping parades. On the approach to the town centre at Howard Park Corner a development of flats, and a complex of surgeries and flats on Norton Way North consolidated a late 1980s revival of a style of architecture related to the origins

118. Pedestrianisation proposals for Station Place, 1989. Over the years many proposals have been made to remove traffic from the main shopping streets. The development of rear servicing in the Letchworth centre, Arena Parade and The Wynd has now made the removal of traffic a more practical possibility. This 1988 proposal by the Pentangle Design Group of Hitchin seeks to reinforce the character of the town centre.

of the Garden City. In 1987 a report by Conran Roche discussed the future of the town centre. Action priorities included improved management through a town-centre association and traffic management for pedestrian priority, the latter an objective which had been on the agenda since the 1965 appraisal. In 1988 the Council commissioned indicative proposals for environmental upgrading. Trees and landscaping played a major role, with some radical suggestions including water gardens along Eastcheap. Some proposals lost the clarity of Unwin's townscapes, formed from articulated building lines, in a welter of reproduction Victoriana. One of the most successful concepts was a perspective, by Pentangle Design, a Hitchin architectural practice, showing a small tile-roofed 'market cross' near the site of the present Station Place roundabout, with comparatively simple paving along Eastcheap and Leys Avenue. It remains to be seen whether this concept, close to Unwin's own informal approach to town centre design, will be adopted as Letchworth moves into the 1990s.

Letchworth caught the national affliction of double yellow lines in September 1965: a cartoon from the front page of the 'Citizen'.

Chapter Fifteen

Back to the Future

Silver Jubilee In 1987 the Silver Jubilee of the promotion of the Letchworth Garden City Corporation Act was celebrated, with a programme of events in September, and a Jubilee Business Exhibition held at the North Herts Leisure Centre 8-10 October. A pioneer party for all those who had lived in the town between 1903-18 was organised, Standalone Farm held an Open Day and there were tours of the Garden City Corporation Enterprises. The Corporation Chairman, Sidney Melman, looked forward to 'the support of everyone who lives or works in the town making sure that Silver eventually turns to Gold'.[1] Already £7,000,000 had been paid to the town out of Section 32 surpluses, and the accounts revealed cumulative revenue surpluses of £2,540,000 for 1986/87 and £2,570,000 for 1987/88. As the spectacular Jubilee firework display was held on Norton Common on 11 September 1987, lighting up the sky for miles around, it seemed that Howard's dream had been realised. Commentators as diverse as Bernard Shaw, H.C.C. Treasurer John Alexander, and Oliver Smedley, one of the Directors of F.G.C. Ltd. who opposed the Bill in 1960-2, had referred to Letchworth as a potential goldmine in terms of its revenue-producing potential. The value of the estate was increasing by leaps and bounds. The estate agents, Bidwells, had produced valuations of £41,712,000 on 31 March 1987, and £52,055,000 a year later. By contrast, the Council had been through a period of governmental pressure on local government spending, which began in the early 1970s when the economic crisis provoked by oil price rises was acutely felt, and continued through a period of sharp inflation in mid-decade, to post-1979 when the newly elected Conservative Government under Margaret Thatcher announced its intention of curbing the role of local government, and progressively reduced the rate support grant.

The Corporation itself had been the creation of a Conservative Government, but the Conservative administration of the 1980s was very different from its predecessor of the early 1960s, under Harold Macmillan. The dismemberment of ' Q.U.A.N.G.O.S.' (Quasi Autonomous Non-Governmental Organisations) became the order of the day. The remaining development corporations which had provided the vehicle for the implementation of the post-war New Towns Programme, together with the Commission for the New Towns, in which the assets had been vested prior to their transfer to local control, were disbanded. The dispersal of assets to the highest bidder, in the manner of the rogue actions of First Garden City Limited, was actively encouraged, to provide revenue for the government. Less immediately profitable assets were transferred to local authorities — thus in April 1983 the Welwyn Hatfield District Council received assets which included town centre sites, the Development Corporation housing having been transferred seven years previously. But although the role of landlord and local authority were now merged, the estate was not the unified entity which had been preserved at Letchworth, whilst the local authority area included a second New Town at Hatfield and rural margins, as at North Herts. Ironically, the Letchworth Garden City Corporation was initially protected through its never having been absorbed into the New Towns legislative structure, but it potentially fell victim to the provisions of the Local Government Act 1972, which had created the expanded district councils including N.H.D.C. in 1974. Under S262 of the 1972 Act, local Acts applying to non-Metropolitan areas were to have been inoperative after 21 December 1986. The Jubilee might not have happened at all! However, in May 1986, the Department of the Environment confirmed that an order would be laid exempting the Corporation from the Provisions of S262. Once again the integrity of Letchworth had been preserved, by a Government whose politics were, on the face of it, antipathetic.

Town and Country Tomorrow   Almost since the inception of Letchworth itself there had been speculation as to where the Garden City movement would lead after the first 'object lesson' had been undertaken. Welwyn Garden City, the Greater London Regional Plan and the state-developed New Towns formed an impressive lineage, particularly as chronicled by Purdom, Osborn and Whittick. However, from the mid-1970s it was recognised that the New Towns Programme, in terms of massive injection of capital by Government for extensive developments on green field sites, was winding down. Milton Keynes, designated in mid-Buckinghamshire in 1967, with a multi-centred master plan by Llewellyn Davies and Walter Bor, covered an immense area with low density development and included a vast glazed shopping centre at its heart which bade fair to update Howard's Crystal Palace concept. Yet to some it appeared to be unduly consumerist in its heavy reliance upon motor access, despite original mini-bus and light transit proposals, whilst the decision to build the shopping centre as the first phase of the town centre evoked Bellamy's *Boston 2000 A.D.*, rather than the Co-operative harmony which underlay the earliest interpretation of Howard's vision in built form at Letchworth. Due to the energy crisis of the early 1970s, plus concern with the quality of life, conservation of natural resources and self-sufficiency began to assume primacy in discussions about the ideal form of new communities.

The Garden City Corporation had always maintained close links with the Town and Country Planning Association (T.C.P.A.). In September 1975, the Corporation, in conjunction with the T.C.P.A., R.I.B.A. and R.T.P.I. organised an open ideas competition, to present ideas for 'Town and Country Tomorrow' (T.A.C.T.).[3] The themes were 'places fit to live in and how to create them', the start of a search for a contemporary Peaceful Path to Real Reform, focussing upon improvement of quality of life, conservation of energy and resources, the relevance of planned dispersal, and the application of Howard's social city concept. The assessors' panel was chaired by Brian Redhead, the journalist and broadcaster. 180 entries were received, and exhibited not only in Letchworth, but also at T.C.P.A. in London and at the 'Habitat' Conference in Vancouver in June 1976. The professional prize winners were concerned with low energy self-sufficiency, whilst the schools entries also brought forward promising ideas, which encouraged the promotion of a Hertfordshire Schools Ideas Competition the following year. In order to develop the ideas, the T.C.P.A. convened a New Communities Committee, which examined the winners' proposals in the context of a possible development of two grid squares of Milton Keynes, but little resulted.

In the late 1970s the economic recession which affected the older inner city areas, and the engineering industries, in addition to the traditional heavy industries of the north, called into question the policies of decentralisation and dispersals. In addition, the first wave of inner city riots at Toxteth, Liverpool and Brixton, London in 1981, and the appointment of Michael Heseltine, Secretary of State for the Environment, as Minister with special responsibilities for master minding the regeneration of Merseyside, removed state funding of dispersed communities from any priority. The New Town concept was applied to the reconstruction of inner city areas, through Urban Development Corporations, in which Government funding was to be regarded as pump priming to attract private investment. The Merseyside initiative was backed through a spectacular Garden Festival in 1984, whilst the London Docklands Development Corporation, with its enterprise zone status, circumventing normal planning controls, controversially attracted massive Cityfinanced office developments such as Canary Wharf, and conversion of dock buildings to expensive housing. This digression, setting the development scene of the mid 1980s, is relevant for two main reasons. The first is that Howard himself was concerned with the reconstruction of London which was the subject of the final chapter of *Tomorrow*. His reactions to the form it took in the 1980s may well have been critical, although he would hardly have regarded the L.C.C. and Inner Borough policies of high density, high rise housing as an unmixed blessing, either.

> Elsewhere new cities are being built: London must then be transformed. Elsewhere the town is invading the country: here the country must invade the town. Elsewhere cities are being built on the terms of paying low prices for the land, and then vesting such land in the new municipalities: in London the corresponding arrangements must be made or no one will consent to build ... Easy comparatively it is to lay on virgin soil a plan of a magnificent city ... of far greater difficulty is the problem — even if all vested interests freely effaced themselves — of rebuilding a new city on an old site.[4]

Secondly, this digression is relevant due to the emphasis placed on private sector participation. Whilst Howard had envisaged that the L.C.C. would have assumed the leading role in the redevelopment of London, his own First Garden City Limited had been a private venture, circumscribed by its constitution to apply its surplus for the benefit of the community. Undoubtedly the Trust model which involved private investment would have continued to hold its attractions for him, given his pragmatic and undogmatic outlook, and his suspicion of government bodies.

The continued pressure for development in the South East has once again brought to the fore the possibility of the promotion of privately developed new country towns. The major strands of the discussion will be set out in a later section, but it is also necessary to consider the future of Letchworth itself.

The Future of Letchworth   On 7 February 1989, the Royal Town Planning Institute East of England Branch and the T.C.P.A. held a Conference at Plinston Hall, Letchworth on the theme of 'Garden Cities of Tomorrow?'. The day's business was divided into two parts. The author spoke about the early development, followed by Andrew Egerton-Smith, Chief Executive of L.G.C.C. reflecting upon the past 25 years of the Corporation with some comments about its future. The afternoon presentations by David Hall and David Lock dwelt upon more general matters about the continued relevance and application of the Garden City model to the increasing demand for housing in the South East. The tenor of Egerton-Smith's presentation followed the topics discussed in Chapter Fourteen. Letchworth was indeed a success story and vindicated Howard's concept and his faith in its viability. Yet it was essentially a finite settlement, permanently protected by its own agricultural area and the Metropolitan Green Belt. Demographically the population was ageing, which had brought about the growth of demand for smaller housing units. The amount of land remaining for housing development was small, with prices of £400,000 per acre or above. The redevelopment of housing within the town area had proved controversial. The town's recent success in restructuring its economic base had underscored the demand for housing. The Corporation's own rental scheme in Green Lane represented a modest contribution to a situation which was becoming more acute.

The balance between economic activity and housing had been a recurrent planning theme in post-war Hertfordshire. Looking to the future what evidence was there that the two might be brought back into equilibrium? The pace of economic revitalisation had essentially been Corporation led, using land which had been industrially allocated since the 1958 County Development Plan. The Council had, perhaps, become more dominant in the housing sector, following the completion of the large new public and private sector estates in the 1970s. The search for housing sites for allocation in the District Plan was difficult, and objections were raised to even the modest extensions of the town area in Green lane and the development of the surplus school playing fields land between Jackmans and Letchworth Gate. A possibility not catered for in the plan was the redevelopment of obsolete industrial land within the town area, represented by the 'Tabbs' site in Icknield Way, a smaller piece of the old Shelvoke and Drewry site nearby, and, in 1988, the residential redevelopment of the former Country Gentleman's Association seed testing grounds further west in Icknield Way, long since converted to a garden centre, and approved by the Council with the retention and conversion of the impressive Tudor-style office block.

As the 21st century approached, what scope was there for the expansion of Letchworth and its further adaptation to the changing economic and social trends, an adjustment which had had painful and not fully resolved consequences in the past decade? Howard's original view was that the assets of the completed town would be turned over fully to its residents. In one sense this has happened through the creation of the Corporation, yet it also had the danger, due to its constitution and membership, of remaining remote from the ideas and aspirations of many, a point brought out in research undertaken in 1981-3 by Dr. Gillian Stamp of Brunel University. Howard also envisaged that the completion of the First Garden City would result in a pioneer group banding together to acquire the land for another settlement, building up the social city. The intervening 90 years have brought about an armoury of controls, many based on the concepts which the planning and development of Letchworth itself pioneered.

Could development pressure possibly bring about peripheral expansion of Letchworth itself in the next decade? In the face of the Metropolitan Green Belt status of its setting this seems unlikely, and would fly in the face of Howard's concepts. However, a few miles away Stevenage has promoted expansion in the face of public and local authority opposition over the past 20 years. The latest modifications to the County Structure Plan announced in 1988 confirmed the removal from the Green Belt and the housing allocation of a large site around Botany Bay Farm on the north-west outskirts of the new town, and partly within North Hertfordshire District. Perhaps pressure for development could bring about comparable incursions around Letchworth when the District Plan for the 1990s is prepared. In addition, the announcement in the Government's 1989 White Paper *The Future of Development Plans* that the County Structure Plans were to be replaced by advisory statements for County Planning Policies, could make the District Plan Inquiry a forum for developer pressure to secure allocation of housing of marginal sites.

Historically, the expansion of Letchworth was examined as early as 1921 by Thomas Adams, who considered radial corridors of development fanning out from Letchworth, separated by thick agricultural wedges.[7] Possibly a rationalised form of ribbon development, the expansion of Letchworth would have joined to Baldock on the east, a virtual *fait accompli* today with only the A1(M) providing tenuous separation of the main industrial area from Baldock's western flank. The south-eastern sector within the A1(M) looks particularly vulnerable, given the possibility of revival of an improved access road running from Letchworth Gate to the A505 to lead into the industrial area and business park. Westward Adams saw Letchworth joined to Hitchin, which continued suburban development along the Cambridge Road brought to within the width of the Harkness Nursery on Rosehill, immediately outside the Garden City Estate. Adams' third corridor led northwest towards Arlesey upon open land between the Stotfold Road and Arlesey Road, projecting outwards the thrust of the Bedford Road which was developed in the 1930s. This land also lay beyond the Garden City Estate and across the County boundary in Bedfordshire. Coincidentally, it included the grounds of the Fairfield Hospital, an immense Victorian mental institution programmed for closure and possible redevelopment in the 1990s.

If Adams's model is rejected, the alternative proposition must be based upon Unwin's

The · Garden · City · Principle · applied · to · Suburbs.

119. The Garden City Principle applied to the Suburbs, 1912. Raymond Unwin, like Howard before him, saw the expansion of the central city by means of related satellite developments separated by green wedges.

'Garden City principle applied to suburbs',[6] itself a reworking of the diagram which Howard used showing the expansion of Adelaide, South Australia, across a park reservation to preserve the amenity of both the original settlement and its new satellite. Unwin first published his diagram in *Nothing Gained by Overcrowding* in 1912. This envisaged that planning would protect parkway belts and natural features, articulating developments outwards towards detached and relatively self-contained satellites, and this was elaborated by Unwin to form the basis of one of his major developments strategies in the 1929 *Greater London Regional Plan*. As the First Garden City moves towards its 10th decade, it is evident that the North Hertfordshire District Council policy makers and the Corporation will need to take fundamental and probably controversial decisions if Letchworth is to progress beyond being an affluent community, a landmark in the museum of planning, recycling its surpluses. Janus-like, all must look to the future by creative examination, discussion and reinterpretation of the principles upon which the First Garden City was conceived and built.

Back to the Future   The continued debate over community development in the South East has focussed attention on the Garden City. In 1985 the Housebuilders Consortium prepared a scheme for a 'new country town' at Tillingham Hall, Essex.[10] Although rejected by the Secretary of State, there have been other proposals, and organisations such as the Town and Country Planning Association are advocating a programme of planned self-contained communities. In 1988, the Secretary of State for the Environment, Nicholas Ridley, although re-affirming commitment to retention of the Metropolitan Green Belt, suggested that new villages should be built outside present green belt, especially where developers were willing to meet infrastructure costs.[11] In January 1988 Professor Peter Hall spoke of the necessity for a positive strategic planning authority for the South East, in place of the advisory, and ineffectual SERPLAN,[12] whilst in October 1988, Geoffrey Steeley, Hertfordshire County Planner, in the Tenth Ebenezer Howard Memorial Lecture, looked towards creating social city clusters.[13] That autumn H.R.H. Prince of Wales announced in his television programme 'Visions of Britain' that he proposed to build a major extension to Dorchester on Duchy of Cornwall land. Whilst attacking the harsh modernity of much 20th-century housing, he commended Letchworth for its humanely-designed residential areas. At the Plinston Hall meeting in February 1989, both David Hall and David Lock spoke of a Garden City revival, from the different viewpoints of public agency and private developer as enabler. There are growing numbers who wish to see such a revival.

What are the essential points to be drawn from Howard's work to assist the promotion of new Garden Cities?[14] Howard's original concept was based on privately sponsored development, relying on known methods of raising venture capital, using a conventional company model, with the important provision of clauses in the Articles of Association limiting dividend to 5 per cent. He admitted that none of the elements was original — it was their cumulative power which was significant.

1. **The idea** The simplest and oldest ideas are best and Howard based his unique combination of proposals upon the simple fact that development of land greatly enhances its value. He turned the speculators gain to community benefit through the original company constitution, sound at the time but, as already noted, subverted in the 1950s. However, the quasi-public body or trust still appears to be an appropriate vehicle to temper the natural inclinations of market forces to maximise their own returns.

2. **A broad appeal** Despite the sceptics Howard had something for everyone — co-operative and private housing, free enterprise and co-operative industry, which appealed both to Utopian idealists and practical men. Through the efforts of Adams and Neville at the Garden City Association, and subsequently industrialists and developers who were prepared to invest in the scheme, the dream was translated to reality.

3. **Words and action** Howard was determined to press for the development of a prototype and stated that it would be futile to await state action. Howard's direct action cannot be emulated today due to the complexity of regional guidance, structure and district local plans, and most of the sites considered by the Garden City Pioneer Company would now be classed as Green Belt or Rural Priority Areas. However, his determination that the book should not remain a theoretical utopia, and his predilection for entrepreneurial flair is being matched in the latter day determination of developers to succeed. What is required is a mechanism for harnessing developmental initiative to community benefit.

4. **Use of tried and tested methods** Although the concept of a new ideal community sounded revolutionary, it was to be brought into being by well known techniques — the limited liability company raising capital on the security of the land, and using landlord covenants over the lessees to secure high quality of development; it resembled 'town planning' in the respect of the basis of a master plan and development control, but it differed fundamentally in that it was exercised by the landowner, and not by a local

authority as a democratically elected body. Both Steeley and Hall have emphasised the existence of mechanisms which could bring about the social city. Whilst no new community, unless wholesale urban or rural enterprise zones were created, would have the ability to bypass development control exercised through district councils, the direct landlord role has the potential to underpin design standards in the context of changing planning legislation.

5. **A professional approach**   The process of evaluation of various sites for the First Garden City included assessments by Adams, Unwin and other professionals, canvassing of manufacturers to learn whether they were locationally mobile, and detailed surveys of the Letchworth site, with reports on its geology, water supply and suitability for industry, before the limited competition for the layout plan was organised. Together with the complex process of land assembly, undertaken with such success as to be the envy of modern developers, the quality of professional advice was elevated to a status in community design which it has retained ever since.

6. **Persistence and pragmatism**   Howard and subsequently Adams as estate manager were not afraid to bring in others. Adams persuaded the Company to host the 1905 Cheap Cottages Exhibition, a remarkable undertaking which attracted many visitors to see 'Garden City in the making'. Whilst some purists were offended, the publicity value was enormous at a time when the Company was overstretched through providing basic infra-structure. Likewise, Cottage Societies, the equivalent of today's Housing Societies, were encouraged to build in Letchworth at a time when the Company's finances did not permit its building. The attraction of industrialists to a fully serviced trading estate, although borrowed from Trafford Park in Manchester, promoted the concept of a ready serviced industrial area where firms could locate and develop working relationships with each other. This concept has remained unchanged in essence, though updated in the late 20th century as the modern business park. The pragmatic aspects of the implementation of the First Garden City perhaps stresses the necessity for an overall body with the ability to involve a wide range of developmental skills, rather than a house builder where the emphasis would, not unnaturally, be on building a large residential development, as exemplied in some of the new village proposals. Such a body would have a greater ability to take the long-term view of development which was so necessary at Letchworth and which still tempers the enthusiasm of modern developers.

7. **A model for emulation**   Imitation is the sincerest form of flattery — the lesson of Letchworth, and of Hampstead Garden Suburb and Welwyn subsequently, was felt in state response through legislation. It also created a model which was popular in the best sense as it appealed to a deep rooted desire for individual homes and gardens which the super rational high density high rise 'radiant cities' derived from Le Corbusier could never satisfy for the British. This deep seated atavistic appeal, as much a reflection of Unwin's reworking of Howard's vision as the original, helps to explain the success of the often derided suburban estates of the inter-war period which followed basic Garden City layouts and densities, but without their overall concern for community development. The basic principles are reflected equally in the imagery prepared for the abortive Tillingham Hall scheme, as in the continued visual appeal of Letchworth itself.

The lessons of Letchworth should be regarded as models for future community development. Physically, Letchworth represents a seductive model for town planning. In 1909 Frederic Law Olmsted Jnr., son of the doyen of American landscape architects, visited Letchworth. He made a far-sighted assessment of its strengths and weaknesses. He found the road network of Letchworth almost too closely reminiscent of the ubiquitous grid iron of the American city but 'the number of ill-considered designs seems to be no more than is reasonably to be expected as the price of a healthy state of active experimenting'. He concluded 'age is what Letchworth seems mainly to need; age, the growth of vegetation, and the quality which comes from a house or a garden or a town only as the result of long-continued painstaking care in the common place work of maintenance, repair, and adaption to use on the part of those who live in it'. In the intervening 80 years the Garden City has attained the mellowness of Arcadia, aided by Unwin's original respect for natural environment and subsequent high standards of planting and landscaping. From the air the sinews of the plan still stand out, revealing their strength, but clothed in a greenery which now conceals many of the errors of judgement which seemed so significant at the time of their commission. At ground level, if the overall impression now seems to be overwhelmingly suburban in character, this itself is a measure of the universal influence of Unwin's plan and policies and the lush greenery which vividly evokes Howard's original objectives of a synthesis of town and country, the greening of the Garden City.

Ebenezer's Magnetic Dream Town — Summer '89
Howard's earliest biographer, Dugald MacFadyen, included vignettes of Letchworth at ten-yearly intervals, describing the commonplace events which constituted everyday life, standing out in relief against the implementation of Howard's grand design. In the First Garden City, the long hot summer of 1989 emphasised the verdure and shade of the mature tree planting, though greenswards and lawns inevitably hardened into dusty yellow-brown patches, with the water shortage and hosepipe ban acutely felt by keen gardeners. Elderly residents began to find the generous plots too difficult to manage, and the North Herts Council for Voluntary Service appealed for helpers.

The leasehold reversion controversy continued to make headline news and was featured on Radio Four's *You and Yours* on 18 July, when residents spoke of financial difficulties over freehold purchases through second mortgages and had arranged for independent valuation of selected test cases, legal costs of which were funded by the Corporation. Property sales remained static. By contrast, Letchworth Garden City Corporation's residential development, east of Green Lane, of 59 units for rental attracted over 150 applicants. The first keys were ceremonially handed over by Sidney Melman, the Corporation Chairman. Meanwhile, North Herts Council announced their decision to proceed with environmental up-grading of the Westbury Estate, built in the 1920s.

Arguments over the success of the town centre continued. It was revealed that 70 per cent of local residents spent their money outside the town, bringing fresh concern over the quality of shopping facilities. The Corporation's business consultant, Sue Cheshire, sought to bring groups of retailers into discussions at the Business Centre. Traders in The Wynd complained of lack of promotion of their refurbished precinct, and the Corporation acknowledged problems with The Arcade. One of its most attractive features, the coffee shop, announced impending closure. On 17 July, five North Herts Councillors buried their political differences and sought to promote the town through the Council's Town Centre sub-committee. Yet the town centre was not without its attractive features, and the refurbishment of 50, Leys Avenue, a parade of shops, won a Civic Award commendation from the Council.

In the business sector, closure of I.C.L.'s Icknield Way and Blackhorse Road plant by the end of 1989 necessitated counselling on the formation of new businesses and self employment. In July, Spirella announced the final closure of its Letchworth operations by the end of October, with redundancy for the remaining 47 employees. New businesses were diverse, although not often labour intensive. Muskaan, in Flint Road, manufacturers of ethnic snacks which provided employment for 60, won the title of East Anglian Business

Woman of the Year for its proprietor, Meera Taneja. Letchworth had become a multi-cultural community, with Asian and Black councillors. Research conducted locally for the Department of Education revealed that some local schools had in excess of 20/30 per cent pupils of ethnic minorities. Language and curriculum support ensured common achievement by G.C.S.E. stage but there had been noticeable falling behind at ages 12 and 13. Education 2000, with its involvement with the six secondary schools, reported that the external funding of one and a half million pounds would be spent by September 1989 and appealed for local support. In July 1989, the St Christopher school honoured the memory of Laurence Olivier, who first acted at the school in 1924.

July 1989 marked the first national strike of local government officers, affecting the Orchard Hostel for the mentally handicapped, the Kennedy Gardens Day Centre for the elderly and Noel Family Centre. Libraries and museums were closed and 290 of the 506 council staff supported the first of their action on 4 July.

Nevertheless, the summer brought a carnival atmosphere to the streets. On 1 July, 40 floats paraded through Letchworth on the Hitchin and Letchworth Round Table's twelfth annual carnival to raise over £3,000 for local charities. The following week, the eleventh annual One Day Funday organised by the Letchworth Garden City Society filled the Kennedy Gardens with the colour and bustle of an outsize Edwardian garden party, with stalls, bands and choirs. Period costumes worn by many recalled the pioneer fêtes and pageants in which Howard had participated. Looking forward to the 1990s, it was announced that the Ideas Fair, first held in 1979, would feature an environmental theme, linked to growing national concern with 'green issues'. As the first industrial town where avoidance of pollution and conservation of natural features were prime objectives, 'Ebenezers's Magnetic Dream Town' seemed likely to remain a model settlement for the new decade, and indeed the century ahead.

Abbreviations used in Notes, References and Bibliography

A.R. :	*Architectural Review*, London
(B.A.L.) R.I.B.A. London:	British Architectural Library, Royal Institute of British Architects, London
F.G.C. Ltd. :	First Garden City Ltd., Letchworth. The original development company floated 1 September 1903
F.G.C. Mus. :	First Garden City Heritage Museum, Letchworth
G.C. :	*The Garden City*, London, journal of the Garden City Association
G.C.A. :	Garden City Association, London. Founded 1899 by Ebenezer Howard
G.C. &. T.P. :	*Garden Cities and Town Planning*, London, journal of the Garden Cities and Town Planning Association
G.C.T.P.A. :	Garden Cities and Town Planning Association; renamed from Garden City Association
H.C.C. :	Hertfordshire County Council
H.C.C. D/EHo :	Hertfordshire County Record Office, Ebenezer Howard Papers
J.R.I.B.A. :	*Journal of the Royal Institute of British Architects*, London
J.(R.)T.P.I. :	*Journal of the (Royal) Town Planning Institute*, London
L.G.C. Corp. :	Letchworth Garden City Corporation, created by Act of Parliament in 1963
L.U.D.C. :	Letchworth Urban District Council, created 1919, dissolved 31 March 1974
N.H.D.C. :	North Hertfordshire District Council, the extended local authority, based on Letchworth, created 1 April 1974
Parker Coll. :	Collection of papers and drawings of Barry Parker in the First Garden City Heritage Museum, Letchworth
R.U. :	Raymond Unwin
T. & C.P. :	*Town and Country Planning*, journal of the Town and Country Planning Association, London
T.C.P.A. :	Town and Country Planning Association, successor in name to G.C.A. and G.C.T.P.A.
Unwin Coll. :	Unwin material deposited at the Library of the Royal Institute of British Architects, London (British Architectural Library)

Notes

Chapter One: Coketown Rebuked

1. The quotation opens Chapter Five of Dickens's novel. The style reflects the author's concern at the harsh triumph of material values over the more humane society, reflected in the book by the circus people. Coketown was regarded as the paradigm of the Victorian industrial city; for example Mumford (1961) concludes that 'in a greater or lesser degree every city in the urban world was shaped with the characteristics of Coketown'. Ashworth (1954), Bell (1961), and Cherry (1988) all contain detailed accounts of the rise of the industrial city, and palliative measures taken to control its environmental consequences.

2. Ashworth (1954) Ch. II and III and Cherry (1988) contain useful summaries of Chadwick's pioneering work. An early and comprehensive appraisal was contained in B. W. Richardson, *The Health of the Nations: A Review of the works of Edwin Chadwick* (2 Vols.), London, 1887.

3. Tarn (1973) provided a detailed history of the Trust movement, and charted its fusion with the Garden City movement. For a comprehensive account of the pioneering role of Henry Roberts (1803-76) in the design of working-class housing see Curl, J. S., *The Life and Work of Henry Roberts*, Phillimore, 1983.

4. Armytage (1961) taps the rich stream of Utopianism setting the idealistic context for Owen's experimental communities. Owen's two major reports were reprinted in 1970. Owen, R., *A new view of Society*, 1813-14, 1970 Edn. Harmondsworth, Penguin Books, and *Report to the County of Lanark*, 1821, 1970 Edn. Harmondsworth, Penguin Books. Creese (1966) and Bell (1972) contain useful accounts of New Lanark.

5. Creese (1966), Bell (1972) and Tarn (1973) all include good accounts of the West Yorkshire industrial settlements.

6. Ruskin's lectures on political economy grew out of his work on architecture and art history. *Unto this last* (1862), *Sesame and the Lilies* (1865) and *The crown of wild olive* (1866) developed his views that social questions were inextricably linked with art. Morris developed overtly into a committed socialist; see Thompson, E. P., *William Morris: Romantic to Revolutionary*, London, Merlin (1977).

7. Howard (1898) and Howard (1902) heading Chapter One. Mumford (1961) also used the same quotation, which vividly prophesies Garden City housing. It is not, despite Howard's attribution, to be found in *Sesame and the Lilies*.

8. William Morris, 'Art and Socialism: The aims and ideals of the English Socialist of Today', a lecture delivered before the Secular Society of Leicester, 23 January 1884, *Collected Works* 23, p.127.

9. Creese (1966), Darley (1975) and Tarn (1973) all include Bedford Park. For a discussion in the context Shaw's work, see Saint, A., *Richard Norman Shaw*, New Haven and London, Yale (1976). Life in the pioneer garden suburb is discussed in Bolsterli, M. J., *The Early Community at Bedford Park*, London, Routledge and Kegan Paul (1977).

10. General accounts of Port Sunlight are included in Creese (1966), Darley (1975) and Tarn (1973). An excellent detailed account of the architecture and design by Hubbard, E., and Shippobottom, M., is included in *Lord Leverhulme. Catalogue of an Exhibition presented by Unilever to mark their Golden Jubilee*, London (1980), pp.149-99.

11. General accounts of Bournville are included in Creese (1966), Darley (1975) and Tarn (1973). Harvey, W. A., *The Model Village and its cottages*, London (1906), contains a good account of the early housing by the consultant architect.

12. Beevers (1988), p.17.

13. The pioneering work of the L.C.C. Architects Department in the design and construction of Council housing was described in Beattie (1980). The influence of Raymond Unwin on the design of the pioneering cottage estates was brought out, see also Unwin (1902).

Chapter Two: An Ideal City Made Practicable

1. Quoted in MacFadyen (1933), p.1. The origin of this material lies in typescript notes in Hertfordshire County Council Record Office, Howard Papers (H.C.C. D/EHo/F17). Apart from MacFadyen, the

published biographical references include Moss Eccardt (1973), Fishman (1977) and Beevers (1988). The latter is by far the most comprehensive account — 'a critical biography' in the best sense.
2. H.C.C. D/EHo/F17.
3. Beevers (1988), pp.17-18, 24. Howard cited Kropotkin's *Factories, Fields and Workshops* (1899) in *Garden Cities of Tomorrow* (1902), p.31. This work also appeared under Swan Sonnenschein's imprint.
4. Howard (1898), p.103. Chapter Ten of *Tomorrow* was titled 'A Unique Combination of Proposals'. For discussion of the major editions of *Tomorrow* see Note 13 below.
5. Purdom (1913), pp.9-14 discussed the relationship between Victoria and Hygeia, and Howard's intial concept.
6. Chadwick (1966). This account also records the exchange of ideas on urban parks between Paxton and Olmsted. See also Chadwick, G. F., *The Works of Sir Joseph Paxton*, London, Architectural Press, 1966.
7. Armytage (1961) and Darley (1975) contain accounts of the chartist communities, the latter includes their surviving buildings.
8. MacFadyen (1933), p.20.
9. 'News from Nowhere' was originally published in serial form in *Commonweal*, Morris's Socialist League newspaper, 11 January-4 October 1890. First authorised edition London, 1891. See Morris, William, *News from Nowhere*, ed. Redmond, J., London, Routledge, 1970. The publisher, Reeves and Turner, had also published, with Howard's assistance, *Looking Backward* in an English edition.
10. H.C.C. D/EHo/F3. Early drafts of the material are dated 1892. The 'Master Key' diagram is in D/EHo/F1; the draft chapter in D/EHo/F3. Beevers (1988) believes that 'The Master Key' was originally intended as Howard's overall title.
11. The surviving original diagrams in Howard's hand are in H.C.C. D/EHo/F1.
12. *Tomorrow: A Peaceful Path to Real Reform* was republished by Swan Sonnenschein in 1902 in revised form as *Garden Cities of Tomorrow*, a title that has become part of the lore of community design in the 20th century. In 1946 the book was republished, edited by F. J. Osborn, with an Introductory Essay by Lewis Mumford (London, Faber and Faber). The first edition will be cited below as Howard (1898).
13. Howard (1898), p.10.
14. Ibid. Chapter One, 'The Town Country Magnet'. The chapter was appropriately headed with the final quatrain of Blake's 'Jerusalem', and a quotation from Ruskin's *Unto this Last* on 'the necessity of beauty'.
15. H.C.C. D/EHo/F4. The 'Crystal Way' or 'Great Victorian Way' was included in a survey of glazed arcades by Nikolaus Pevsner in *A History of Building Types*, Washington and London, 1976, pp.262-4.
16. Howard (1898), Chapter 13, 'Social Cities', pp.128-141. The cluster diagram of 'Slumless, Smokeless Cities' appeared on p.130. Its reduction to a fragment for the 1902 revised edition of Howard's book weakened the concept of the overall system and tended to place emphasis on *isolated* Garden Cities, without the mutual symbiosis envisioned originally.
17. Howard (1898). Chapters Two and Three dealt with Revenue from the agricultural and town land, Chapters Four and Five with Expenditure, and Chapters Six, Seven, Eight with Administration, 'Semi-Municipal Enterprise' and 'Pro-Municipal Work'.
18. Ibid., pp.84-5.
19. Ibid., pp.96-7.
20. Howard's intent is clear from a draft, 'Rurisville', H.C.C. D/EHo/F1, which states 'It is usual in announcing an invention to give a clear description of its essential features (accompanied by drawings if necessary); and thirdly, if such an invention requires special instruments or appliances for its construction or working, to give a full and lucid description of such . . . The invention which is the subject of this book is, very fortunately, not of a value which can be protected by letters patent . . . Besides, the specification I am filing is a Provisional Specification, and the claims of the inventor are not set forth till the complete specification is put forward.'

Chapter Three: Utopia Limited
1. Howard collected the reviews in a scrapbook of press cuttings, now in Welwyn Garden City Central Library. The *Fabian News* verdict is quoted by Osborn in his preface to Howard (1946). Howard himself discussed the reviews in his 'Postscript' to Howard (1902), pp.161-71.
2. From the selection of 'Press Opinions' appended to Howard (1902), pp.188-91.
3. Ibid., p.163.
4. Ibid., p.170.

5. Lawrence, Dan H., *Bernard Shaw, Collected letters 1898-1910*, London, 1965, pp.188, 199.

6. MacFadyen (1933), p.38.

7. Ibid., pp.40-3; Howard (1902), p.166.

8. Simpson (1985); Chapter Two 'Launching the First Garden City, 1901-6' contains a full account of Adams's key role.

9. Garden City Association (1901) contained a full transcript of the proceedings.

10. Ibid., p.1 (title page).

11. Ibid., pp.13-14.

12. Ibid., pp.23-9, Neville spoke to his paper, reproduced pp.46-9, which contained the pre-requisites.

13. Ibid., pp.34-5.

14. Reproduced in full, ibid., pp.47-74.

15. The Pressbooks are now in First Garden City Heritage Museum, Letchworth. Burns's speech was reported in the *Morning Leader*, 6 January 1902; Adams's rejoinder appeared on 23 January.

16. Howard (1902), p.171.

17. The Company's Prospectus and a Share Application were bound into Howard (1902), pp.173-83.

18. Purdom (1913), p.29.

19. Whilst Purdom (1913) and others published partial accounts of the selection process, it can best be pieced together from the Minute Books and Correspondence of the Garden City Pioneer Company, and subsequently First Garden City Ltd. These are now in the possession of the Letchworth Garden City Corporation. The author is indebted to the late Horace Plinston, former L.G.C. Corporation Chief Executive for access to the correspondence for extensive study. Plinston (*c*.1980) also contains reference to the material. The sections dealing with the selection of the site and commissioning of the layout plan in the present work are based upon this material.

20. Hine, R. L., *Confessions of an Uncommon Attorney*, (London 1951), p.45.

21. Purdom (1913), pp.29-31, Purdom (1951), p.39, and Hare, W. L., 'A Part of Rural England', *G.C. & T.P.*, 20(6), June/July 1930, pp.147-50.

22. Adams to Parker 17 July 1903, L.G.C. Corp.

23. Purdom (1913), pp.31-35.

24. F.G.C. Ltd., Directors' Minutes, Resolution 14, 12 November 1903, L.G.C. Corp.

25. H.C.C. D/EHo/F3.

26. Purdom, C. B., 'At the inception of Letchworth', *T. & C.P.* 21(113), September 1953, p.427; see also Purdom (1951), pp.40-42.

27. Composed on 18 March 1905, and cited in Johnson (1976), p.50.

Chapter Four: Letchford Manor

1. MacFadyen (1933), p.49.

2. Ibid., p.51.

3. The topography, flora and fauna of the Garden City are described in The Letchworth Naturalists' Society, *In and Around Letchworth*, Letchworth, The Museum, 1963.

4. Johnson (1976) summarises pre-historic and pre-conquest settlement, see also Lane, W. H., 'Prehistoric and primitive man', *Coronation Booklet*, Letchworth U.D.C., 1937, pp.10-16.

5. Moss-Eccardt, J., 'An Anglo-Saxon Cemetery at Blackhorse Road, Letchworth, Hertfordshire', *Bedfordshire Archaeology Journal*, 6 (1971), pp.27-32.

6. Histories of the three parishes are summarised in Purdom (1913), Hine, 'The Village history of Letchworth, Willian and Norton', pp.17-34 in *Coronation Booklet*, and Johnson (1976), pp.16-41.

7. The excavations and preliminary findings were described in Matthews, K. and Burleigh, G., 'A Saxon and Early Medieval Settlement at Green Lane, Letchworth', *Hertfordshire's Past*, 26, (Spring 1989), Letchworth, pp.27-31, and North Herts. Museums, *A Saxon Site in Letchworth*, N.H.D.C., 1989.

8. The plebiscite for the name was described in Purdom (1913), p.45.

9. The most exhaustive study of Letchworth street names was compiled by Kenneth Johnson for the loose-leaf Local History Index in Letchworth Library.

Chapter Five: The Layout Plan

1. The detailed material which records the commissioning of the plan is contained in the Garden City

Pioneer Co. and First Garden City records and correspondence, L.G.C. Reference was made to these sources in compiling the present account.

2. A copy of Humphreys' Report is in the First Garden City Heritage Museum.

3. G. C. Pioneer Co. Engineering Committee Minutes, 12 October 1903.

4. F.G.C. Ltd., Directors' Minutes, Resolution 32, 12 October 1903. Warren wrote enthusiastically to Adams that Webb was 'absolutely the best man for preparing the scheme', 6 November 1903, F.G.C. correspondence, L.G.C. Corp.

5. Sennett, A. R., *Garden Cities*, (2 Vols.), London, Bemrose, 1905.

6. For biographical material on Parker and Unwin see Creese (1966), Miller (1981a), (1981b), Day (1981).

7. Recorded by Unwin in 'The Royal Gold Medal — Presentation to Sir Raymond Unwin', *J.R.I.B.A.* 3ss. 144(12), 24 April 1937, p.582.

8. Carpenter's description of Unwin in *My Days and Dreams* (London, George Allen and Unwin, 1916), pp.131-2.

9. R.U. to Ethel Parker, 9 August 1981, Hitchcock Collection.

10. Barry Parker and Raymond Unwin (1901) contained a paper by Unwin, 'Co-operation in Building', pp.91-108, which contained the seeds for his planning work to 1914.

11. Ibid., pp.82-5.

12. 'On the Building of Houses in the Garden City', in Garden City Association (1901), pp.69, 72.

13. Unwin (1902), p.3.

14. Plans of Starbeck are in Parker Coll. F.G.C. Mus. Letchworth. Parker and Unwin published a booklet *Cottages Near a Town*, Manchester, 1903, based on their Northern Artworkers Guild exhibit. A copy is in F.G.C. Mus.

15. The foundation of New Earswick is described in Waddilove (1954). Accounts of the design of the early phases of cottage development are in Creese (1966), Miller (1980), (1981), Day (1982), Jackson (1985).

16. B. B. Moffat, R.I.B.A. Membership File, No.1464 (L), (B.A.L.), R.I.B.A., London.

17. Raymond Unwin, 'The Planning of Garden City', Appendix B in Purdom (1913), p.228.

18. F.G.C. Ltd. Directors' Minutes, 28 January 1904.

19. Ibid., 11 February 1904. The 'original' plan presented to the Board by Unwin is not readily identifiable. A fragmentary photoprint crudely labelled 'Mr. Unwin's Plan' (*sic*) survives in F.G.C. Mus. Letchworth, together with a modified version, drawn on linen which was also used as the basis for the first published version.

20. The Lucas/Cranfield plan is represented by a photoprint in F.G.C. Mus. Letchworth. The Lethaby/Ricardo plan was illustrated in Adams (1934) and Purdom (1963), but is not in F.G.C. Mus. Its present whereabouts is unknown. Adams's letter to Ricardo dated 29 November 1910 praising the plan is in F.G.C. Mus.

21. Unwin described his plan in Appendix B, Purdom (1913), pp.222-9, and in 'Making the Plan of Letchworth', *G.C. & T.P.* 20(6), June/July 1930, pp.156-9. Whilst Mabel Barry Parker credited her late husband with a leading role in preparation of the layout plan, available contemporary evidence does not appear to corroborate this.

22. R.U. to Adams, 22 February 1904, L.G.C. Corp.

23. R.U. to Adams, 11 July 1904, L.G.C. Corp.

24. Purdom (1913), p.69 and Purdom (1951), pp.52-3.

25. Unwin Papers, UN 12, (B.A.L.) R.I.B.A. London. The published Building Regulations were included as Appendix K in Purdom (1913), pp.302-15.

26. Purdom (1913), p.69.

27. The infrastructure was described by A. W. E. Bullmore, F.G.C. Ltd. Engineer in 'The Public Services of Garden City', Appendix D to Purdom (1913), pp.242-60. The account was updated in Chapter Five, 'The Public Services' in Purdom (1925), pp.11828.

28. In 1905 Parker and Unwin prepared a 'Plan of Present Development' for F.G.C. Ltd. This was periodically updated and reprinted. The formal centre of the town was destined to remain a paper concept until after the First World War, as will be discussed below.

29. Unwin (1909) and Purdom (1925) illustrated representative road sections showing the variety of treatment and planting.

30. The earliest Parker and Unwin drawing showing the central roundabout is dated July 1908, F.G.C. Mus. Unwin described the *'carrefour à giration'* in *Town Planning in Practice* (London, 1909).

31. Timetables were included in all the early Garden City guides and commuting was encouraged. The railway was to play an important role in bringing visitors to Letchworth, particularly for the 1905 Cheap Cottage Exhibition (see below).

32. Bullmore, 'The Public Services of Garden City', pp.249-53.

33. Ibid., pp.253-5.

34. H.C.C. D/EHo/F3. Extract from a paper given at The Mansion House, London, 11 July 1905, in which Howard described progress to date on building Letchworth.

Chapter Six: Garden City Homes

1. F.G.C. Ltd. Minute Books, L.G.C. Corp.

2. Johnson (1976), p.50.

3. Accounts in Miller (1978), Miller (1979a) and Miller (1980) describe the organisation, entries and impact of the Exhibition. *The Book of the Cheap Cottage Exhibition*, County Gentleman and Land and Water Ltd., London, 1905, contained a comprehensive description of the entries (copies in F.G.C. Mus., Letchworth). The Technical Press carried copious articles — for example see *Architectural Review*, *The Builder*, *Builder's Journal*, *Building News* issues over Summer 1905.

4. Purdom (1913), pp.50-1.

5. UN 9/3, Unwin Papers, (B.A.L.) R.I.B.A. London.

6. Brodies system was described in detail in Moore, R., 'An early system of larger panel building', *J.R.I.B.A.*, September 1969, pp.383-6.

7. F.G.C. Ltd. published an attractive illustrated Guide, *Where Shall I Live?* which contained full details of the exhibits, an up-to-date progress report on the development of Letchworth, and essays by Howard, Gaunt, Unwin and others.

8. Vivian wrote about the Garden City Tenants' schemes in *Where Shall I Live?*, pp.55-7. For modern accounts see Miller (1979a), (1979b).

9. Barry Parker and Raymond Unwin (1901), Plate 11. The scheme was illustrated in Plate 38, with a wider range of housing than was subsequently included in the Co-partners' developments. The above publication included Unwin's description of the proposals in his paper 'Co-operation in Building', pp.96-102.

10. Unwin (1906b). The event marked his emergence as a national spokesman for housing and town planning.

11. Unwin (1906b), p.111.

12. Ibid., p.109.

13. Published by Garden Cities and Town Planning Association (London, 1912). See also Note 24 below.

14. Letchworth Cottages and Buildings Ltd. and Howard Cottage Society Ltd. are discussed in Miller (1979a), (1979b). The author had access to their archives, from which the letters from Howard to Osborn are taken.

15. A wide ranging study of co-operative housing was undertaken in Pearson (1987). Beevers (1988), Chapter Nine deals with Howard's interest in the subject. Howard himself wrote about the concept in 'Co-operative Housekeeping, A Suggestion by Ebenezer Howard', *The Garden City* 1, ns (8) September 1906, and 'A New Outlet for Woman's Energy', *G.C. & T.P.* ns 3 (6), June 1913, pp.152-9. Purdom (1913) discussed the scheme and illustrated the plans, pp.98-103.

16. Benoit-Levy (1911) and Purdom (1913) both contained a selection of the most progressive architect-designed houses in Letchworth. From 1974 onwards the author undertook detailed research into the buildings of Letchworth using N.H.D.C., L.G.C. Corp. and F.G.C. Mus. Archives. A working paper, N.H.D.C. (1976), was compiled. Biographical details of the Letchworth architects, many of them one-time Parker and Unwin assistants, were compiled using R.I.B.A. Membership Records, (B.A.L.) R.I.B.A., London. Creese (1966) included a chapter on the architecture of Parker and Unwin, whilst Hawkes (1986) is based on an edited version of Parker's own essays on his architecture, originally published 1910-12 in the U.S. Arts and Crafts periodical, *The Craftsman*.

17. Moffat, B. B., R.I.B.A. Membership File No. 1464 (L), (B.A.L.) R.I.B.A., London.

18. For an exhaustive discussion of Baillie Scott's architecture (which however omits 29 Norton Way

North) see Kornwolf, J. D., *M. H. Baillie Scott and the Arts and Crafts Movement* (Baltimore, John Hopkins Press, 1972).

19. Parker spoke about his methods at a discussion on 'Control of Elevations in Practice', *J.T.P.I.* 18(7) May 1932, p.164. 'What he [Parker] got officially at Letchworth was not a hundredth part of what he got unofficially. Builders and architects came to him . . . and frequently he was able to make suggestions [for design improvements] . . . which was the most valuable part of the whole thing'. Sketches in Parker Coll. F.G.C. Mus. Letchworth confirm this practice.

20. Notes on the local contractors have been compiled with the assistance of Kenneth Johnson's Local History Index, Letchworth Library.

21. Berlepsch Valendas (1912) and Benoit-Lévy (1911, First edition 1908) were perhaps the most comprehensive of the early accounts. F. L. Ackerman and Thomas Adams were responsible for the spread of the Garden City movement to U.S.A. and Canada, whilst Pavel Mizhuev and Aleksandr Block transferred the concept to Russia. International planning conferences, such as that held at the R.I.B.A. in 1910 invariably included a visit to Letchworth, preparing the ground for the foundation of the International Garden Cities and Town Planning Federation in 1913.

22. Cherry (1974), Sutcliffe (1981), and Miller (1984) deal with the emergence of planning from 19th-century bye-law and public health practice, assisted by the Garden City movement. Miller (1981a, 1981b) details Unwin's key role in the promotion of planning, whilst Swenarton (1981) concentrates on the housing-domination of planning from 1915 onwards.

23. Unwin (1909), p.320.

24. The idealised layout, based on housing blocks with communal backland, stemmed from Unwin's early housing quadrangles in *The Art of Building a Home* and *Cottage Plans and Common Sense*, developed through such practical examples as his layouts at Pixmore, Letchworth, Brentham and Hampstead Garden Suburb. A discussion of its evolution is contained in Miller (1981).

Chapter Seven: The Spirit of the Place

1. Brunt (1942), originally published as separate articles in *The Citizen*, is probably the most comprehensive guide to the early social history of Letchworth. Purdom (1951), Chapter Two 'Garden Cities' is a personal account which catches the mood of the community. Charles Lee, 'From a Letchworth Diary', pp.434-442 in *T. & C.P.* 21(113), September 1953 (The Letchworth Jubilee), embellishes the past, whilst Ethel Henderson, 'Letchworth then and now', pp.457-61 in *Ibid.* is naively gushing in style, evoking the essential innocence of the pioneer years. Miss Henderson later privately published an extended account as *The Ideals of Letchworth, the First Garden City*, Letchworth,(*c*.1975).

2. Foreword to Brunt (1942), p.viii.

3. M. J. Pritchard, 'The First Garden City', unpub. M.A. Thesis (University of London Courtauld Institute, 1970), p.64.

4. Peggy Curtice Hitchcock (née Unwin), letter to the author.

5. Carpenter described Millthorpe in *My Days and Dreams*, London, George Allen and Unwin, 1916. A more recent appraisal of Carpenter and his influence is Tsuzuki, Chuschinchi, *Edward Carpenter Prophet of human fellowship* (Cambridge, Cambridge University Press, 1980).

6. 'From a Letchworth Diary', pp.435-6.

7. Orwell, George, *The Road to Wigan Pier* (London, Gollancz, 1937). The reference to Letchworth occurs on pp.152-3 of the Penguin reprint, Harmondsworth, 1962.

8. Howard (1898), Chapter Seven, 'Semi-Municipal Enterprise — Local Option — Temperance Reform', pp.72-81.

9. Brunt (1942) and Purdom (1913), (1925), deal with the polls in detail.

10. Furmston (*c*.1940), Chapter Six, 'Landlord of The Skittles'.

11. Brunt (1942) contains the most comprehensive account of early religious life.

12. Armytage (1961) sets the Alpha Union in context with the mainstream of Utopian-religious thought.

13. Purdom describes his conversion and marriage in Purdom (1951), Chapter One. He described the interior of St Hugh with evident affection in Purdom (1913), pp.121-4.

14. Buchan, John, *Mr. Standfast* (Edinburgh, 1919). The reference occurs on p.51 of the Nelson reprint (Edinburgh, 1923).

15. Brunt (1942) and *The Citizen* (Letchworth), 'Jubilee Supplement', 25 January 1963, pp.xvi-xvii, give good accounts of early education in Letchworth.

16. Brunt (1942) and 'Jubilee Supplement', pp.xiv-xv.

17. Recalled by a female pioneer at one of the author's lectures in 1978.

18. *The 'Borough' Pocket Guide to Letchworth* (Cheltenham, 1908), pp.20-2.

19. Brunt (1942) and Letchworth National Library Week Committee, *Letchworth: a town built on a book* (Letchworth, 1966).

20. Miles (1967) and Cowlishaw (1908) give detailed accounts of Miss Lawrence and the building, and subsequent history of 'The Cloisters'.

21. Miles (1967), pp.21-3.

22. F.G.C. Mus. Letchworth contains copies of both *Letchworth Magazine* and *The City*.

23. The poems appear on pp.69-70 and 199-200 of Betjeman, John, *Collected Poems*.

24. Connett, Maureen, 'Harold Gilman and Letchworth', *Hertfordshire Countryside*, 39(299), March 1984, pp.21-3.

25. Strone, D., 'Two Paintings by Spencer Gore', *National Art Collection Fund News*, Jan. 1984, pp.143-4.

26. Local History Index, Letchworth Library.

27. Brunt (1942) catalogues the early 'street theatre' in Letchworth. F.G.C. Mus. contains several examples of the Arbor Day Certificates, including one presented to Howard.

28. Purdom (1913), pp.135-8, Purdom (1951), pp.169-75, and Brunt (1942).

29. Purdom, Lee, Brunt, op. cit. Copies of the scripts are in F.G.C. Mus.

30. Wadowska, Audrey, 'The oldest purpose built cinema', *Hertfordshire Countryside* 25(135), July 1970, pp.44-6.

31. Johnson (1976), pp.75-7, *The Citizen*, '75th Anniversary 1906-81 Souvenir Edition' (Letchworth, October 1981), p.3.

32. Buchan, op. cit., pp.37-61 chronicles the 'Biggleswick' interlude.

33. Purdom (1951), pp.20-30.

34. Whittick, Arnold, *F.J.O. Practical Idealist*, Town and Country Planning Association (London, 1987), pp.22-8.

Chapter Eight: Industry and Commerce

1. Plinston (1980), p.8.

2. A copy of Humphreys' Report is in F.G.C. Mus., Letchworth.

3. Purdom (1963), pp.15, 21.

4. Benoit-Lévy (1911), p.141. The example referred to was Dent's — see below.

5. Simpson (1985), pp.36-8.

6. Purdom (1951), pp.52-4.

7. Brunt (1942), pp.1-2, 62-3; Benoit-Lévy (1911), pp.136-8.

8. J. M. Dent, *The Memoirs of J. M. Dent, 1849-1926* (London, Dent, 1928), pp.127-30; Benoit-Lévy (1911), pp.140-1.

9. Benoit-Lévy (1911), pp.138-40.

10. Ibid. (1911), pp.141-3.

11. Brunt (1942), pp.65-6.

12. Plinston (1980), pp.49-50.

13. Purdom (1913), p.150; Purdom (1925), pp.113-4.

14. Benoit-Lévy (1911), pp.144-5.

15. Hard, F., 'An Industry Moves', *T. & C.P.*, 21(113), Sept. 1953, pp.449-50.

16. Benoit-Lévy (1911), pp.147-9, and personal information from John Hunter, the grandson of Edmund Hunter.

17. Spirella Co., 'Silver Jubilee Album', F.G.C. Mus., Letchworth.

18. Benoit-Lévy (1911), pp.149-52.

19. *Spirella Monthly*, 1(16), June 1912, p.89.

20. 'Album Presented to H.R.H. Duke of York by Spirella Employees, 9 June 1926', Duplicate Copy, F.G.C. Mus., Letchworth.

21. *Spirella Monthly*, (1), January 1912, p.1.

22. 'Letchworth's Diamond Jubilee Year', supplement to *The Citizen*, 25 January 1962, p.ix.

23. Brunt (1942), p.67.
24. Ibid., pp.67-9; Henderson (c.1975), 'Memories of early shopkeepers'.
25. *Letchworth Garden City Directory* (Letchworth, Wheeler Odell & Co.), 1907.
26. Purdom (1925), pp.98-103.
27. Brunt (1942), pp.8-12; *Citizen 75th Anniversary 1906-1981 Souvenir Edition*, 1 October 1981, pp.2-3.

Chapter Nine: Company, Council and Community
 1. Brunt (1942), pp.26-7, Benoit-Lévy (1911), pp.187-91.
 2. Ibid., p.117, and Ibid., pp.191-4. The latter included the detailed budget.
 3. Brunt (1942), pp.27-33; Brunt dealt with the 'cost of economies' on pp.35-9 of Ibid.
 4. Benoit-Lévy (1911), p.177.
 5. Brunt (1942), p.40.
 6. Ibid., pp.40-7.
 7. Purdom (1963), pp.15-30; Purdom (1951), pp.56-8.
 8. 'The Town Planning Conference: Visit to Letchworth', *The Building News* (2910), 14 October 1910, p.539.
 9. 'Letchworth's Convincing Record', *G.C. & T.P.*, 3ns(2), February 1913, pp.37-8.
10. Gaunt, W., 'The Town Square at Letchworth', *G.C. & T.P.*, 3ns(3), March 1913, pp.75-9.
11. Purdom (1913), p.70.
12. Brunt (1942), p.35; 'Letchworth's Diamond Jubilee Year', p.iv.
13. 'Letchworth's Diamond Jubilee', p.iv.
14. Ibid., p.iv.
15. A general history of the evolution of state aided, local authority housing is given in Swenarton, M., *Homes Fit for Heroes* (London, Heinemann, 1981).
16. Letchworth U.D.C. housing programmes were discussed in Purdom (1925), pp.69-72.
17. Ibid., pp.118-23.
18. Plinston (1980), pp.66-7.
19. The Garden Cities and Town Planning Association adopted a formal definition of the term 'Garden City' in 1919: 'A Garden City is a town designed for healthy living; of a size that makes possible a full measure of social life, but not larger; surrounded by a permanent belt of rural land; the whole of the land being in public ownership or held in trust for the community'. Purdom, C. B. (Ed.), *Town Theory and Practice* (London, Benn, 1921), p.34.
20. Purdom (1913), pp.176-82; Purdom (1925), pp.77-8.
21. For general histories of planning see Cherry (1974), Cherry (1988).
22. Cited in MacFadyen (1933), pp.95-6. Bonham-Carter had made similar statements in 'Garden Cities and Satellite Towns and Decentralisation', *J.T.P.I.*, November 1929, p.14. The relationship between landlord and local authority planning at Letchworth was discussed by the author in *Background Statement No.4* (N.H. 74), presented in evidence to the North Hertfordshire District Plan Public Local Inquiry, November 1982.

Chapter Ten: A Living from the Land
 1. Howard (1898), p.17.
 2. Ibid., p.25.
 3. Purdom (1913), Appendix F, 'Agriculture and Smallholdings in Garden City', pp.272-83 (written by H. Burr, F.G.C. Ltd. Surveyor).
 4. Simpson (1985), p.24.
 5. Ibid., p.25.
 6. Purdom (1949), p.144.
 7. Simpson (1985), p.25.
 8. Furmston (194?), pp.18-20, 33-4; MacFadyen (1933), pp.91-2.
 9. Benoit-Lévy (1911), pp.157-60.
10. Brewer, H., 'Home Gardens and Their Value', *T. & C.P.*, 21(113), September 1953, pp.453-5.
11. Plinston (1980), pp.60-2.

Chapter Eleven: Garden City Comes of Age

1. Howard's final years are described and an assessment of his achievements are made in Beevers (1988), Chapters 11-14.
2. Purdom (1951), pp.64-8; see also Beevers (1988), Chapter 13, and for a comprehensive history of Welwyn Garden City see de Soissons, Maurice, *Welwyn Garden City: A town designed for healthy living* (Publications for Companies, Cambridge, 1988).
3. Told by Lewis Mumford to the author, in conversation at Amenia, New York, June 1978.
4. Howard, Ebenezer (trans. L. E. Creplet), *Ville Jardins de Demain* (Paris, 1904).
   Howard, Ebenezer (trans. Maria Wallroth-Unterlip), *Gartenstadte in Sicht* (Jena, 1907).
   Howard, Ebenezer (trans. Aleksandr Black), *Goroda Budushavo* (St Petersburg, 1911).
   Howard, Ebenezer (trans. Dr. B. Murck and R. Svoboda), *Zatradni Mesta Budoucnosti* (Prague, 1924).
5. G. B. Shaw to A. C. Howard, 25 May 1928, HCC/EHo/F17.
6. Purdom (1925), Chapter Seven; Purdom, C. B., 'The Finance of Letchworth', *G.C. & T.P.*, 12(2), February 1922, pp.24-6.
7. Purdom (1963), p.33.
8. *I.C.T.*, International Computers and Tabulators Ltd., London, March 1960, copy in Letchworth Reference Library.
9. *Letchworth Official Guide* (Cheltenham, n.d., c.1952), p.69.
10. Local History Index, Letchworth Library and Purdom (1925).
11. Coaten, H. C., 'The Industries of Letchworth', *G.C. & T.P.* (20)6, June/July 1930, p.172.
12. Ibid., p.174.
13. Parker, R. B., 'Presidential Address — Where we Stand', *J.T.P.I.*, 14(2), November 1929, p.8.
14. Purdom (1925), Chapter Three; 'Letchworth of Today', *G.C. & T.P.*, 16(2), February 1926, p.88.
15. The following examples are culled from issues of *The Citizen* in the author's collection, and *Hullabaloo*, the 1935 Civic Week Programme.
16. *Hertfordshire Regional Planning Report 1927* (London, W. R. Davidge), pp.53, 83.
17. Wadowska, Audrey, op. cit., Note 30 to Chapter Seven above, and local press advertisements.
18. *The Citizen*, 20(1026, 1027), Letchworth, 4 and 11 June 1926, Civic Week numbers: 'Letchworth's Coming of Age', *G.C. & T.P.* 16(2), February 1926, and 16(6), July 1926.
19. *The Citizen*, 20(1027), 11 June 1926.
20. *Hullabaloo*, 'The Official Magazine of Letchworth Civic Week', Letchworth, June 1935.

Chapter Twelve: Post War Expansion

1. Johnson (1976), pp.97-8.
2. In the possession of Letchworth Garden City Corporation, see below, Chapter Fourteen.
3. Plinston (1980), pp.91-2.
4. Ibid., p.75.
5. Plinston (1981), pp.10-11; Purdom (1962), pp.34-9.
6. Purdom (1949), pp.137-9.
7. Abercrombie, Patrick, *Greater London Plan 1944* (London, H.M.S.O., 1945).
8. For early history of Stevenage New Town see Purdom (1949), pp.391-4, 420-2; Mullan, Bob, *Stevenage Ltd. Aspects of the Planning and Politics of Stevenage New Town, 1945-78* (London, Routledge, 1980), pp.39-62.
9. Cullingworth, J. B., *Town and Country Planning in England and Wales* (London, Revised Third Edition, 1970), pp.247-8.
10. de Soissons, op. cit., pp.112-21.
11. Plinston (1981), pp.16-18, Purdom (1963), pp.35-6.
12. Purdom (1963), pp.37-8.
13. Cullingworth, op. cit., pp.147-58.
14. Purdom (1980), p.69.
15. Abercrombie, op. cit., para. 353, pp.140-1.
16. Howard (1946), p.105.
17. The pre-1974 structure of planning authorities was described in Cullingworth, op. cit., pp.43-6, 120-36.

18. Doubleday, E. H., *Hertfordshire County Development Plan Written Statement* (Hertfordshire County Council, 1951).
19. Plinston (1981), pp.11-16.
20. Cullingworth, op. cit., pp.254-8.
21. Plinston (1981), pp.35-8; *The Citizen*, No. 2628, Letchworth, 23 November 1956.
22. Stein, C., 'Toward New Towns for America', *Town Planning Review*, 20(3), October 1949, pp.219-29, gives the early history. As the present author discovered, Unwin was informally consulted over the original Radburn Plan, see Miller (1981b), p.528.
23. *T. & C.P.* ('The Letchworth Jubilee'), 21(113), September 1953, p.400.
24. *The Citizen* ('Letchworth Jubilee Edition'), No.2459, Letchworth, 28 August 1953. The section on consumer goods and local events is drawn from this source.
25. *Letchworth. The First Garden City*, *Official Guide* (Cheltenham, Burrow, n.d., *c*.1951) contains a useful survey of the major industries, supplemented by *T. & C.P.* ('The Letchworth Jubilee') and *The Citizen* ('Letchworth Jubilee Edition').
26. The author compiled an account, including buildings constructed 1945-75, for the revision of Pevsner, N. (ed. Cherry, B.), *The Buildings of England — Hertfordshire*, Second Edition (Harmondsworth, Penguin, 1976), pp.224-34.
27. For a comprehensive and sympathetic account of the Hertfordshire Schools programme see Saint, A., *Towards a Social Architecture* (London and New Haven, Yale, 1987).

Chapter Thirteen: Save Letchworth Garden City

1. The essential accounts of the remarkable take-over struggle and its outcome are contained in three major references to which the reader is directed for a more detailed history of the period: Plinston, H., *Letchworth — A Record of Events* (typescript, F.G.C. Mus., Letchworth, n.d., *c*.1980); Plinston, H., *A Tale of One City* (Letchworth Garden City Corporation, 1981); Purdom, C. B., *The Letchworth Achievement* (London, Dent, 1963).
2. The full text of the Act is given as Appendix E to Plinston (1963).
3. *The Garden City Estate of Letchworth. Scheme of Management*, L.G.C. Corp.

Chapter Fourteen: The Old Order Changeth

1. The key documents were: Doubleday, E. H., *Letchworth Central Area Appraisal Plan* (H.C.C., December 1965); Kitching, L. C., Such, F. H., and Leigh, J. V., *People and Traffic. A Study of Conflict and Congestion in Letchworth* (H.C.C./L.U.D.C., September 1970); Overton, D., *Hertfordshire 1981 — Policy Statement* (H.C.C., September 1972).

   The latter represented a continuation from the First Review of the County Development Plan, approved May 1971, which extended the time horizon of County Planning Policy from the terminal date of the County Development Plan by eight years to 1981, by which time it was anticipated that the County Structure Plan would be in operation, see below.
2. For a general review of the 1968 Act and the subsequent 'two tier' development plans see Cullingworth, op. cit., pp.109-117.
3. Ibid., pp.136-42 reviews the complex interrelationship between the modification of the form of development plans and local government reorganisation.
4. Kelly, M. J., '1919-74', *Letchworth Garden City Official Guide* (Letchworth), p.6.
5. Cullingworth, op. cit., pp.174-8 contains a general introduction to the strengthening of historic building and conservation legislation. Department of the Environment Circular 8/87 *Historic Buildings and Conservation Areas — Policy and Procedures* (London, H.M.S.O., 1987) contains the latest updated policy statement on preservation and enhancement of the historic built environment.
6. Creese, W. L., *The Search for Environment. The Garden City: Before and After* (New Haven and London, Yale, 1966). See also Creese (1967) for a selection of Unwin's writing on planning. Hughes, M. (ed.), *The letters of Lewis Mumford and Frederic J. Osborn: A transatlantic dialogue 1938-70* (Bath, Adams and Dart, 1971) contained much seminal material appraising and reinterpreting the Garden City movement.
7. Parker, C. M., *Material available for a memoir of R. B. Parker at 296 Norton Way South*, Letchworth, 1970. She noted that the catalogue had been made 'in response to a request from Lewis Mumford'.
8. *The Book of Letchworth*, Johnson (1976) retains its appeal as an exhaustive catalogue of incidents in the history of Letchworth, recounted in the author's characteristically idiosyncratic style. 'K.J.' has also

written extensively in the local press over the past 30 years and continues to lead walks around the Garden City. His *Local History Index* in the Letchworth Library is an invaluable *Vademecum* for an Odyssey into virtually any aspect of Letchworth's history.

9. Miller (1975), pp.253-5.

10. The author compiled the research on individual sheets for each building or group to form a 'Letchworth Building Index'. This aimed at recording basic data for each building with architectural or historic significance in the development of Letchworth to 1914. A mimeographed summary in the form of a Working Paper was prepared by North Hertfordshire District Council in 1976, and used by the author as the basis of discussions with the Department of the Environment inspectorate.

11. Department of the Environment, *List of Buildings of Special Architectural or Historic Interest. District of North Hertfordshire (Letchworth Area)* (London, 1979).

12. North Hertfordshire District Council (Planning Officer B. G. Hull), *Letchworth Conservation Area Broadsheet*, 1977. The text and illustrations were prepared by the present author during his tenure as Principal Planning Officer (Conservation and Design) in the N.H.D.C. Planning Department.

13. For an itemised catalogue of the exhibition see Miller (1978).

14. Johnson (1976), p.118.

15. This section is based upon 'Letchworth — the past 25 years: and what next?', an account given by Andrew Egerton-Smith, L.G.C. Corp. Chief Executive, to a joint R.T.P.I. East of England Branch/ T.C.P.A. Conference held in Letchworth on 7 February 1989. Financial details and descriptions of the major projects are taken from the L.G.C. Corp. *Annual Report and Accounts* (Letchworth, 1964-   ).

16. The Hertfordshire County Structure Plan was prepared under Part II of the T. & C.P. Act 1971, as amended. The 'Commencement Order' was made on 21 March 1973. A first phase of public involvement took place in Spring 1973, followed by a second in Winter 1973/4 on major issues, which produced heightened public support for green belt policies. A third phase of consultation on the basis of 'Planning means choosing' followed in early 1975. The District Councils which came into being on 1 April 1974 were extensively consulted; the *Hertfordshire County Structure Plan Written Statement* was published in 1976. The plan was approved in modified form by the Secretary of State, after lengthy public hearings, on 21 September 1979.

17. Preparation of the N.H.D.C. District Local Plan involved extensive work. 'Topic Studies' on related subject areas were published in 1978-9, a draft plan was published for comment over Jan.-Sept. 1981, published as a formal plan in January 1982, and examined at a Public Local Inquiry between Oct. and Dec. 1982. The Inspector's report was received in Summer 1983, approving the plan with modifications. The plan was formally adopted on 6 March 1984. See N.H.D.C., *District Plan Written Statement* (Letchworth, March 1984).

18. The author was extensively examined at the Public Local Inquiry over the inclusion of sites such as the Creamery Playing Fields at Letchworth Gate. See N.H.D.C. Evidence in 'Background Statement No.4' (NH 74) and (NH 147), and the Inspector's *Report on the Public Local Inquiry*, 7 June 1983, paras. 197-253.

19. 'Letchworth — the first 25 years: and what next?', para. 12.

20. 'Helping Your Business To Succeed', *The Business Centre* (L.G.C. Corp., n.d., *c*.1985), and L.G.C. Corp *Business News*, 1984-. The A1 'Corridor' project was the subject of a promotional leaflet 'Hertfordshire's A1 — we've been in business for years', published by H.C.C. County Planning and Estates Dept. (n.d., *c*.1987).

21. N.H.D.C. *District Plan Monitoring Report, Housing*, 1983.

22. Information from N.H.D.C. Housing Department, April 1989.

23. Information on the vicissitudes of the agricultural enterprise is contained in the Corporation's *Annual Reports*. They were also summarised by Andrew Egerton-Smith in 'Letchworth — the past 25 years: and what next?'. The 'In Hand Farming Master Plan' was prepared by Bidwells in Autumn 1987. The long-distance walks are described in *Six Countryside Walks around Letchworth Garden City* (L.G.C. Corp., 1986). The Corporation publishes various brochures and information packs on the Standalone Farm Centre.

24. Education 2000 was described in the Corporation *Annual Reports* for 1986 and 1987. Briefing documents were issued to local businesses at a series of working breakfasts in Spring 1987. See also 'Education 2000, Educating People for Change' (Letchworth, n.d., *c*.1988).

25. The development and its opening were illustrated in *Tenth Report and Accounts* (L.G.C. Corp., 1975).

The Corporation also issued a descriptive brochure on the project. Subsequent *Annual Reports* charted progress on The Wynd and other town centre refurbishment.

26. 'Letchworth Shopfronts', prepared by Conran Roche in conjunction with L.G.C. Corp. and N.H.D.C., April 1987.

Chapter Fifteen: Back to the Future

1. 'Corporation Milestone', *Insight*, 37, 3 September 1987, L.G.C. Corp. *Insight*, published quarterly, is the Corporation's own newspaper, delivered to all Letchworth residents. The estate valuations were reported in the *Annual Reports*.

2. 'Letchworth Garden City Stays in Business', *Planning*, (670), 30 May 1986, p.1.

3. 'TACT', *Competition Conditions* (L.G.C. Corp., September 1975).

4. Howard (1898), pp.148, 150.

5. Andrew Egerton-Smith's paper, 'Letchworth Garden City Corporation — 25 years: and what then?' has been cited in skeleton form. Hall's paper was essentially that released by the T.C.P.A. as 'Policies for Urban Development' on 16 January 1989. The East of England R.T.P.I./T.C.P.A. issued the collected papers of the Conference in *Garden Cities of Tomorrow*, H.C.C. Planning and Estates Department, 1989.

6. Stamp, G., *The Letchworth Garden Study* (mimeo., London, Brunel Institute of Organisation and Social Studies, July 1983).

7. Adams, Thomas, 'Reserving productive areas within and around cities. A proposal to substitute agricultural wedges for zones', *Journal of the American Institute of Architects*, 9(10), 1921, pp.316-9.

8. Unwin (1912), Diagram VII, p.10; Howard (1902), Diagram 4, facing p.128. The author drew attention to the relevance of these models in the context of the problems of continued pressure for expansion of Letchworth, in Miller (1983).

9. For detailed discussion of the Greater London Regional Plan see Miller (1989).

10. As the first of the Housebuilders 'New Towns', Tillingham Hall attracted a great deal of publicity. See especially: (i) *Tillingham Hall — Outline Plan*, prepared for Consortium Developments by Conran Roche, Milton Keynes, May 1985; (ii) Shostack L. and Lock, B., 'New Towns in the South East: a planned response to a regional crisis', *The Planner (J.R.T.P.I.)*, 71(5), 1985, pp.19-22; (iii) 'Tillingham Hall — the new country town proposal', *The Planner (J.R.T.P.I.)*, pp.6-7.

11. 'Housing in Rural Areas', *A Statement by the Secretary of State for the Environment* (London, Department of the Environment, 5 July 1988).

12. Hall, P., 'The Coming Revival of Town and Country Planning', *R.S.A. Journal* (Royal Society of Arts), 136(5302), 1988, pp.41730.

13. Steeley, G., *The Path to Real Reform. The Tenth Ebenezer Howard Memorial Lecture*, given at Royal Society of Arts, London, 27 October 1988 (L.G.C. Corp., 1988).

14. The following section is based upon the conclusions of the author's paper given at the R.T.P.I./T.C.P.A. Conference held at the Plinston Hall in February 1989.

Appendix One

Local Authority Chairmen 1919-89; Chief Officers 1974 and 1989

a. Chairmen, Letchworth Urban District Council 1919-74

1919-24 Cllr. C. F. Ball, C.B.E.
1924-27 Cllr. Dr. N. MacFadyen
1927-30 Cllr. W. H. Gaunt, C.B.E.
1930-33 Cllr. A. W. Brunt
1933-36 Cllr. R. W. Tabor
1936-40 Cllr. F. Nott
1940-45 Cllr. L. W. Bennett, M.B.E., J.P.
1945-47 Cllr. Mrs. M. M. Harvey, J.P.
1947-49 Cllr. G. F. Woodbridge
1949-50 Cllr. E. G. Gardiner
1950-51 Cllr. G. F. Woodbridge
1951-52 Cllr. E. G. Gardiner
1952-55 Cllr. G. F. Woodbridge
1955-56 Cllr. Dr. J. Clay
1956-60 Cllr. H. S. Day
1960-63 Cllr. A. C. Bywaters
1963-64 Cllr. J. A. Talbot
1964-66 Cllr. D. Kennedy
1966-68 Cllr. N. C. Martin
1968-70 Cllr. Mrs. M. M. Gavin Jones
1970-74 Cllr. C. W. Sax

b. Chairmen, North Hertfordshire District Council 1919-89

1973-75 Cllr. W. Miller
1975-76 Cllr. R. A. Lodge
1976-77 Cllr. C. J. Marshall
1977-78 Cllr. Mrs. B. F. Wearmouth
1978-79 Cllr. F. J. Smith
1979-80 Cllr. D. W. C. Winch
1980-81 Cllr. R. D. Bloxham
1981-82 Cllr. J. A. Rafell
1982-83 Cllr. Mrs. P. A. Rule
1983-84 Cllr. G. Woods
1984-85 Cllr. K. F. Emsall
1985-86 Cllr. M. K. Tatham
1986-87 Cllr. R. P. Evens
1987-88 Cllr. A. G. Burrows
1988-89 Cllr. A. A. Evens
1989   Cllr. P. W. MacCormack

c. North Hertfordshire District Council Chief Officers, 1 April 1974

Chief Executive: M. Kelly, LL.B., D.P.A., M.B.I.M.
Secretary: F. W. Hammond, F.C.I.S.
Solicitor: D. A. Woolston, LL.B.
Treasurer: K. Sutton, I.P.F.A., A.R.V.A.

Technical Officer: F. H. Such, C.Eng., F.I.Mun.E., M.Inst.H.E., A.M.B.I.M.
Housing Officer: T. A. C. Thompson
Planning Officer: B. G. Hull, M.R.T.P.I., Dip.T.P.
Environmental Health Officer: D. Coyne, M.A.P.H.I.

d. North Hertfordshire District Council Chief Officers, 1 June 1989

Chief Executive: K Sutton, I.P.F.A.
Director of Legal and Administrative Services: B. J. Hunt
Director of Finance: S. MacDonald, B.S.(Econ.), I.P.F.A.
Director of Engineering and Leisure Services: S. L. Williams, C.Eng., M.I.C.E.
Director of Housing and Environmental Health: D. Coyne, M.I.E.H.
Director of Planning: P. Archard. Dip.T.P., F.R.T.P.I., M.B.I.M.
Director of Contact Services: R. MacLachrie, C.Eng., M.I.C.E.

Appendix Two

Letchworth Garden City Corporation Chairmen 1963-89; Board Members and Chief Officers 1963 and 1989

a.   Chairmen

Robert Humbert, O.B.E., T.D., D.L., J.P., F.R.I.C.S., 1963-1978
Sidney Melman, J.P., F.C.I.S., 10 October 1978-

b.   Board Members

i)   1 January 1963

R. A. Humbert (Chairman)
C. C. Barker
L. W. Bennett
Sir Harold Fieldhouse
C. W. Sax
D. G. Haddow (from 30 April 1963)

ii)   1 June 1989

S. A. Melman (Chairman)
Prof. G. C. Cameron
K. F. Emsall
M. O. Kearns
E. Lyall
Mrs. A. D. Woods

c.   Chief Officers

i)   1 January 1963

H. Plinston, M.B.E., LL.B. (Secretary/Solicitor)
J. A. J. Barrett, F.L.A., A.T.I.I. (Accountant)
T. W. Freeman, A.R.I.C.S., Q.A.L.A.S. (Estates Officer)

ii)   1 June

A. J. D. F. Egerton-Smith (Chief Executive)
M. C. Davies (Property Manager)
P. Franklin (Accountant)
H. A. Patterson (Corporation Secretary)

Appendix Three

Garden City Trees

The tree-lined roads of Letchworth have always been regarded as symbolising the Garden City concept of housing layout. Initially an attempt was made to plant a distinctive species for each road, but this was later modified after the Urban District Council took over the responsibility for highway maintenance. In more recent years there has been the problem of renewal, for many of the early specimen trees have reached the end of their life-span. Both the North Hertfordshire District Council and the Letchworth Garden City Corporation have spent large budgets on maintaining the town's arcadian character.

The following list, taken from the 1951 L.U.D.C. *Official Guide*, gives an indication of the variety of planting up to the Second World War. Some roads have subsequently been replaced with fewer species.

Road	Trees Planted	Country of Origin
Baldock Road	Sycamore	Europe
	Limes	Central and Southern Europe
Bedford Road	Schwedler Maple (Variety of Norway Maple)	Europe
Birds Hill	Round-headed Locust tree	East U.S.A.
Broadway, North	Sugar or Birdseye Maple	Canada, U.S.A.
	Silver Birch	Great Britain and Europe
	White Ash	East U.S.A.
Broadway, Middle	Small-leaved Lime	Northern Europe
Broadway, South	Manna Ash	South Europe and Asia Minor
Broughton Hill	Mountain Ash	Great Britain and Europe
Cashio Lane	Purple Plum	Central Asia
Common View	Scarlet Thorn	Europe and U.S.A.
Cowslip Hill	Silver Birch	Great Britain and Europe
The Crescent	Almond	West Asia
Cross Street	Mountain Ash	Great Britain and Europe
The Dale	Horse Chestnut	North Greece, Albania
Eastcheap	False Acacia	East U.S.A.
Field Lane	Red Horse Chestnut	Hybrid of English Horse Chestnut and American Red Buckeye
Gernon Road	Broad-leaved Lime	Europe
Glebe Road	Manna Ash	South Europe and Asia Minor
	Sycamore	Europe
	Cherry Laurel	South-East Europe and Asia Minor
Green Lane	Sycamore	Europe
Hillshott	Almond	West Asia
Hitchin Road	Norway Maple	Europe
Icknield Way East	Almond	West Asia
Icknield Way West	Double Cherry	
	Purple Plum	Central Asia

Letchworth Gate	Red Horse Chestnut	Hybrid of English Horse Chestnut and American Red Buckeye
Leys Avenue	Mountain Ash	Great Britain and Europe
Lytton Avenue	Simple-leaf Ash	England
	Single-leaf Ash	England
	Manna Ash	South Europe and Asia Minor
Meadow Way	False Acacia	East U.S.A.
Nevells Road	Schwedler Maple	Europe
Norton Way North	Norway Maple	Europe
	Sycamore	Europe
Norton Way South	Horse Chestnut	North Greece, Albania
	Lime	Central and Southern Europe
Pixmore Avenue	Broad-leaved Lime	Central and Southern Europe
	Sycamore	Europe
Pixmore Way	Weeping Elm	Great Britain and Europe
	Norway Maple	Europe
Pixmore Way East	Maple	Europe
The Quadrant	Schwedler Maple	Europe
Ridge Avenue	Lombardy Poplar	Southern Europe
	Lime	Central and Southern Europe
Ridge Road	Norway Maple	Europe
Rushby Mead	Broad-leaved Lime	Central and Southern Europe
Sollershott East	Horse Chestnut	North Greece, Albania
Sollershott West	Sycamore	Europe
Souberie Avenue	Pear	Europe and North Asia
	Mountain Ash	Great Britain and Europe
	Hawthorn	Great Britain, Central Asia, Syria and North Africa
South View	Silver Birch	Great Britain and Europe
	Indian Beam	East U.S.A.
	Common Hawthorn	Great Britain, Central Asia, Syria and North Africa
	Hawthorn	
Spring Road	False Acacia	East U.S.A.
	Common Lime	Central and Southern Europe
Station Place	Lime	Central and Southern Europe
Station Road	Silver Birch	Great Britain and Europe
Town Square	Hornbeam	East England and Central Europe
	Deodar Cedar	Himalayan Mountains
	Common Beech	Great Britain
	Lombardy Poplar	Southern Europe
	Cornish Elm	Great Britain
Willian Way	Red Horse Chestnut	Hybrid of English Horse Chestnut and American Red Buckeye
Works Road	Maple	Europe
	False Acacia	East U.S.A

Bibliography

1. Archives

First Garden City Heritage Museum, Letchworth: Garden City Association pressbooks and correspondence, Parker Collection, plans, photographs and practice records.

Hertfordshire County Council Record Office: Ebenezer Howard Papers.

Hitchcock Collection: Correspondence between Raymond Unwin and Ethel Parker.

Letchworth Garden City Corporation: First Garden City Ltd., Minute Books and correspondence.

Letchworth Public Library: Local History Collection, Local History Index.

North Hertfordshire District Council: Bye-law records and plans of the former Letchworth Urban District Council.

Royal Institute of British Architects, British Architectural Library: Membership records and Unwin Papers.

Town and Country Planning Association: Minute Books.

University of Manchester: Department of Town and Country Planning, Unwin Papers, photographs and slide collection.

Welwyn Garden City Library: Osborn Papers.

2. Theses and Dissertations

Day, Michael, 'Sir Raymond Unwin (1863-1940) and R. Barry Parker (1867-1947): A Study and Evaluation of their contribution to the development of Site Planning Theory and Practice', unpub. M.A. Thesis, Manchester University, 1973.

Miller, Mervyn, 'To Speak of Planning is to Speak of Unwin: the contribution of Sir Raymond Unwin (1863-1940) to the Evolution of British Town Planning', unpub. Ph.D. Thesis, University of Birmingham, 1981.

Pritchard, Mark, 'The First Garden City', unpub. M.A. Thesis, Courtauld Institute, University of London, 1970.

3. Official Publications

Local Government Board, *Manual on the Preparation of State-aided Schemes*, 1919.

Local Government Board, 'Report of the Committee Appointed by the President of the Local Government Board and the Secretary for Scotland to consider questions of Building Construction in connection with the provision of dwellings for the working classes in England, Wales and Scotland and to report upon the methods for securing economy and despatch in the provision of such dwellings', Cd. 9191, 1918 (*The Tudor Walters Report*).

Ministry of Health, 'Garden Cities and Satellite Towns, Report of the Departmental Committee' (*The Marley Report*), 1935.

4. Books and Articles

Abercrombie, Patrick, *Greater London Plan 1944* (London, H.M.S.O., 1945).

Adams, Thomas, *Design of Residential Areas*, Harvard City Planning Series, No.IV (Cambridge, [Mass], 1934).

Adams, Thomas, *Recent Advances in Town Planning* (London, Churchill, 1932).

Armitage, W. H. G., *Heavens Below: Utopian Experiments in England, 1560-1960* (London, Routledge and Kegan Paul, 1961).

Ashworth, William, *The Genesis of Modern British Town Planning: A Study in economic and social history of the Nineteenth and Twentieth Centuries* (London, Routledge and Kegan Paul, 1954).

235

Atkinson, George, 'Aus Englischen Gartenstadten' (with substantial sections by Bernard Kampffmeyer), *Deutsche Gartenstadt Gesellschaft* (Berlin, Renaissance-Verlag Robert Federn, 1910).

Beattie, Susan, *A Revolution in London Housing* (London, Architectural Press, 1980).

Beevers, Robert, *The Garden City Utopia: A Critical Biography of Ebenezer Howard* (London, Macmillan, 1988).

Bell, Colin and Rose, *City Fathers: the early history of Town Planning in Britain* (London, Pelican, 1972).

Benoit-Lévy, Georges, *La Cite Jardin* (Paris, Editions Cite Jardins par Charles Gide, 2nd ed., 1911).

Berlepsch-Valendas, B.D.A., *Die Gartenstadtbewegung in England, ihre Entwickelung und ihr jetziger Stand* (Munchen und Berlin, Druck und Verlag von R. Oldenburg, 1912).

Bonham-Carter, Sir Edgar, 'Planning and Development of Letchworth Garden City', *T.P.R.*, January 1951, pp.362-376.

'Borough' Guide, *Letchworth Garden City* (Cheltenham, Burrows, 1908).

Brunt, Arthur William, *Pageant of Letchworth* (Letchworth, n.d., *c*.1942).

Cherry, Gordon E., *Town Planning in its Social Context* (London, Leonard Hill, 1970).

Cherry, Gordon E., *The Evolution of British Town Planning* (Leighton Buzzard, Leonard Hill, 1974).

Cherry, Gordon E., *Pioneers in British Planning* (London, Architectural Press, 1981).

Cherry, Gordon, *Cities and Plans* (London, Edward Arnold, 1988).

Cowlishaw, W. H., 'The Cloisters, Letchworth' *A.R.*, January 1908, pp.198-207.

Craske, Harold, 'Letchworth Garden City 1903-1909', *G.C.*, NS4(35), November 1909, pp.250-2.

Creese, Walter L., 'Parker and Unwin: Architects of Totality', *Journal of the Society of Architectural Historians*, 22 (3), Oct. 1963, pp.161-70.

Creese, Walter L., *The Search for Environment: the Garden City Before and After* (New Haven, Yale, 1966).

Creese, Walter L., *The Legacy of Raymond Unwin: a human pattern for planning* (Cambridge [Mass], M.I.T., 1976).

Culpin, Ewart G., *The Garden City Movement up to Date* (London, G.C.T.P.A., 1913 and 1914).

Culpin, Ewart G., 'The Garden City and the Manufacturer', *G.C. & T.P.*, V(2), February 1915, pp.30-8.

Culpin, Ewart G., 'The Lesson of Letchworth: Garden Cities and Reconstruction', *G.C. & T.P.*, VII(4), December 1917, pp.66-71.

Darley, Gillian, *Villages of Vision* (London, Architectural Press, 1975).

Day, M. G., 'The contribution of Sir Raymond Unwin (1863-1940), and R. Barry Parker (1867-1940) to the development of site planning theory and practice', in Sutcliffe, Anthony (ed.), *British Town Planning: The Formative Years* (Leicester University Press, 1981).

Dent, J. M., *The Memoirs of J. M. Dent (1849-1926)* (London, Dent, 1928).

Edwards, Arthur M., *The Design of Suburbia* (London, Pembridge, 1981).

Evans, Paul, 'Raymond Unwin and the Municipalisation of the Garden City' in Steadman, P. and Owers, J., *Transactions of the Martin Centre* (Cambridge, Woodhead-Faulkner, 1976).

First Garden City Ltd., *Garden City in the Making* (Garden City Press, Hitchin, 1905).

First Garden City Ltd., *Guide to Garden City* (London, n.d., *c*.1906).

First Garden City Ltd., *Letchworth Garden City in Pictures* (n.d., *c*.1912).

First Garden City Ltd., *Letchworth: Where Town and Country Meet* (Letchworth, n.d., *c*.1935).

Fishman, Robert, *Urban Utopias in the Twentieth Century: Ebenezer Howard, Frank Lloyd Wright and Le Corbusier* (New York, Basic Books, 1977).

Furmston, W. G., *Ancestral Jottings* (Letchworth Printers Ltd., n.d., *c*.1940).

Garden City Association, *Conference at Bournville . . . Report of Proceedings* (London, 1901).

Garden City Association, *Garden Cities: Report of a public meeting at the Holborn Restaurant, June 2, 1902* (G.C.A., London, 1902).

Gaunt, W. H., 'The Town Square at Letchworth', *G.C. & T.P.*, III (3) March 1913, pp.75-9.

Hare, William L. *et al.*, 'A Part of Rural England. North Hertfordshire before the Garden City', a series of articles commemorating the 25 years of development of Letchworth, *G.C. & T.P.*, June/July 1930, pp.147-77.

Hawkes, D. (ed.), *Modern Country Homes in England. The Arts and Crafts Architecture of Barry Parker* (Cambridge, Cambridge University Press, 1986).

Henderson, Ethel, *The Ideals of Letchworth: The First Garden City* (private publication, Letchworth, n.d., *c*.1975).

Hebbert, Michael, 'Frederic Osborn, 1885-1978', pp. 177-202 in Cherry, G. E. (ed.), *Pioneers of British Planning* (London, Architectural Press, 1981).

Hine, Reginald L., 'The Village History of England', in *Coronation Booklet* (Letchworth U.D.C., 1937).

Howard, Ebenezer, *Garden Cities of Tomorrow* (London, Swan Sonnenschein, 1902).

Howard, Ebenezer, *Garden Cities of Tomorrow*, new edition, ed. F. J. Osborn with introduction by Lewis Mumford (London, Faber, 1946)

Howard, Ebenezer, 'The Land Question at Letchworth', *The City* (Letchworth) I (7), July 1909, pp. 153-7; I (8) August 1909, pp.177-84.

Howard, Ebenezer, *Tomorrow: A Peaceful Path to Real Reform* (London, Swan Sonnenschein, 1898).

Jackson, Frank, *Sir Raymond Unwin: architect, planner and visionary* (London, Zwemmer, 1985).

Johnson, Kenneth, *The Book of Letchworth* (Barracuda, 1975).

Joseph Rowntree Village Trust, *New Earswick* (York, 1912).

Lanchester, H. V., 'Letchworth Jubilee' (with contributions by Osborn, Mumford, Purdom, Feiss *et al.*), *T. & C.P.*, 21(113), Sept. 1953.

Letchworth Chamber of Trade, 'Letchworth: England's First Garden City' (Letchworth, n.d., *c*.1933).

Letchworth Citizen, 'Letchworth's Diamond Jubilee Year' (Letchworth, 1963).

Letchworth Civic Week Committee, 'Hullabaloo', *Civic Week Official Programme* (Letchworth, 1935).

Letchworth Garden City Corporation, *Annual Report and Accounts* (Letchworth, 1963-).

Letchworth Garden City Directory (Letchworth, Wheeler Odell, 1907).

The Letchworth Naturalists' Society, *In and Around Letchworth* (Letchworth, The Museum, 1963).

Letchworth Printers Ltd., *Letchworth: England's Most Progressive Garden City* (Letchworth, n.d., *c*.1923).

Letchworth Urban District Council, *Official Guide*, 1951, 1963, 1974.

Lyon, T. Findlay, 'Sir Raymond Unwin 1863-1940', *J.R.I.B.A.*, 3ss 70(9), September 1963, pp.356.

Matthews, Keith and Burleigh, Gilbert, 'A Saxon and Early Medieval Settlement at Green Lane, Letchworth', *Hertfordshire's Past*, Spring 1989, pp.27-31.

Mawson, T. H., 'The Meaning of Letchworth', a series of articles on the celebration of Letchworth's coming-of-age, *G.C. & T.P.*, 16(6), July 1926, pp.127-47.

Miles, V. W., *The Cloisters, Letchworth* (Letchworth, Lawrence Cloisters Trust, 1967).

Miller, Mervyn, 'Letchworth Conservation Area', *T. & C.P.*, 43(5), May 1975, pp.253-5.

Miller, Mervyn, 'Letchworth Revisited: Cheap Cottages from 1905', *Housing Outlook*, (4), 1978, pp.10-14.

Miller, Mervyn, 'Letchworth Garden City 1903-78', *Catalogue of a Commemorative Exhibition, 22 July-22 December 1978*, First Garden City Museum, Letchworth.

Miller, Mervyn, 'Garden City Influence on the Evolution of Housing Policy', *Local Government Studies*, 5(6), November/December 1979, pp.5-22.

Miller, Mervyn, 'The Howard Cottage Society: Pioneers of Garden City Housing', *Housing Outlook* (5), 1979, pp.13-16.

Miller, Mervyn, 'In Search of the £150 Cottage', *T. & C.P.*, 49(2), February 1980, pp.48-50.

Miller, Mervyn, 'Raymond Unwin, 1863-1940', pp.72-102 in Cherry, G. E. (ed.), *Pioneers in British Planning* (Architectural Press, 1981).

Miller, Mervyn, 'Letchworth Garden City — Eighty Years On', *Built Environment*, 9(3/4), 1983, pp.167-184.

Miller, Mervyn, 'The Roots of Planning', *The Planner*, (J.R.T.P.I.), 70(9), September 1984, pp.11-15 (1984).

Miller, Mervyn, 'The elusive green Background: Raymond Unwin and the Greater London Regional Plan', *Planning Perspectives*, 4(1), January 1989, pp.15-44.

Moss-Eccardt, John, *Ebenezer Howard* (Aylesbury, Shire, 1973).

Mumford, Lewis, *The City in History* (London, Secker and Warburg, 1961).

MacFadyen, Dugald, *Sir Ebenezer Howard and the Town Planning Movement* (Manchester University Press, 1933).

Nettlefold, J. S., 'Ideals and Results and Letchworth', *G.C. & T.P.*, 3(4), April 1913, pp.89-91.

New Townsmen, *New Towns After War* (London, Dent, 1918).

North Hertfordshire District Council (M. K. Miller), 'Letchworth Buildings Index', Working Paper, 1976.

North Hertfordshire District Council, 'Letchworth, Baldock and District Guide', 1976.

North Hertfordshire District Council, 'Letchworth Conservation Area Broadsheet', 1977.

Olmsted, Frederick Law (Jr.), 'Through American Spectacles', *G.C. & T.P.*, NS 4(34), May 1909, pp.198-200.

Osborn, F. J., *Green-Belt Cities: The British Contribution* (London, Faber and Faber, 1946).

Parker, Barry, 'Our Homes', B.N., 19/26 July 1895, private offprint, Buxton, 1895.

Parker, Barry, 'On the Planning of a Small House', *The City* (Letchworth), I(6), June 1909, pp.139-44.

Parker, Barry, 'Presidential Address: Where We Stand', *J.T.P.I.*, 16(1), November 1929, pp.1-10.

Parker, Barry, 'Site Planning As Exemplified at New Earswick', *T.P.R.*, 27(2), February 1937, pp.79-102.

Parker, Barry, 'The Life and Work of Sir Raymond Unwin', 26 (5), *J.T.P.I.*, August 1940, pp.161-2.

Parker, Barry, 'Memoir of Sir Raymond Unwin', *J.R.I.B.A.*, 15 July 1940.

Parker, Barry and Unwin, Raymond, *The Art of Building a Home* (London, Longmans, 1901).

Parker, Barry, and Unwin, Raymond, 'Cottages Near a Town', *Catalogue of the Northern Artworkers Guild Exhibition* (Manchester, H.C.D. Chorlton, 1903), pp.34-43.

Pearson, Lynn F., *The Architectural and Social History of Cooperative Living* (London, Macmillan, 1987).

Pepper, Simon, 'Introduction: The Garden City Legacy', *A.R.*, 163 (976), June 1978, pp.321-324.

Plinston, Horace, 'Letchworth: A Record of Events', unpub. typescript, First Garden City Heritage Museum, Letchworth, n.d., *c.*1980.

Plinston, Horace, *A Tale of One City* (Letchworth Garden City Corporation, 1981).

Purdom, C. B., *The Garden City* (Dent, 1913).

Purdom, C. B., *Garden Cities and Satellite Towns* (Dent, 1925, Rev. 1949).

Purdom, C. B., *The Building of Satellite Towns* (London, Dent, New Edition 1949).

Purdom, C. B., *Life Over Again* (London, Dent, 1951).

Purdom, C. B., *The Letchworth Achievement* (London, Dent, 1963).

Purdom, C. B., 'Unwin and the Garden City Movement' *T. & C.P.*, 21 (11), November 1963, pp.429-33.

Sennett, A. R., *Garden Cities in Theory and Practice* (London, Bemrose, 1905).

Simpson, Michael, 'Thomas Adams, 1871-1940', pp.19-45 in Cherry, G. E. (ed.), *Pioneers in British Planning* (Architectural Press, 1981).

Simpson, Michael, *Thomas Adams and the Modern Planning Movement* (London, Mansell, 1985).

'Sir Freshwater Spray', (Fitzwater-Wray, William), *How Sir Gadabout came to Garden City*, Letchworth (reprint from *The Worker*), 1922.

Sutcliffe, Anthony (ed.), *British Town Planning: The Formative Years* (Leicester University Press, 1981).

Swenarton, Mark, *Homes Fit for Heroes* (London, Heinemann Educational Books Ltd., 1987).

Tarn, J. N., *Five per cent Philanthropy: An Account of Housing in Urban Areas, 1850-1914* (Cambridge University Press, 1973).

Taylor, Nicholas, *The Village in the City* (Temple Smith, London, 1973).

Thompson, E. P., *William Morris: Romantic to Revolutionary* (Revised Edition, London, Merlin, 1977).

Unwin, Raymond, 'On the Building of Houses in the Garden City', *The Garden City Conference at Bournville . . . Report of Proceedings*, G.C.A. (London, 1901), pp.69-74.

Unwin, Raymond, 'Cottage Plans and Common Sense', *Fabian Tract No.109* (Fabian Society, London, 1902).

Unwin, Raymond, 'The Cheap Cottage: What is really needed', G.C., 1(4), July 1906, pp.55-7, (1906a).

Unwin, Raymond, 'The Planning of the Residential Districts of Towns', (i) Transactions of the Seventh International Congress of Architects, R.I.B.A., London, pp.417-25; (ii) *The Builder*, 91 (3311), 21 July 1906, pp.99-100 (1906b)

Unwin, Raymond, *Town Planning in Practice* (London, T. Fisher Unwin, 1909).

Unwin, Raymond, *Nothing Gained by Overcrowding: How the Garden City type of development may benefit both owner and occupier* (London, G.C.T.P.A., 1912).

Unwin, Raymond, 'The Planning of Garden City', Appendix B in Purdom (1913).

Unwin, Raymond, 'Making the Plan of Letchworth', *G.C. & T.P.*, 20(6), June/July, pp.156-9.

Waddilove, L. E., *One Man's Vision: The Story of the Joseph Rowntree Trust* (London, Allen and Unwin, 1954).

Index

Figures in bold refer to illustrations.